Injustice

Injustice

Political Theory for the Real World

MICHAEL GOODHART

OXFORD
UNIVERSITY PRESS

OXFORD
UNIVERSITY PRESS

Oxford University Press is a department of the University of Oxford. It furthers the University's objective of excellence in research, scholarship, and education by publishing worldwide. Oxford is a registered trade mark of Oxford University Press in the UK and certain other countries.

Published in the United States of America by Oxford University Press
198 Madison Avenue, New York, NY 10016, United States of America.

Library of Congress Cataloging-in-Publication Data
Names: Goodhart, Michael E., 1969– author.
Title: Injustice : political theory for the real world / Michael Goodhart.
Description: New York, NY : Oxford University Press, 2018. |
Includes bibliographical references and index.
Identifiers: LCCN 2017053288 (print) | LCCN 2018006408 (ebook) |
ISBN 9780190692445 (Updf) | ISBN 9780190692452 (Epub) |
ISBN 9780190692421 (hardcover : alk. paper) | ISBN 9780190692438 (paperback : alk. paper)
Subjects: LCSH: Justice—Philosophy. | Political ethics. |
BISAC: POLITICAL SCIENCE / Civics & Citizenship. |
POLITICAL SCIENCE / History & Theory. | PHILOSOPHY / Political.
Classification: LCC JC578 (ebook) | LCC JC578 .G648 2018 (print) |
DDC 172/.2—dc23
LC record available at https://lccn.loc.gov/2017053288

for Carole Pateman

my teacher and friend

CONTENTS

ACKNOWLEDGMENTS

I have benefited from a lot of help in writing this book. First and perhaps foremost I want to thank the Alexander von Humboldt Foundation for its generous support, in the form of a year-long residential research fellowship in Berlin in 2008–2009; I am pleased at last to deliver this long-overdue return on its investment. I also thank the Hertie School of Governance in Berlin for hosting me during that year in Germany and for providing a collegial atmosphere conducive to research and reflection. The University of Pittsburgh has aided me in ways large and small; I want to explicitly acknowledge the support I received during that fellowship year and two subsequent sabbatical leaves, as well as an award from the European Studies Center that facilitated a return to Berlin in 2010.

Thoughtful and engaging audiences have kindly entertained preliminary versions of various parts of the argument that follows; I am grateful to members of the Global Governance Colloquium at the Hertie School, the research unit on Transnational Conflicts and International Institutions at the Wissenschaftszentrum Berlin für Sozialforschung (WZB), the Economic Rights Group at the University of Connecticut's Human Rights Institute, the Humanities Center at Carnegie Mellon University, the Center for Global Ethics and Politics at the City University of New York, the Monash Politics Research Workshop at Monash University in Melbourne, the School of Social and Political Sciences Seminar Series at the University of Melbourne, and the Vanderbilt Political Theory Colloquium. I very much appreciate the insightful and unvarnished critiques offered by the students in my fall 2012 capstone seminar on global justice. Audiences and discussants at various meetings of the American Political Science Association, the Association for Political Theory, and the International Studies Association have also provided helpful feedback. I can't recall or repay the innumerable helpful conversations over coffee or drinks—though I can thank my friends at Make Your Mark coffeehouse for the dark roast and warm welcome they always provide.

In addition, many friends, colleagues, and students have given me various kinds of support along the way; I especially want to acknowledge Patricia Donohue, Lisa Ellis, Carol Gould, Carole Pateman, Jackie Smith, Michael Zürn, and everyone in the Global Studies Center. The comments and suggestions of the readers enlisted by Oxford University Press to review this manuscript were enormously helpful; likewise, a paper based closely on chapter 7 appeared in the *Journal of Political Philosophy*, and I am grateful to Bob Goodin and to reviewers for the journal for their valuable suggestions (and for permission to reuse that material here). I owe even greater debts to several interlocutors who have been immensely giving of their time, wisdom, and support: Eva Erman, Anja Görnitz, Terry Macdonald, Jeannie Morefield—and especially Brooke Ackerly and Roger Rouse, whose generosity in repeatedly offering me astute and constructive feedback and support has been humbling. Thanks to all of them I've improved the argument and its presentation immeasurably; they are model colleagues and valued friends. Angela Chnapko, my editor at Oxford, shepherded the book to publication with great dexterity, and I appreciate her unwavering enthusiasm and encouragement about the project.

As always, my family and friends have been supportive throughout. I recognize that this "as always" has made many things possible in my life, and I am deeply grateful for it. I want to thank my parents, Judy and Butch Goodhart, my sister Deb, Donna and Warren Hoppe, and Gordon Denny for their patience and understanding. For very helpful help, I thank my cats, Shadow, Bert, and Cecilia, without whom the book would have been finished sooner but also been lonelier to write. Finally, to Susan Hoppe, for whom the book probably couldn't have been finished soon enough (though she would never say so): thank you for everything.

The image on the cover is entitled *Injustice*; it is one of a pair of angels (the other is called *Justice*) painted by Croatian artist Maxo Vanka. *Injustice* belongs to a group of 25 murals Vanka created that adorns the interior walls of St. Nicholas Croatian Catholic Church in Millvale, PA, just across the Allegheny River from Pittsburgh. The murals, created in two phases in 1937 and 1941, are outstanding examples of the social realist style popular at the time. They speak to themes of faith and family, the immigrant experience in America, social justice and injustice, and the horrors of war. I first saw the murals several years ago (I have seen them many times since), and I immediately knew that this was the image I wanted for the cover for this book. It testifies powerfully to the enduring injustices of war, violence, imperialism, greed, hunger, and indifference.

I am deeply grateful to The Society to Preserve the Millvale Murals of Maxo Vanka for permission to use this image. (That permission does not imply any endorsement of the arguments in this book.) Vanka's murals are a local treasure, and I am happy to be able to highlight them here. I invite you to visit http://vankamurals.org/ to learn more about Vanka and the Millvale murals; better yet, I invite you to come to Pittsburgh to see them for yourself!

Injustice

Introduction

In 2008, I went to Berlin to write a book about global economic justice. I thought then that the rapidly growing debate on this topic lacked sufficient attention to democracy—in particular to economic democratization—and it was my intention to craft an account of global justice that would address this shortcoming. In the intervening years I have not wavered in my conviction that democratization of the global economy is of paramount importance, yet the book before you is not the one I first set out to write. The more I read and reflected on global justice, the more it became clear to me that I would instead write a very different book, one that questioned the dominant approach to the subject and rejected the parameters of the established debates.

The dominant approach, which I call *ideal moral theory*, or IMT, conceives of global justice as a problem of moral philosophy. The theorist's task is to work out what an ideally just society would look like as a way of clarifying our moral obligations and guiding reforms meant to realize that ideal. Theorizing in this mode is ubiquitous within political theory and political philosophy generally and within global normative theory in particular (especially in the Anglo-American tradition)—so much so that one of the main challenges I face in articulating an alternative is to show that IMT is not simply what political theory is or does.[1] In the chapters that follow, I develop a radically different approach, one that seeks to change the way theorists think about justice and injustice.

Just as this book is not the one I expected to write, this introduction may not be the one you are expecting to read. Typically, an introduction sets up a puzzle or problem through the use of examples, by telling a story. Next, it explains the source of the puzzle, pointing to mistakes, omissions, or contradictions within or among the leading scholarly accounts before finally previewing how the book will resolve the problem, change the story, and advance the debate. My primary concern in this book is with IMT as an approach to political theory, not with any specific puzzle as such. The book does not seek to resolve any of the myriad problems arising within the paradigm of IMT but rather to present an alternative to that paradigm.

So I shall begin with a different kind of story, the story of my growing intellectual frustration with IMT. It comprises four anecdotes that offer some insight into the influences that have shaped my thinking in the years I have been laboring on this project. I then explain the backstory of my argument, situating it within the field of global normative theory and as a reaction against the dominant approach within that field. Next, I provide an overview of the argument, which attempts to *unthink* IMT, to *reconceptualize* the problem of injustice, and to *show* how we might do better. Finally, to help orient readers to what is to come, I discuss several important and somewhat unusual features of the book.

FRUSTRATIONS OF IDEAL MORAL THEORY

I was very fortunate to receive a residential research fellowship from the Alexander von Humboldt Foundation in 2008–2009. I arrived in Berlin on the same day as presumptive Democratic (US) presidential nominee

Barack Obama, whose inspiring remarks to adoring masses bathed in brilliant July sunshine in the city's Tiergarten are now overshadowed in my mind by the looming global financial crisis, a storm that was then gathering on the horizon. During that year, literally trillions of dollars were spent to shore up teetering financial markets and tottering banks and corporations, even as millions of people lost their jobs, their homes, their savings, their health, and some even their lives. The suffering was, and remains, broad and deep. I was particularly struck by the irony of watching the same governments that repeatedly bemoan their penury and incapacity when pressed to address poverty and widespread human misery in our world act so swiftly and decisively, and on such a massive scale, to preserve "the global economic system" and the fortunes of the global elite. The theories of justice I was reading and writing about at the time seemed depressingly unhelpful in making sense of what was going on.

The global financial crisis ground on long after my return to Pittsburgh. In September 2011, popular outrage and frustration erupted into the streets in the United States, with protestors occupying New York's Zuccotti Park—and soon many other public spaces—to denounce the inadequacy of the response to the crisis as well as the massive inequalities in wealth and the corrupting influence of money in our political system. The Occupy movement, modeled on uprisings in Tunisia and Cairo's Tahrir Square and echoing burgeoning protest movements in such disparate places as Chile, Spain, Wisconsin, and Indonesia, quickly spread across the country and throughout the world. In Pittsburgh, I helped to organize a monthly event, Occupy Your Mind, that brought scholars and activists together in open community forums to discuss important issues of injustice within and beyond our city. We talked a lot about power and ideology and democracy at those meetings and very little about ideals of justice. One of our biggest challenges was to find ways to clarify the interconnectedness of various local struggles and to situate them within the broader context of the global financial crisis and neoliberal globalization—connecting the dots, as we called it. These connections, I came to realize, are central to understanding and combating injustice, though they are mostly absent from the political theory literature on justice.

The Occupy moment faded, and when I probably should have returned to working more intently on this book, I instead embarked (in January 2013) with a colleague and fourteen wonderful University of Pittsburgh undergraduates on a unique study abroad program called PittMAP (Multiregional Academic Program). During that spring semester we spent about five weeks each in Brazil, India, and China studying the politics of global inequality. We worked hard inside the classroom, but the most meaningful and unique learning took place outside of it. Through the efforts of our colleagues in Pittsburgh and our partners abroad, we met frequently with scholars, activists, journalists, government officials, and representatives of nongovernmental organizations (NGOs) involved in or knowledgeable about social justice work in all three countries. I taught two courses that term: a core course on the politics of global inequality and a seminar on theories of global justice. While the former was primarily a lecture combining normative and empirical perspectives on inequality and the politics it engenders, the latter was taught mainly as an advanced seminar in political theory. Our direct encounters with injustice and our conversations with people working to end it challenged me to rethink the texts we were reading for the seminar and to revamp my approach to teaching them. The disconnect between those texts and our experiences was significant and maddening for all of us; my inability to persuade my students that the theories of justice we were dissecting had relevance for the real world literally just outside the door left a deep impression on me as a teacher and as a scholar.*

Recently, as I've come nearer to completing the book, my "civilian" friends and acquaintances have naturally asked me what it's about. My attempts to outline the argument for them frequently get derailed at an early stage because they are somewhat incredulous about IMT: as outsiders, they have no need of the "operation of Brechtian defamiliarization" that Charles Mills recommended for philosophers immersed in that approach. They simply leap right to the conclusion that Mills anticipates as the likely

* Of course, injustice resides just outside the door in Pittsburgh too, though for various reasons (that reflect poorly on us), it's harder for us to see and easier to ignore.

result of such an exercise: *how on earth could anyone imagine that that's a sensible or appropriate way to think about these problems?*[2] I have come to view this reaction as shockingly predictable.

I recount these four anecdotes because they shed some light on this book's evolution and on the kind of intervention that it makes in the global justice debates within political theory. The first part of the book can be read as my attempt to walk readers through an operation of estrangement or defamiliarization analogous to the one I experienced in the "real world"; the second part reconceptualizes justice and injustice in the space created by this operation; the third tries to show why and how it matters if one adopts this alternative approach.

THE BACKSTORY: GLOBAL NORMATIVE THEORY

Contemporary global normative theory (theorizing about global justice) took off with two seminal publications in the early 1970s. The first was John Rawls's *A Theory of Justice*, which popularized a constructive method of reasoning about ideal principles of justice that admiring followers applied almost immediately to global problems, arguing that both Rawls's methods and his conclusions could be applied straightforwardly to the global context.[3] Not long after *Theory*'s appearance, Peter Singer published his powerful essay "Famine, Affluence, and Morality," which used the memorable analogy of a child drowning in a shallow pond to argue that the rich have extensive obligations to aid the poor when they can do so without sacrificing anything of (comparable) moral significance.[4]

Since then, debate has raged about the nature and extent of the obligations citizens of rich and powerful countries have toward the poor and about how to determine responsibility for the injustices that plague our world. Interestingly, however, there has been very little debate about how to approach these questions—at least until recently. While Singer's consequentialism has certainly been influential,[5] the overwhelming majority of theorists and philosophers working on problems of global justice today have followed in the broad Rawlsian tradition, regardless of whether they have adopted Rawls's own "social liberal" (statist) views or followed the more cosmopolitan leanings of the "global Rawlsians."[6]

Rawls's constructivism exemplifies an approach to problems of justice and injustice that, again, I shall refer to as *ideal moral theory*. IMT is *ideal* in that it seeks to work out an account of pure or perfect justice, which its practitioners regard as essential for identifying injustice and providing practical guidance for the transition from our radically unjust circumstances to a more just society. IMT is *moral* in that it conceives of its principles of justice as moral principles that engender categorical obligations and responsibilities. IMT thus conceives the core problems of justice as problems to be solved through philosophical reflection on ideal moral principles of justice and on the nature and extent of the obligations and responsibilities that follow from them.[†] Throughout this book I use the acronym IMT to emphasize both the *ideal* and the *moral* aspects of the approach and to differentiate IMT *as an approach* from "ideal theory" as a step or stage in theorizing justice (see chapter 1). Insisting on this distinction also serves as a constant reminder that my critique of IMT differs fundamentally from that of the so-called nonideal theorists, who have recently questioned IMT's reliance on abstraction and idealization and worried about its relevance. I share these concerns, but as will become clear soon enough, I believe that IMT's problems go much deeper, and my critique therefore goes much further.

Rawls began *Theory* with the bold assertion that justice is the first virtue of social institutions,[7] and while his work has been subjected to trenchant and voluminous criticism from nearly every conceivable angle, only a handful of thinkers has questioned this fundamental claim about the

[†] In his later work, Rawls characterized his conception of justice as "political, not metaphysical." This "political turn" reflects a shift in his *justificatory* strategy; Rawls never renounced the constructivist methodology of *Theory*, which remains the basis of his substantive conception of justice. Overlapping consensus brackets metaphysics rather than abandoning it; it embraces "many metaphysics" rather than none; K. Anthony Appiah, "Grounding Human Rights," in *Human Rights as Politics and Idolatry*, ed. Amy Gutmann (Princeton, NJ: Princeton University Press, 2001), 201. I have always found it curious and somewhat worrisome that the later "political" account leaves all of the key substantive conclusions of the earlier arguments unchanged. In any case, my concern is less with Rawls than with debates he helped to initiate.

primacy of justice. Not surprisingly, then, most global normative theorists begin, as Rawls did, by attempting to work out ideal moral principles of justice. These principles guide the design of (proposed) social institutions, enable critique of existing arrangements, and guide reform. The first task for political theorists, on this approach, is to determine what justice is and requires, a task essential and prior to questions of institutional design, critique, and reform.[‡]

For reasons I shall explain later on, my approach does not recognize a neat differentiation between domestic and global injustice. Throughout this book, however, I engage primarily with global normative theory and theorists. I do so partly because this project was originally conceived as a more conventional contribution to that literature. Probably like many others, I was drawn to global normative theory by its discussion of matters such as the tremendous inequality and staggering poverty that characterize our world today; here were leading political theorists speaking passionately and intelligently to those very issues! Yet as I worked through what's been written on these topics, I became increasingly frustrated not just with the answers IMT was generating but also with the questions it was asking. These answers and questions do not, in my experience, prove very helpful in understanding or combating concrete injustices; often they impede clear thinking about injustice.

In this book I propose a radically different approach. I do so because I am interested in problems different from those IMT addresses. I care less about divining the requirements of spotless justice than about

[‡] Gerald Gaus argues against too close an association between Rawls and IMT, tracing the discussion of ideal theory back through the work of 19th-century utopian socialists to Thomas More and ultimately to Plato; Gerald Gaus, *The Tyranny of the Ideal: Justice in a Diverse Society* (Princeton, NJ: Princeton University Press, 2016). He makes a fair point: ideal thinking has been around for a long, long time. Because I'm concerned primarily with global normative theory, however, it is more appropriate to start with the work of Rawls and Singer in the 1970s and the critical reaction to it. Other important historical sources of global normative theorizing include world federalism (Luis Cabrera, ed., *Global Governance, Global Government: Institutional Visions for an Evolving World System* [Albany: State University of New York Press, 2011]) and the cosmopolitan theories of self-determination advanced by leading black and anticolonialist thinkers after the Second World War (Adom Getachew, *Worldmaking after Empire: The Rise and Fall of Self-Determination*, forthcoming).

getting to grips with the concrete injustices people struggle against daily. I care less, that is, about working out an ideal moral conception of justice and deriving its institutional requirements than about finding ways to challenge and transform unjust social arrangements and the ideologies that sustain them. Put differently, I have come to believe that injustice is primarily a political rather than a philosophical problem and come to doubt that IMT is a helpful or even an adequate way of conceptualizing it.

My primary aim and motivation in writing this book is to do better with respect to injustice—to do better in making sense of it and in bringing theory to bear on it in ways that might help to advance the work of people struggling against injustices of all kinds. To be clear, I'm not suggesting that political theory has to be about social transformation; I'm proposing an approach to injustice that regards social transformation as central to combating it. Likewise, I'm not arguing that IMT is somehow wrong. I offer a critique of IMT and develop an alternative approach because I find IMT unhelpful in addressing real-world injustice. That said, I do maintain that some of IMT's premises or assumptions are *mistaken*, by which I mean *taken wrongly to be necessary to sound theorizing about injustice*. Showing that core elements of IMT are mistaken in this specialized sense is essential to my project because IMT is so ubiquitous within global normative theory that proceeding otherwise can easily seem like an error. Some brush-clearing is therefore required to open up the alternative path I intend to follow; without it, I fear that path won't be visible or appealing to theorists accustomed to following the more familiar route worn by IMT.

OVERVIEW OF THE ARGUMENT

That brush-clearing takes place in the book's first two chapters (Part I: "Unthinking Ideal Moral Theory"), where I dig deeper into the nature and theoretical sources of the frustrations recounted in this introduction. My aim in these chapters is to question IMT *as an approach to theorizing justice and injustice* by defamiliarizing readers with it. That is, I aim to unthink its familiar assumptions and procedures to open up space for the imagination of alternatives. In the next three chapters (Part II: "Reconceptualizing the Problem") I propose what I call a bifocal approach to injustice, an alternative way of thinking about the politics of injustice that integrates realistic analysis of conflict, power, and politics with substantive normative critique and prescription. It does so by conceptualizing claims about justice and injustice as ideological claims and relying on a hypothetical conception of political normativity to make sense of them. Finally, in the last two chapters (Part III: "Political Theory for the Real World"), I consider what practical difference it makes if one adopts the approach I recommend, discussing the work political theory and political theorists can do to combat injustice and showing how this approach transforms our thinking about responsibility for it.

One of my chief concerns in the first part of the book is to show that, irrespective of the substantive accounts of justice that it yields, IMT is a problematic *approach* for theorists concerned, as I am, with understanding and combating injustice. In chapter 1 ("The Trouble with Justice"), I begin to estrange readers from IMT through a review and critique of its core assumptions and procedures, stressing two assumptions that are rarely made explicit but which are central to the approach. IMT conceptualizes injustice as the absence or opposite of justice, and it presumes that only justified moral principles can provide an adequate and reliable guide for critique and reform. These assumptions are problematic in themselves, I argue, and they contribute to three pathologies that cripple IMT: analytical paralysis, a reflex to subordinate politics to morality, and a disposition to distortional thinking. The search for justified principles of justice leaves IMT stuck at the first (ideal) stage of theorizing, making it hard to tackle concrete problems of injustice. Conceptualizing principles of justice as moral principles means that politics becomes a threat, leading to a diminished role for democracy in ideal conceptions of justice, even as IMT relies on hypothetical consent and pseudodeliberation to justify its claims. Heavy reliance on idealization introduces various kinds of distortion into ideal conceptions of justice; these distortions reveal that justice is prone to function ideologically in ways that undermine the two core assumptions and raise damning questions about the utility and coherence of IMT as a way of theorizing injustice.

In chapter 2 ("Barking up the Wrong Trees"), I show that three of the central debates within global normative theory are afflicted by these pathologies. Constructivist methods for identifying principles of justice are both blatantly undemocratic and severely distortional; debates about the scope of justice are depoliticizing, question-begging, and philosophically irresolvable; claims about how the global order affects the poor depoliticize and distort power relations in the global economy and ignore the ideological context in which the claims themselves operate. My argument is not that IMT gives problematic answers to these questions but that the questions themselves are unhelpful and unnecessary, artifacts of the approach. Again, in making these arguments, my aim is to defamilarize readers with IMT—to make it seem less like a natural, sensible, coherent, and necessary approach to theorizing injustice than like a strange, bewildering, and profoundly problematic one.

The second part of the book develops a radical alternative to IMT. I begin, in chapter 3 ("Getting Real?"), through an engagement with realist political theory, which shares many of my concerns about IMT and offers an alternative approach (or approaches) of its own. Through critical dialogue with Amartya Sen's nonideal realism, the liberal realism of Bernard Williams, and the critical realism of Raymond Geuss, I show that realist political theory is much more susceptible to conservatism, distortion, and idealization than its proponents typically acknowledge. It is often not very realistic, and it is not supportive of normative critique. While critical realists in particular insist that their approach is compatible with critique, what its proponents mean by this is the critical analysis of political norms—the analysis of power and unmasking of ideology. A realistic approach to the politics of injustice requires such a critique, I agree, but it also depends on the critical-normative *evaluation* of society, the aim of which is to offer substantive critique that can guide transformative social change. These two types of critique must, I argue, be integrated in a single theoretical framework for theorizing and combating injustice.

I propose such a framework in chapter 4 ("The Bifocal Approach"), where I argue that conceptualizing justice claims as ideological claims facilitates the reconciliation and integration of realistic and normative analysis within a single framework. This proposed bifocal approach combines an analytical and a "partisan" lens within a single theoretical apparatus, providing a more comprehensive understanding of injustice than its competitors by integrating two crucial functions of political theory: the analysis and critique of ideologies and substantive normative critique and political prescription. This approach depends on a conception of political normativity as hypothetical rather than categorical; I defend this conception of normativity as theoretically plausible, motivationally adequate, and crucially enabling for theorizing justice and injustice.

In chapter 5 ("A Democratic Account of Injustice"), I work within a particular substantive approach to articulate a democratic account of injustice from the core principles of freedom and equality for everyone. This account locates injustice in deformities of power relations—in domination, oppression, and exploitation—and recommends specific feminist epistemological tools and dialectical methods of inquiry appropriate for developing a democratic conception of injustice. I use this discussion to illustrate the advantages of the bifocal approach, to show how it changes the way we think as theorists about the type and purpose of the normative work we undertake as ideologists. This discussion also equips me with a particular substantive perspective I will use in the final part of the book in considering the implications of my broader approach.

That final part of the book tries to show what practical difference it makes for political theory and political theorists if one adopts the proposals outlined above. Chapter 6 ("Political Theory and the Politics of Injustice") focuses on the work that political theory and political theorists might do in support of an effective political response to injustice. I argue that most conflict about injustice arises from ideological disagreements about the meaning of (in)justice itself. The politics of injustice—of these conflicts, and of efforts to change things—must be counterhegemonic politics. It must, that is, be a politics that challenges the dominant ideology, questioning its values, ideas, and interpretations of the world, and that disrupts prevailing understandings of justice and injustice. Its success depends on building countervailing power through discursive political engagement, efforts enabled by the work of articulation and translation. The goal of this transformative, emancipatory politics is to establish a reflexive, open-ended, and continual process of repair, renewal, and (re)generation—to establish the conditions for the realization of many diverse utopias.

Finally, chapter 7 ("Taking Responsibility for Injustice") puts many of the ideas outlined here to work in considering the problem of responsibility for systemic injustice. I argue that responsibility must be reconceptualized as a political rather than a philosophical problem and that its solution depends on counterhegemonic political struggles over the meaning of injustice itself.

SETTING THE STAGE

I want to make clear from the outset that this book is meant to be provocative. It tries to unsettle familiar ways of thinking and doing things in global normative theory. It will not deliver what many readers have come to expect from typical interventions in the literature: it defines no ideal principles of justice, offers no elaborate moral and philosophical justifications of its key normative arguments, and proposes no concrete policy or institutional reforms designed to guide us toward a just world. What it primarily offers is a new and distinctive *approach* to problems of injustice in politics and in political theory, one designed to make theory relevant for and useful in the real world.[§]

Again, there are many ways of doing political theory and many purposes for which it might be done. In this book, I am primarily concerned with how political theory can help in understanding and combating injustice.

[§] By "the real world" I don't mean (as some realists seem to) an objective world of "facts." The inescapability of interpretation is a central premise of my approach. Rather, I use "the real world" to refer *our* world—characterized by power, conflict, politics, and rival interpretations—as opposed to the idealized world of IMT.

That is, I am interested in developing a theoretical approach to the politics of injustice that can contribute to emancipatory social transformation. Theorists intent on seeking moral foundations for ideals of spotless justice and devising philosophical justifications for such principles will probably dislike much of the argument that follows (and certainly dislike my characterization of that work as ideological). This shouldn't be surprising: our concerns are divergent. To be clear, my point in this book is not to argue that others should share my concerns; it is rather to argue that, for those who *do* share them, we need to do things differently. What I propose here is not a substitute for IMT but an alternative to it, one designed to clarify what political theorists might do to challenge injustice and to advance emancipatory change. That said, I argue forcefully throughout the book that IMT is not, despite the protestations of many of its advocates, a necessary or even particularly useful approach to injustice.

One of the things I do differently is to insist on the distinction between *moral* and *normative* claims. For reasons I can't address here, these distinct notions have become deeply and problematically conflated in global normative theory and indeed throughout political theory and philosophy generally. In this book, I use the term normative to refer to *ought-propositions* of any kind, including but not limited to moral claims. The latter are a subset of normative claims purported to be categorical—that is, to carry special motivational and normative force related to their supposedly being true, valid, reasonable, self-evident, nonrejectable, logically indispensable, whatever—and thus to entail categorical or universally binding duties, obligations, or responsibilities.

I shall have much more to say about this distinction between normative and moral claims, about the supposed categorical normativity of the latter, and about the theoretical leverage to be gained by insisting on and operationalizing this distinction in chapter 4. One of the reasons I adopt the unusual nomenclature of ideal *moral* theory is to constantly remind readers that the dominant approach to global normative theorizing does typically conflate these terms, using moral and normative interchangeably. I do not want or need to take a position on whether categorical moral principles might exist or how one might attempt to discover or justify them. I am only arguing that claims about justice and injustice can be usefully conceived differently, as ideological claims. I am careful to use the term "normative" to refer to ought-propositions generally and to use "moral" to refer only to this allegedly special subset of claims. Doing so allows me to highlight some of the distinctive mistakes and difficulties that arise because IMT conflates them while consistently conceptualizing its principles of ideal justice as moral principles possessed of this mysterious categorical force.

Another distinctive feature of my argument is its sustained (if somewhat episodic) critique of neoliberalism. Neoliberalism is an economic and political doctrine originating in the Austrian school (Hayek, von Mises) in the years following the First World War. It intermixes a theoretical design for the reorganization of international capitalism with a political project of restoring the power and influence of capital and refashioning the state in ways supportive of that aim.[8] The economic doctrine of neoliberalism promotes uninhibited trade, unregulated markets, and the unrestricted movement of capital, all in the name of stimulating economic growth. This economic doctrine rests on three core political beliefs: in the sanctity of freedom from government interference and property rights ("liberty"); in the creative power of entrepreneurialism and individuals' responsibility for their own economic success or failure ("individualism"); and in the unparalleled fairness and efficiency of the market as a mechanism for allocating benefits and burdens in society ("the free market"). The corresponding political doctrine advocates a minimal role for the state, which should be limited to providing institutions necessary to uphold liberty, individualism, and free markets—including a strong military, an independent but constrained judiciary, and an extensive domestic police function.

These doctrines engender several distinctive institutional logics, including economic deregulation as well as *re*regulation to promote the spread of market mechanisms; welfare state devolution, retraction, and recomposition; and, the creation of an expansive, intrusive, and proactive penal and security apparatus. The cultural tropes of liberty and individualism provide a kind of glue that holds these fissiparous elements together,[9] binding free markets to an authoritarian moralism that disciplines those at the lower end of the class structure by maintaining a characteristic form of social insecurity consisting in precarious employment, heavy-handed policing, mass incarceration, and widespread monitoring and surveillance of the poor.[10]

Neoliberalism is typically identified with the economic project of establishing free markets, yet it is equally concerned with the political project of restoring class power.[11] As Harvey notes, these economic and political projects frequently prove incompatible in practice, and when they collide, it's typically the political project that prevails. Recognizing this tension helps to explain why neoliberalism tolerates and often promotes corporate welfare, crony capitalism, growing economic inequality, and the upward redistribution of wealth, all of which advance the restoration of class power at the expense of liberty, individualism, and free markets.[12]

Neoliberalism emerged as a potent political force following the period of economic "stagflation" in the 1970s in northwest Europe and North America. The elections of Margaret Thatcher in the United Kingdom and of Ronald Reagan in the United States marked the advent of a period of neoliberal economic and political transformation that continues essentially unabated.[13] By the 1990s, neoliberalism had solidified into a specific set of policy prescriptions known as the Washington Consensus because of its promotion by three pivotal global economic actors based in the US capital: the World Bank, the IMF, and the US Treasury Department.[14] These policy prescriptions were promoted aggressively through so-called structural adjustment programs designed to remake national economies and societies. The first major experiment in structural adjustment took place in Chile following the CIA-backed Pinochet coup d'état, under the guidance of Milton Friedman's "Chicago Boys." Structural adjustment has subsequently been implemented by other authoritarian regimes (e.g., China), through electoral triumph (e.g., the United States, the United Kingdom, New Zealand, Germany, Canada, arguably South Africa), through "conditionality," which makes international financial and development assistance dependent upon adoption of neoliberal reforms (e.g., in the global South, the formerly Communist countries of Russia and Eastern Europe, and, more recently, in the southern half of the EU), and through "disaster capitalism," including by means of direct military conquest (notably in Iraq).[15] Today, neoliberalism has risen again from the ashes of the global financial crisis—more vulture- than phoenix-like—in the guise of "austerity."

In this book, I use the term neoliberalism to refer to the *ideology* animating these economic and political projects as well as to the projects themselves. By ideology I mean "a set of ideas by which men [*sic*] posit, explain and justify ends and means of organized social action, and specifically political action, irrespective of whether such action aims to preserve, amend, uproot or rebuild a given social order."[16] Simply put, ideology is a constellation of values and ideas people use to interpret the world and to orient themselves and their actions within it. Again, that set of ideas within neoliberalism comprises liberty, individualism, and free markets. Today neoliberal ideology suffuses our social norms, our civic institutions, and our political life. It has become a hegemonic discourse, one that has no serious rivals and "has pervasive effects on ways of thought to the point where it has become incorporated into the common-sense way many of us interpret, live in, and understand the world."[17]

Some readers have objected to this characterization of neoliberalism, so let me clarify that in calling it hegemonic I don't mean to imply that it is completely dominant or uncontested. As Gramsci maintained, hegemony is always aspirational, always in process, always being negotiated and rearticulated in light of changing social realities and the inevitable cracks and contradictions that emerge in its facade.[18] I call neoliberalism hegemonic to emphasize how deeply it structures the thinking of policymakers, scholars, and citizens alike, how it constricts and constrains our political imagination. This is not to suggest a shortage of critical assessments of its policies and their adverse and sometimes egregious effects: global normative theory is replete with such criticisms. The problem, as I describe in chapter 2, is that many of those criticisms (unconsciously) assume and reproduce core neoliberal assumptions about and interpretations of the world and as a result deny or neglect the deeper relations of domination, oppression, and exploitation that structure our contemporary social and economic arrangements. This problem is amplified by IMT's reliance on idealization, which normalizes these power relations and the institutional structures underlying them, shielding them—though not necessarily the particular outcomes they generate—from thoroughgoing critique.

My emphasis on neoliberalism throughout this book is a response to its hegemonic status, which must be thematized if we are to get to grips with injustices like poverty and inequality that concern me deeply. Returning to neoliberalism repeatedly throughout the book also provides some cohesion to the argument and allows me to deepen my critique of it through various examples in different contexts. In stressing it, I don't mean to suggest that neoliberalism is the only or necessarily the primary source of injustice in our world or that it poses a unique problem for IMT. It permits me to illustrate the limitations of IMT, which has the same difficulty thematizing and theorizing race, gender, (dis)ability, and other social relations of domination. To be clear: the problem is not that IMT can't or doesn't *recognize* racism or misogyny or poverty as injustices; the problem is that its method and assumptions preclude an adequate critique of the power relations through which these and other injustices are produced and thus preempt a radical, socially transformative approach to them.

The book before you is written mainly for global normative theorists, a large and eclectic group, and for theorists at various stages of their intellectual careers. I've thus tried to write in a clear and accessible, even informal, style and to avoid jargon and highly technical argument where possible. I've also tried to make the book accessible by being explicit about why I'm doing what I'm doing when I'm doing it. Another technique for increasing accessibility is the dialogical mode of argument I adopt throughout. I often proceed through sustained critical engagements with authors whose work I have learned a lot from; these discussions are meant to lay bare the thinking behind my own positions and to clarify key points of divergence and disagreement. These engagements are also intended as a way of showing respect and gratitude for the efforts of scholars I respect, even when my criticisms of those efforts may seem severe.

I am not shy about signaling my agreement with others or about borrowing their good ideas; I won't try to reinvent wheels or to downplay similarities in the pursuit of originality for its own sake. This way, I avoid tedious hairsplitting, honor the work of those on whom I build, and model the kind of collaborative political theory I believe is essential for challenging injustice. This practice gives my argument a broadly synthetic quality. I don't mind that at all; while there are numerous innovations in the pages that follow—the bifocal theoretical approach, its hypothetical conception of political normativity, the sustained attention to the politics of injustice—what's most distinctive and important is the overall approach. One way to put it is that I'm really calling for a paradigm shift in global normative theory, a radical departure from the methods and assumptions of IMT (and of realist political theory).

I don't mean this to sound pompous: as Thomas Kuhn argued, a new paradigm is not necessarily better—and there is no guarantee that it will be more productive—than its predecessor. One paradigm gives way to another when a discipline begins to exhaust the constellation of questions it set out to answer and starts to pile up anomalies that can't easily be addressed within the boundaries of "normal science." New paradigms pose different questions and enable new kinds of inquiry; they ultimately take hold and prove successful when they allow scholars to tackle important problems that the previous paradigm proved unable or ill-suited to address. The advent and advocacy of a new paradigm neither proves nor requires that previous ones were wrong; rather, it signals that, at least in the view of some critics, it might be valuable to reexamine our basic assumptions, reconceptualize familiar problems, ask new questions, and adopt alternative ways of thinking about them.[19] That's the work I undertake here.

In advocating for a new paradigm, I'm joining nonideal theorists, realists, republicans, critical theorists, and others concerned with the limitations of IMT and eager to make political theory more relevant and useful in struggles against injustice. I've borrowed heavily from, synthesized, and built upon key aspects of their work, in an effort to push further. Whether the approach I'm advocating proves useful for others—either as a model or a foil—remains to be seen, but I hope this book opens up space for new and creative thinking about injustice and about how political theory can be more effective in and for the real world.

PART I

Unthinking Ideal Moral Theory

1

The Trouble with Justice

In this and the following chapter I attempt to defamiliarize IMT for readers by questioning its fundamental assumptions and procedures. I've called Part I of this book "Unthinking Ideal Moral Theory" to emphasize the depth of the questioning I have in mind: I invoke *un*thinking to highlight "a contrast with familiar calls for *re*thinking that often leave fundamental epistemological issues untouched. . . . [T]he challenge consists not merely in reassessing what we know but also in interrogating the *ways of knowing* upon which our 'knowledge' rests."[1] In these chapters, I develop a critique of IMT as an approach to global normative theorizing, rather than criticizing the conclusions of particular authors working within the approach or joining the debates about how best to implement it. My focus in this chapter is on the approach itself—on its methods and procedures, its core assumptions, and on the theoretical pathologies it engenders. In the next chapter, I show that some of the key questions of procedure and substance frequently debated within global normative theory are artifacts of IMT and argue that focusing on them severely and unnecessarily constrains our thinking about injustice.

I begin with a brief, schematic overview of IMT. Next, I consider two troubling assumptions at the core of this approach: that injustice must be conceived as the absence or opposite of justice, and that the aim of political theory is to provide ideal guidance for reform. Each of these assumptions, I argue, is problematic in itself; together, they encourage three distinctive pathologies in IMT: theoretical paralysis, a reflex to subordinate politics to morality, and a proclivity to distortional thinking. Among the key conclusions of this chapter is that justice—both in its ideal and in its instantiated forms—can function ideologically in ways that compromise the arguments and conclusions of IMT and demonstrate the need for an alternative approach.

IMT, BRIEFLY

The following overview of IMT is necessarily a composite sketch drawn from many sources, including the work of contemporary proponents and practitioners of IMT and of its critics. As such, it emphasizes common features rather than presenting an accurate portrait of any particular thinker or theory. It is not, however, a caricature: I attempt to limn those commonalities as faithfully as I can. I make no attempt in the discussion that follows to characterize or generalize about the many and varied substantive theories of justice produced by ideal theorists; I assume that readers who want to be are already familiar with them. Again, my concern is not with the conclusions of any particular theory of justice but rather with the approach that yields them.

Among the fundamental methodological assumptions of IMT is that political theory requires ideal moral principles of justice to enable critique and guide reform. These principles are *ideal* in that they depict justice in its pure or perfect form, uncontaminated by specific considerations of context and circumstance. They are *moral* principles in that they are conceived as having categorical normative force—that is, as engendering or entailing binding duties and responsibilities. The primary tasks in theorizing justice are the discovery, articulation, and justification of such principles and the derivation of obligations and responsibilities from them. In justifying principles of justice, IMT relies on philosophical techniques designed to establish their impartiality or nonrejectability, to show that they would command hypothetical assent, or to derive them analytically from purportedly obvious or unobjectionable premises. These philosophical techniques are employed because pure principles of justice must, in some sense, be true, valid, or correct if they are to carry categorical force. According to Gaus, this "naive" understanding that IMT aims at the truth, "alas, seems widely embraced in political philosophy."[2]

Within IMT, the overriding emphasis is on defining and defending these ideal moral principles of justice: "the current literature on social justice is mainly concerned with working out, revising, refining, and debating the relative merits of different ideal principles of justice, and the justifications of those principles."[3] The aim is to establish what justice is and requires in its pure form. Virtually all ideal theorists agree that principles of justice should be determined without consideration of actual injustice.

> "[M]oral theories of social justice, political authority, political legitimacy, and many other moral-political concepts are not shown to have any defect in virtue of the fact, if it is one, that the alleged requirements or preconditions of these things are not likely ever to be met." More succinctly, ". . . the truth about justice is not constrained by considerations of the likelihood of success in realising it. . . ." According to ideal theory, the objective of political philosophy is to take up a perspective on politics that, through abstraction and idealization, is unencumbered by facts pertaining to the plausibility that a theory might ever be realized in practice. These are quite irrelevant to the philosophers' task of getting at the truth of the matter.[4]

As one enthusiast sums it up, only "abstract, pure, context-free philosophy" provides an adequate basis for thinking about justice in our current circumstances.[5]

Theorizing proceeds in two stages. The first stage is concerned with the working out of ideal moral principles of justice. Rawls explained the conceptual and procedural priority of ideal theory, the name that technically belongs to this first stage of theorizing within IMT, by arguing that "a deeper understanding [of the pressing and urgent matters we confront in everyday life] can be gained in no other way."[6] Ideal theory is necessary for and prior to social reform; it provides guidelines for the design and construction of an ideally just society.* Progressive reform is only possible once we have clearly specified principles of justice in hand.[7] Simon Caney argues that theorists need ideal principles because, without them, we have no basis for deciding that the status quo is terrible and no basis for knowing that a better state of affairs is possible or how to attain it.[8] Ideal theorizing is thus "an essential piece of the work to be done," a necessary "precursor" to identifying injustice and thinking about remediation.[9]

Nonideal theory is the name given to the second(ary) stage of theorizing within IMT, in which theorists use principles of justice developed in the first stage to take the measure of injustice in our society. In this stage, theorists also identify responsibility for the practical realization of justice, again relying on the principles developed at the ideal stage and on the facts of particular cases. Ideal theory establishes the target, and nonideal or "transitional" theory works out a path from our present unjust circumstances toward that ideal.[10] Good policy is only "good" in relation to the overall ideal of a perfectly just society; seemingly desirable changes might turn

* Caney maintains that universal principles of the kind employed by IMT "often specify background constraints on what can be done rather than detailed outlines of how society must be arranged down to the last detail"; Simon Caney, *Justice beyond Borders: A Global Political Theory* (Oxford: Oxford University Press, 2005), 41. This certainly may be true, as in the work of Onora O'Neill, whom Caney cites. Often, however, as in Rawls or in Caney's own work, such principles do more: while not necessarily full blueprints, they specify the important features of the ideal precisely by ruling things out. Telling a builder that a structure must be accessible to people with disabilities, must contain only sustainable building materials, may not block neighbors' views or have fewer than one restroom per floor, etc.—while not a blueprint—substantially constrains the final design.

out to be obstacles to further necessary reforms. Piecemeal initiatives won't do, since all transitional steps must be morally permissible, feasible, and effective in relation to the goal of realizing the integrated conception of justice.[11] As A. John Simmons puts it, "to dive into nonideal theory without an ideal theory in hand is simply to dive blind, to allow irrational free rein to the mere conviction of injustice and to eagerness for change of any sort."[12]

TWO TROUBLING ASSUMPTIONS

Justice and Injustice

There are two important assumptions informing IMT that are rarely spelled out or defended. The first is that injustice can only be conceived as the absence or opposite of justice. The assumption itself is clear enough, once we look for it, in Rawls's assertion that we can understand injustice "in no other way" than through an ideal moral conception of justice, in Caney's insistence that there is "no basis" for determining when existing social arrangements are intolerable or for thinking about how to improve them apart from such a conception, and in Simmons's fears about the "mere conviction of injustice," which he considers irrational and maybe even licentious. Crucially, this unarticulated assumption motivates (in part) the search for ideal moral principles of justice and determines IMT's distinctive two-stage procedure: a method is required to elucidate what justice is and requires before it's even possible to think carefully about injustice. Strangely, despite the significance of this assumption and the adamant insistence on it, I have found no explicit argument for or even discussion of the idea that injustice must be conceived in this way in the literature.

There are good reasons to think that it need not be. Judith Shklar provocatively suggested that injustice might be theorized on its own terms, maintaining that the urgency and the phenomenological distinctiveness of injustice argue for conceiving it independently of justice.

> Why should we not think of those experiences that we call unjust directly, as independent phenomena in their own right? Common sense and history surely tell us that these are common experiences and have an immediate claim on our attention. . . . Why then do most philosophers refuse to think about injustice as deeply or as subtly as they do about justice? I do not know why a curious division of labor prevails, why philosophy ignores iniquity, while history and fiction deal with little else, but it does leave a gap in our thinking.[13]

One thing that disappears into this gap is the "phenomenological distinctiveness" of injustice (which Shklar ultimately located in inequality and in the experience of being "denied one's dignity as a human being").[14] Conceiving of injustice as the absence or opposite of justice renders distant, static, and cerebral something that many people experience as immediate, dynamic, and visceral—as a denial or violation, an existential threat. Theorizing injustice as an aberration or departure from ideal justice fundamentally mischaracterizes people's sense and experience of injustice and misses or misapprehends its political character and significance.

Shklar was fascinated and disturbed by the realization that injustice survives and even thrives within the context of what she called normal justice.[15] Most injustices, she observed, occur *within* the framework of an established polity and an operative system of law in normal times; often, it is the very officials entrusted with upholding justice who commit, in their official capacities, the gravest injustices.[16]

> In every historically known society, the rich dominate the poor with the latter's hapless consent, since they accept their fate for the sake of peace. That is the real meaning of recognizing thine and mine and of the normal model of justice. . . . In a radically unequal society the rules cannot but encourage unlawful conduct among the deprived and their exploiters. The former are desperate, the latter can get away with it. Law naturally falls very differently upon them. The normal model of justice is thus revealed as the expression of the inequality

> that is the real fountain and origin of injustice, which has an exuberant life of its own and which no system of justice, however fair, can ever expect to eliminate.[17]

It's revealing that Shklar focuses on economic domination and exploitation rather than the state oppression often held (perhaps too biographically) to animate her "liberalism of fear." Her assertion that the "normal model of justice" benefits the rich and the strong seems unsurprising to anyone who studies politics, yet for practitioners of IMT it must be highly disorienting. Because they regard justice as an impartial moral principle, even the suggestion that it might serve the interests of some at the expense of others is anathema, almost literally inconceivable. In addition, that justice and injustice often coexist within society also suggests—though this does not seem to have been Shklar's focus—that the meaning of justice itself is *contested* within society, that justice might function ideologically. If a "just" society can be riven by injustice, injustice cannot be merely the absence or opposite of justice; it must in some sense also be a critique of it. I shall return to this crucial point later on.

The Ideal Guidance Assumption

The second significant assumption that I want to challenge is that the role of political theory and theorists is to provide "ideal guidance," by which is meant something like using ideal moral principles of justice to criticize existing social arrangements, to evaluate (normatively and comparatively) the status quo and possible alternatives to it, and to recommend reforms (policies, institutional changes) intended to make society more just (more like the ideal). Holly Lawford-Smith observes that while ideal guidance is not a requirement or objective of all kinds of normative theory, most ideal theorists believe that theories of justice should be action-guiding.[18] Likewise, Erman and Möller maintain that "it is agreed that if a theory of justice would not help us to 'get things done' this would be a major cause for concern."[19]

One might agree, as I do, that theory should be action-guiding and that getting things done with theory is important; one might nonetheless object, as I do, to the notion of ideal guidance. Ideal theorists assert, again mostly without argument, that the only way to guide action and to get things done is with ideal moral principles of justice. The implicit argument seems to be that fully justified ideals provide reliable and impartial bases for evaluation and action and that without such ideals, evaluation and action are impossible or indefensible.

I find at least two features of this logic troubling. The first is that it has a distinctive whiff of Platonism about it: questions about what justice is and requires are questions for *philosophers* to answer. It goes unasked why this should be so, why the knowledge and experience of people who suffer injustice directly shouldn't also inform our thinking about these questions. This logic also entails a momentous epistemological assumption about how philosophers come to know and understand what justice is and requires. The second troubling feature of this logic is the way it allows ideal theorists to have their cake and eat it too. IMT is deeply prescriptive: it defends substantive political values and recommends policies and institutional designs informed by them. But it also insists that it is rational, objective, above the fray. So ideal theorists make substantive normative recommendations *and* also insist on their neutrality. They square this circle by appealing to the impartiality of recommendations based on justified moral principles. Put succinctly: *ideal* guidance, and only ideal guidance, transmogrifies partisanship into impartiality. Shklar helps us to see, however, that justice and theories of justice often function ideologically. If that's right, or even if it's a possibility, then it's a mistake to begin with the assumption that theory can be simultaneously impartial and prescriptive. Where does that leave us with respect to acting and doing? I must postpone an answer to that question until the second part of this book. For now, the salient point is that *that is the question*: whether theory can be rigorous and action-guiding without reliance on moral ideals, and if so, how we should understand the nature of its prescriptions and the activity of theorizing itself.

Some readers of this book have complained that I am not saying anything new about IMT here. The so-called nonideal theorists have already questioned whether the principles of justice in which IMT trades are too abstract and whether IMT pays sufficient attention to concrete injustices. I must reject this criticism emphatically. Nonideal theory *by definition* accepts the framework of IMT, including its assumptions that injustice is the absence or opposite of justice and that ideal guidance is the only sound way to address injustice. What nonideal theorists have done—and I have learned a great deal from their critiques—is to question how IMT formulates ideals and to propose ways in which it might get on with the second-stage work of identifying and addressing the injustices made visible by those ideals, might shift its emphasis from the first to the second stage of theorizing. It is an *internal* critique of IMT. In questioning IMT as an approach, I am offering an *external* critique of its assumptions and operation far more radical than anything nonideal theorists have proposed. Yet unlike most realists, I don't simply reject IMT's concern with substantive critique and prescription out of hand. Indeed, I regard both as vital functions of political theory. My careful attention to how IMT conceives and handles these matters indicates my desire to remedy critique and prescription of the pathologies with which IMT infects them.

THREE PATHOLOGIES

These pathologies—theoretical paralysis, a reflex to subordinate politics to morality, and a disposition toward distortional thinking—can be traced back to the two troubling assumptions at the heart of IMT (and the methods informed by them on which IMT relies). In making these links, I go beyond the many critics on whose work I draw in showing that these pathologies are related, congenital, generalized, and disabling.

The "Paralysis of Analysis"

The first pathology I want to discuss is one that Keith Horton diagnosed as the "paralysis of analysis," a tendency to focus on points of disagreement and to imagine that what's needed to solve the most difficult problems is more thinking (by us),[20] leading to seemingly endless debate. Because of the central role that principles of justice play in IMT, ideal theorists are primarily engaged in philosophical disputation over which conception of justice should be adopted. These disputes typically take the form of arguments showing that a particular conception of justice is the (only) one consistent with certain morally justified principles or the one that best reflects and advances them.[21] Such arguments attempt to establish the truth or validity of the principles of justice, without which the principles cannot adequately ground the duties, obligations, and responsibilities they supposedly entail and cannot be defended against rivals (more on this below). Paralysis quickly sets in: arguments about justice involve many, many assumptions, abstractions, idealizations, inferences, and deductions, each of which introduces points of possible disagreement whose disputation itself becomes the subject for further discussion and debate, such that it becomes nearly impossible to move past the first stage of theorizing about justice.

Growing frustration with this paralysis has inspired an internal critique of IMT among theorists concerned about its relevance and its ability to speak to pressing injustices in our world. Often referred to as "nonideal theorists" as a way of indicating their impatience with ideal theorizing and their eagerness for IMT to get on with the second-stage work of critique and reform, these thinkers are an eclectic bunch; if anything unites them, it is their worry that IMT does not pay adequate attention to nonideal considerations and that it is (therefore) frequently irrelevant.

The moniker "nonideal theory" is somewhat ironic in that all nonideal theorists are necessarily also ideal theorists, given the conceptual and procedural relationship between the two stages of theorizing. Another irony is that discussions of nonideal theory, supposedly driven by the urgency of addressing injustice and initiating reform, are overwhelmingly methodological; there is a lot of talk about how to do nonideal theory but comparatively little doing of it. To be fair, some theorists really do engage in nonideal theorizing in their work; a further difficulty, however, is that in IMT, disagreements about what is to be done quickly revert back into disagreements about what is to be thought and how it should be thought about—into disputes about whether the principles of justice have been properly specified, justified, and applied.

The complaint that IMT focuses too much on the first stage of theorizing is also misleading, because it ignores that the approach itself effectively dictates this focus. Everything in IMT hinges on the specification of the conception of justice: ideal moral principles of justice are required for the identification of injustice, for ideal guidance, and for the formulation and comparison of proposals for reform. Thus the paralysis of analysis results from the interaction of the methodological demands imposed by the troubling assumptions of IMT and the difficulty of providing dispositive arguments for any particular conception of justice. In other words, the pathology that Horton diagnosed is congenital. The condition is exacerbated by professional incentives for theorists to do "original" work to enhance their "marketability" and ensure their advancement (which often means introducing clever tweaks or critiques of the theories advanced by leading scholars in the field). It's hardly surprising, then, that after 40-plus years, global normative theory is still by and large debating the same questions with which it began, still seeking to identify what ideal justice is and requires.

To be clear: this inability or unwillingness to move past the first stage of theorizing is not, in itself, a problem—*if* the question one cares about is, "What's the (true) meaning of justice?" It is deeply problematic for anyone primarily concerned, as I am, with the question, "What can be done to challenge and combat injustice?"

The Subordination of Politics to Morality

The second pathology I want to consider is IMT's reflex to subordinate politics to morality. This too can be traced to the core assumptions of the approach; it manifests in atrophied democratic institutions and practices in the ideally just society.

When Rawls called justice the first virtue of social institutions, he was quite clear that "the overriding demand to be made of a social and political system is that it conforms to certain moral requirements, whose content is generated by a philosophical theory."[22] These ideal requirements for political systems are specified in the principles of justice derived in IMT's initial or ideal stage of theorizing. Raymond Geuss refers to this as the "ethics first" approach; Bernard Williams dubs it "political moralism."[23] One

> consequence of undertaking political theory in this moralistic manner is that it starts from outside politics, whereby the demands of morality give content to the principles of cooperation or legitimate political action, or political structures and institutions are designed according to prior moral stipulations.[24]

Evaluating social institutions by their conformity with the strictures of moral philosophy inevitably makes politics appear dangerous. Politics is uncertain, open-ended, unpredictable; it threatens to upend or overturn the sureties of justice. The priority of morality and the heavy reliance on philosophy within IMT have led its so-called realist critics to conclude that IMT "represents a desire to evade, displace, or escape from politics."[25] This conclusion is quite accurate: In IMT, politics is carefully contained and constrained to ensure that it cannot interfere with the dictates of morality and the realization of justice. Limiting politics in this way reduces it to a moral forum for the implementation of theories of justice.[26] Politics cannot be evaded; it must be tamed.

Critics might object that I am overstating or mischaracterizing the case. In a recent article, for example, Erman and Möller contend that no one really endorses the view that politics is an arena for the implementation of morality.[27] I am not claiming, however, that most or even many ideal theorists explicitly endorse this position; my claim is that IMT conceptualizes justice in a way that *entails* the subordination, displacement, and containment of politics. The entire point of developing an ideal moral conception of justice is for its principles to govern the design and operation of basic social arrangements, to shape, delimit, and regulate the political. It's hard to imagine what such a conception of justice might be for if not to define the nature and extent of acceptable political action.

Recall that Rawls was quite explicit about this: "The overriding demand to be made of a social and political system is that it conforms to certain moral requirements."[28]

This subordination of politics is evident in the atrophied understanding of democracy prevalent throughout global normative theory. Of course, ideal theorists routinely endorse democratic political rights and institutions (though typically only at the state level).† The problem is not that IMT rejects democracy outright but rather that there is really nothing much *at stake* in politics on the ethics-first view: everything from the design and functioning of basic institutions to constitutional principles, the content of laws, regulations, and social policy, and the substance and direction of reform is dictated by or derived from moral imperatives. The scope for acceptable controversy is sharply curtailed, with disagreement on the principles of justice necessarily conceived as a kind of mistake (on which more below).[29] At most, disagreement seems permissible only regarding the details of implementation and the identity of the officials who will carry it out. Even the methods of reasoning employed by ideal theorists—the pseudodeliberation and hypothetical consent that pervade initial choice situations—pay homage to democracy while circumventing its actual practice. Genuine democracy plays no part in determining the basic structure of society or defining the values that govern it. There is no consultation of real people, no reliance on political reasons or democratic deliberation and experimentation. Indeed, there is no actual contestation or disagreement admitted in the theorization of principles of justice at all. Democracy is not a source of values or legitimacy for, or even really important to, the functioning of the ideally just society; it is one of the trappings of the ideally just society.

† There's a strange gulf between cosmopolitan approaches to *democracy* and to *justice*. The former do frequently propose global constitutional systems, including forms of global federalism based upon world, regional, and state-level parliaments, while the latter insist that moral cosmopolitanism need not entail political cosmopolitanism (e.g., Charles R. Beitz, "Social and Cosmopolitan Liberalism," *International Affairs* 75, no. 3 [1999]). I don't support world federalist proposals, but I find the differential treatment of democracy revealing; see Michael Goodhart, "Global Democracy through Transnational Human Rights," in *Global Democracy and Its Difficulties*, ed. Anthony Langlois and Karol Edward Soltan (London: Routledge, 2009).

IMT is nonetheless enamored of justificatory strategies that mimic or gesture toward agreement. This fulsome embrace betrays, I think, a deep anxiety on the part of ideal theorists about the kind and quality of validity their methods can deliver. IMT treats justice as a philosophical puzzle; solving it entails reasoning from first principles to substantive conceptions of justice, paying strict attention to conceptual clarity and analytic rigor, in hopes of attaining something like logical irrefutability. Short of that high bar, validity remains doubtful. So in a world where, as Bernard Yack argues, "our disagreements about justice are often just as deep and intractable as our disagreements about the best way to live,"[30] this analytic approach can't deliver what IMT needs. When first principles are themselves in dispute, there's little analytic philosophy can do; it's simply not equipped to adjudicate among rival conceptions.‡

That's where the familiar forms of pseudoagreement come in. Actual agreement is unlikely, given the deep differences Yack cites. The attempt to reach it would anyway be profoundly dangerous for IMT, since allowing meaningful politics in the ideally just society risks the departure from or rejection of the moral conception of justice. Instead we get fake agreement, in the form of arguments about which conceptions of justice people would or could or should endorse based on claims about nonrejectability, hypothetical choice situations, and so on. That real people never get the chance to agree (or not) is steadfastly ignored, an embarrassment akin to a drunken uncle on Thanksgiving. It is as if the differences between real and imagined agreement were merely incidental.

There are good reasons to be suspicious of this substitution of "agreement" for agreement. To begin with, the presumption that agreement on justice is necessary and desirable and that it can be realized through philosophical argumentation encourages us to treat disagreement as some kind of error, depravity, or recalcitrance.[31] This approach denies that

‡ That's because it can't adjudicate among conflicting grounds or premises. It might rule out a conception of justice as improperly derived or justified in light of its own premises (an internal critique of validity), though this would invalidate the specific conception, not the premises themselves.

people's diverse perspectives and social positions could lead them to think differently about what justice is and requires; it thus risks becoming a form of epistemic injustice in its own right, excluding, marginalizing, or diminishing some forms of knowledge and ways of knowing. In addition, agreement—especially fake agreement—can easily silence opposition to dominant understandings of (in)justice and reinforce existing social structures of domination. Besides, talk of "agreement" and "choice" and "consent" lures us into imagining that IMT allows meaningful scope for democracy in the ideally just society when, as we have seen, it does not and cannot do so.

Ideal theorists might object that to adopt a political approach or to permit democratic input into our definitions of justice or allow them to be determined politically would be to concede that might makes right. Without a philosophically defensible, ideal, moral conception of justice to guide and constrain politics, the door is open to tyranny, relativism, even nihilism. If moral and philosophical considerations don't trump political ones, anything goes! I am not of course proposing that we should read off the meaning of justice from existing political arrangements, or that we should allow majorities to determine what justice means. What I am proposing, to foreshadow the argument of Part II, is that if we want to understand and combat injustice, it is vital—analytically and normatively—to take politics seriously. Analytically, that means treating disagreement about justice and injustice as a regular (normal) feature of our world, not as an error or an indication of turpitude, and theorizing it accordingly. Normatively, it means treating claims about justice and injustice as ideological—not moral—claims, and theorizing their normativity and their contingency accordingly.

Once again, the subordination of politics to morality is not, in itself, a problem—*if* one cares about questions like "What would a society governed by my spotless ideal of justice look like?" It is problematic if one is committed, as I am, to giving people a say in determining the principles according to which they are governed and if one is concerned, as I am, with making political theory relevant to the world we live in.

Distortional Thinking

IMT relies heavily on abstraction and idealization in the formulation of ideal moral conceptions of justice. There has been a great deal of discussion about whether IMT is too abstract, whether its use of idealization makes it irrelevant to real-world considerations.[32] Most internal critics of IMT ("nonideal theorists") seem to believe that vigilance is a satisfactory response to these concerns, adopting a "use with caution" position. With Charles Mills, I worry that this optimism may itself represent "a failure to appreciate the nature and magnitude of the obstacles to the cognitive rethinking required" of our assumptions about how the world works and how to theorize it.[33]

All theorization makes use of *abstraction*, which is the distillation of broad empirical tendencies out of the chaos of mere facts for the purposes of generalization and clarification.[34] All abstractions are descriptively inaccurate. That, in many respects, is the point: by misrepresenting the world through silence or simplification, it is sometimes possible to understand it better. There is nothing inherently wrong with abstraction, though it presents theorists with a Goldilocks problem: both too much abstraction and too little diminish the utility of our theories, which can lose contact with the real world or become mere descriptions of it. *Idealization* is the representation of the world as one thinks it ought to be. While abstraction presents a simplified or clarified picture of this world, idealization depicts a world better than this one by some lights. Like abstraction, idealization is inherently inaccurate: any vision of a better world will necessarily be descriptively false of this one.

Charles Beitz argues that whether idealizations misdescribe reality is not a relevant concern; they establish worthy ends at which reformers can aim.[35] This position is right as far as it goes, but unfortunately it doesn't go very far, for two reasons. First, in IMT idealization does not simply establish normative aspirations; it concretizes those aspirations in specific assumptions about the nature and features of the ideally just society, often sanitizing, euphemizing, or just ignoring unpleasant or inconvenient features of our world in the process. Second, those assumptions distort our thinking about justice and inhibit our ability to conceptualize injustice adequately by dismissing it, making it invisible, or treating it as aberrational.[§] In its most extreme forms, Mills maintains, IMT can become "a distortional complex of ideas, values, norms, and beliefs that reflects the non-representative interests and experiences of a small minority" of people.[36]

Onora O'Neill offers some excellent examples of how idealization euphemizes and sanitizes unpleasant features of our world. Arguing that problematic idealizations "abound in discussions of transnational economic justice," she highlights as problematic the "conceptions of fully rational agents, of ideally sovereign states, and of wholly impermeable boundaries, of which no actual cases are to be found." To idealize states as protectors of their citizens' human rights, she laments, is a "grotesque parody" of reality that obstructs theorizing about how best to deal with oppressive regimes.[37] Similarly, she complains that many theories of the global economy employed by ideal theorists make the negative effects of neoliberalism appear to be merely unfortunate byproducts of ineluctable market forces, when in fact they result predictably from economic institutions designed to secure the privileges of the powerful.[38] Her conclusion is that "theories of justice which build on assumptions like these may forfeit practical relevance."[39] I certainly agree, but I also believe that the problems go deeper.

Anne Phillips shows us that idealization can sometimes lead (or permit) theorists to dismiss injustices, taking as her example idealized conceptions of "the market" as a fair and efficient means of allocating resources. Such ideals are often difficult to assess, given that we have only nonideal experiences to inform our thinking about them. As a result, deficiencies in existing markets can always be explained as results

[§] According to Mills, IMT disguises structural domination by silencing oppression (e.g., by ignoring how systematic oppression shapes the basic structure of society), by idealizing social institutions (e.g., by ignoring their impact on the poor or treating it as exceptional), and by idealizing the cognitive sphere itself (e.g., by ignoring how deeply concepts like race shape our thinking); Mills, "'Ideal Theory' as Ideology," 168–69. Distortion of this kind need not be conspiratorial or even conscious in intent (ibid., 172), though it might of course be either.

of deviations from the ideal, even though we have no way to know if the ideal is possible or whether it would work as we anticipate.[40] At the same time, an idealized market theory will often simply dismiss concerns about issues like women's pay inequality by asserting that the inequality exists (only) because the full power of the market has not yet been unleashed. In this case, idealization proves to be an obstacle to understanding because it explains away the problem rather than explaining it, mispresenting how markets actually function in the process.[41]

Idealizations can also render some injustices (theoretically) invisible. Consider Rawls's conceptual map of a world populated by territorially unified and internally homogenous "peoples."[42] Allen Buchanan shows that this idealization makes it impossible to think cogently and critically about certain problems of justice and injustice. The problem is not simply that the concept of "peoples" is false about the world; the problem is that issues like secession and civil war are rendered invisible or illegible by Rawls's assumptions about the social, cultural, political, and territorial unity of peoples, impeding theorists' imagination of institutional and political responses that might address those issues.[43] This invisibility means that Rawls's account can't offer guidance on problems like violence between ethnic or religious groups because the theory itself doesn't recognize the possibility of such conflicts—it has nothing to say about just relations between such groups, whose existence its idealizations deny. Idealizing peoples in this way also makes it impossible to conceive of rebellions or secessionist movements or demands for cultural recognition and autonomy except in ways that presumptively reject the legitimacy of the underlying claims and grievances.

Finally, idealization renders injustice aberrational.[44] This important point is often missed, or misconstrued, in heated debates about Rawls's treatment of race and gender. (To simplify the discussion, I focus solely on race in what follows.) Rawls and his defenders argue that since racial discrimination has no place in an ideally just society, it should not be considered in the formulation of principles of justice—that is, in the ideal theory stage. Ingrid Robeyns maintains that ignoring racism and racial discrimination at this stage is acceptable and even desirable because there shouldn't be any racism in an ideally just society;[45] we don't assume away economic inequality, by contrast, because it is contentious—because what justice requires in this respect is not obvious.[46] Racial inequalities are addressed in nonideal theory, where we confront deviations from or exceptions to the ideal.[47]

It's precisely this treatment of racial injustice as a deviation or aberration that concerns me. There is no doubt that an ideally just society would be free of racism; my doubts relate to how this kind of idealization affects our ability to recognize, theorize, and combat structural racism. The problem is not that IMT won't see racism and its effects as unjust, or even that it won't recognize it as pervasive. The problem is that conceptualizing racism and racial discrimination as aberrational gives us little leverage on how to resolve or even how to think critically about structural racism and white supremacy. If a society is *structured by* racial or other inequalities, those inequalities will shape public thinking, meaning that ideal conceptions of justice will themselves reflect social prejudices and power relationships.[48] Take as an example the ideal of color-blindness, which models the absence of racism in the ideally just society. This ideal reflects deeply racialized thinking: it's probably only possible to imagine ideal justice without reference to race and racism if race and racism have not figured prominently in one's own experience of injustice. To hold that justice need not acknowledge or respond to the brutal and ongoing history of racial discrimination, oppression, and exploitation is to treat that history as irrelevant or incidental to the meaning of justice itself.

Of course, in nonideal theory, the ideal of color-blindness will recognize the mass incarceration of blacks in the United States or the widespread use of violent, often lethal force against them by police and prison officials as injustices. But it is unlikely to be able to formulate adequate responses to such problems because it can only conceive of them as deviations or aberrations from a presumed norm. (This problem is exacerbated by the notorious "strict compliance" assumption, which stipulates that, in ideal theory, all people are presumed to act justly and to do their part in upholding just institutions.)[49] The likely recommendations include policies to correct bias in policing and sentencing and improve training and oversight. It's the ideal of color-blindness that allows officials to blame the problems on "a few bad apples" whose actions do not "reflect our values" or "who we are" when the barrel itself is rotten.[50] Conceptualizing injustice as aberrational makes it impossible to think cogently about power relations—about the ways in which, for example, law enforcement (including the judicial and prison systems) in the United States has historically policed the racial boundary as a way of maintaining inequalities and insecurities fundamental to our basic social and economic arrangements.[51] Moreover, if color-blindness is the ideal, color-consciousness, its opposite, appears as a kind of injustice within IMT; anyone who has watched a well-meaning liberal try to defend affirmative action against the charge that it is discriminatory has glimpsed this problem. This theoretical aversion to color-consciousness makes it easy for white people to ignore a racist past and racist institutions in the present, hard for people of color to initiate discussion of their past or present experiences of oppression, and nearly impossible for society to countenance racial preferences, apology, reparations, or other measures that might begin to address structural racism in a comprehensive way.

Tommie Shelby's work is sometimes cited as proof against such charges by ideal theorists. His essay "Justice, Deviance, and the Dark Ghetto" offers a blistering condemnation of the racial injustices of American society.[52] Shelby's primary aim is to consider how injustice in the basic structure of a society affects the obligations of its citizens—specifically those citizens who suffer the most from that injustice. Ideal theorists cite Shelby, I think, because he relies on broadly Rawlsian notions of justice and fairness—even though he explicitly states that he presumes nothing about "the soundness of the overall Rawlsian apparatus."[53] Shelby shows how racial and geographic discrimination interact in the related domains of housing, employment, and education to rob many black Americans of opportunity, citizenship, and dignity. He argues that there "appears to be a conspiracy to contain, exploit, and underdevelop the black urban poor, to deny them equal civic standing and punish them when they refuse to accommodate themselves to injustice" and that this appearance reflects "an underlying failure of the social scheme to fully embody the value of reciprocity."[54]

Shelby describes two ways in which a society might be unjust. "The first way is when the publicly recognized standards for judging the justice of the basic structure are sound but the institutional arrangement of the society fails to satisfy these standards"; in other words, "society fails to live up to its own professed [worthy] ideals."[55] This is essentially the way that IMT regards the real world, and Shelby's claim that structural racism represents a failure fully to realize the moral ideal of reciprocity seems to suggest that his is a similar assessment. A second way in which a society might be unjust is when "social arrangements may fit the prevailing conception of justice in the society or the political views of the ruling elite but nevertheless be unjust"; in this case, the dominant conception of justice is an ideology that helps to sustain an oppressive regime.[56] This is closer to the way Shklar understood justice, and Shelby's claims about conspiracy, punishment, and "the ill will, selfishness, and callous indifference of many . . . citizens" seem more consistent with this understanding.[57] Shelby's ultimate position remains unclear: he endorses Rawlsian reciprocity and fair equality of opportunity as worthy ideals but also regards appeals to them as futile, fearing that social justice may be out of reach "unless the ghetto poor take on a good deal of the burden in reforming their society."[58] He finally evades the question by arguing that the contrast between the two forms of injustice, "although analytically useful, is too stark for practical purposes"; some aspects of a society, such as its educational and economic institutions, might be regulated by a corrupt ideology, Shelby argues, while others may be reasonably sound.[59]

It seems like a stretch to me to read this essay as a validation of IMT as an approach, even acknowledging that Shelby approves of broad Rawlsian notions of fairness and opportunity. Note that where justice functions ideologically, IMT faces a dilemma: either the ideal conception itself is functioning ideologically, or we must admit that the prevailing conception of justice is unjust. The former case is clearly problematic for IMT; the latter is equally troubling, however, because it shows that injustice is not merely an aberration or departure from ideal justice, as IMT's model of reform assumes. Whatever Shelby's views on Rawls or on IMT, what I find particularly valuable and provocative in his work is his willingness to confront these uncomfortable possibilities in forthright and productive ways.

All of the worries discussed here under the heading of distortional thinking contribute to a deeper theoretical concern that ideal justice can function ideologically in a variety of ways: by reflecting (and protecting) the interests and privileges of those whose experience most closely approximates the ideals and who benefit most from their maintenance;[60] by naturalizing and normalizing injustices associated with dominant or structural injustice, obscuring power relations from view and making them hard to recognize and theorize;[61] and by directly sustaining and promoting injustice. This possibility undermines the two core assumptions of IMT. When justice functions ideologically, it becomes a flawed and fraught standard against which to define and identify injustice. Similarly, when justice functions ideologically, it can't provide reliable or impartial guidance in the way that IMT requires. Again, there needn't be a conspiracy involved. The problem might simply result from our epistemological limitations (bounded experience), or it might reflect unconscious or semiconscious biases (racism or misogyny). Then again, collusion cannot be ruled out. Whatever the case, the key point for now is that IMT lacks the theoretical resources to address injustice when justice functions ideologically, and it may become complicit in exacerbating and perpetuating injustice in such cases.

CONCLUSION

In this chapter I've started to unthink IMT by questioning its core assumptions and methods and highlighting its pathologies and the debilities they cause. I've done so, again, with the aim of defamiliarizing IMT for readers, of making it seem less obvious or necessary. Specifically, I've shown that IMT, as an approach to theorizing about justice, depends on troubling assumptions about injustice and about ideal guidance. These assumptions in turn give rise to several related pathologies—theoretical paralysis, a reflex to subordinate politics to morality, and distortional thinking—that are congenital to the approach itself and thus represent generalized (rather than idiopathic) debilities. Together, I have argued, these pathologies severely disable the project of understanding and combating injustice.

This discussion illustrates the need for an approach that can theorize injustice without the problematic assumption that agreement about justice is a prerequisite for doing so. Such an approach must take politics seriously, analytically and normatively, paying attention to power, conflict, and politics and to the distinctive normativity and contingency of claims about justice and injustice. That is, an alternative approach must grapple with the ideological character or potential of justice, incorporating it into a theoretical framework that can make sense of justice as a contested claim on conflictual political terrain. Finally, to avoid becoming an instrument of injustice, such an approach must allow for and accommodate democratic input into theorizing about justice and must enable meaningful democratic politics. I shall have much more to say about these matters in Part II of the book.

2

Barking Up the Wrong Trees

Chapter 1 identified and criticized the core assumptions of IMT, diagnosed three pathologies traceable to those assumptions, and considered their implications for theorizing injustice. In this chapter I continue the effort to unthink IMT, turning my attention to debates on some of the key questions about global justice typically addressed by ideal theorists. Within IMT, these questions appear natural, straightforward, and necessary to working out what justice requires. I show that these debates are afflicted, to varying degrees, by the three pathologies described in the previous chapter. Moreover, I contend that the questions themselves, rather than being normal or necessary, are really artifacts of the approach—that is, they are important mainly because the core assumptions of IMT make them seem important. Given the problems with those assumptions and their associated pathologies, answers to these questions are unlikely to be of much help in coming to grips with injustice in the real world. Once we have defamiliarized these questions, the dogged determination of ideal theorists to answer them appears like a lot of barking up the wrong trees.

I have selected three familiar questions through which to make these arguments: questions about the selection of principles of justice, about the scope of justice, and about the effects of the global order on the poor. These are certainly not the only big questions taken up by global normative theorists, but anyone familiar with the literature will recognize them as central. I realize that these questions and the wider debates in which they are enmeshed overlap significantly; my discussion of them as separate or independent is thus somewhat artificial. My hope is that whatever misrepresentations this treatment introduces are compensated for, as in cubist painting, by the advantages of seeing the various dimensions of the subject in new and provocative ways that prompt reconsideration of their relation to one another and to the whole.

Again, my aim is to show that some of the standard questions that IMT poses about justice are unnecessary and largely unhelpful in making sense of injustice (at least as typically framed). Fulfilling this aim does not require an extensive overview of the literature, and I won't provide one here.* In fact, I won't engage much with the *substance* of the arguments I consider at all, won't develop systematic counterarguments, and won't defend alternative conclusions. My intention here is not to provide better answers to the familiar questions that IMT poses; it is rather to show that the debates about these questions suffer from the pathologies of IMT and that the questions themselves are not ones to which answers are necessary or particularly helpful in theorizing and combating injustice.

SELECTING PRINCIPLES OF JUSTICE

Within IMT, justifying principles of justice is, for reasons we've seen, the initial and primary task of theorizing justice. Many global normative

* Anyone seeking a good overview might consult Laura Valentini, *Justice in a Globalized World: A Normative Framework* (Oxford: Oxford University Press, 2011), chs. 2–5.

theorists, cosmopolitans and social liberals alike, have followed John Rawls in adopting constructivist reasoning as a method of justifying their preferred principles. The constructivist method[†] relies on shared (if often inchoate) notions about justice to guide the theorist's thinking about its specific demands. These notions are modeled into an initial choice situation, or ICS, a "purely hypothetical situation characterized so as to lead to a certain conception of justice."[1] Rawls was very clear that the role of constructivism "is simply to make vivid to ourselves the restrictions that it seems reasonable to impose on arguments for principles of justice and therefore on these principles themselves."[2] "The crucial thing," he emphasizes, "is not to use principles that are contested"[3] because the point of the exercise is to turn the selection of principles of justice into a problem of rational decision.[4]

I have argued extensively elsewhere that constructivist reasoning is inappropriate in global normative theory because "in the absence of background consensus [about important questions of global justice], constructivism *necessarily* begs key questions: the method only gives us persuasive answers when . . . begging them seems 'natural and plausible' in light of existing widespread agreement."[5] Such agreement manifestly does not obtain globally (and may not obtain domestically); thus, constructivist reasoning fails on its own terms, relying on controversial assumptions that presuppose a substantive view of justice.[6] Although many ideal theorists whistle past this particular methodological graveyard, I regard this criticism as fatal for constructivism—at least in *global* normative theory. Nonetheless, I present another lethal argument here, one showing that constructivist reasoning, as a form of IMT, is mortally debilitated by the three pathologies described in the previous chapter. I do so both to further substantiate my critique of IMT and to help make the search for ideal principles of justice seem a less natural or obvious starting point for

[†] Note that "constructivism" in the philosophical sense is not the same as constructivism in international relations theory, nor should it be confused with what is sometimes called social *constructionism* in the social sciences. For an introduction to the constructivist method in moral theory, see John Rawls, "Kantian Constructivism in Moral Theory," *Journal of Philosophy* 77, no. 9 (1980).

thinking about injustice. My critique focuses on the constructivist account offered by Gillian Brock, whose scholarship I greatly admire. Her work is principled, her proposals creative, and her writing animated by evident concern and compassion for those enduring injustice. In addition, Brock is admirably explicit and precise in modeling her initial choice situation (ICS)—unlike a disconcerting number of theorists who merely gesture toward "what reasonable people would choose." She's an ideal foil precisely because of the rigor of her work.

I won't spend too much time on the first pathology, theoretical paralysis, because its symptoms are less obvious when focusing on a single account. (There will be plenty of evidence of this pathology later on.) Still, Brock herself is clearly aware of the problem. In taking issue with Darrel Moellendorf's argument for a global difference principle, she endorses a broad "Rawlsian" (i.e., constructivist) approach but parts with Moellendorf over whether people would choose a global difference principle.[7] What's interesting about her argument for my purposes is less her reasoning or her conclusions than her frank acknowledgment that in order to reach a different conclusion she'll have to construct her ICS differently; she's well aware that the design of the choice situation determines the "choices" that follow. Brock can (and knows she can) tweak the design of the ICS to alter the results of the "deliberation." As with all contract theories, one gets out what one builds in; this alone makes the prognosis with respect to paralysis grim.

The second pathology, the subordination of politics to morality, is much more evident in Brock's account and foreshadowed by my use of scare quotes above. To see it, we can accept her invitation to imagine ourselves as randomly selected, decision-making delegates to a global conference convened to determine "what would be a fair framework for interactions and relations among the world's inhabitants."[8] As delegates, we are instructed to be self-interested, because people tend to have limited sympathies or impaired moral imaginations (though sometimes we become more sympathetic by imagining ourselves in other people's positions).[9] We are ignorant of our allegiances but appreciate that our decisions will be binding on us, and everyone, regardless of the social positions we occupy (rich or poor, old or young, etc.). We have access to any information we might require about history, psychology, economics, or other subjects but know very little about global demographics; this prevents us from gambling on (for instance) our being part of the sixth of the world's population that is Indian and designing the system to favor Indians.

> We delegates do receive specific information about the world, however, including data about our urgent global collective problems and how we will have to cooperate to solve them . . . about various threats to peace and security, including threats we face as a result of the increasing number of people who have access to weapons (especially weapons of mass destruction) and the activities of terrorists and drug traffickers . . . [and] about environmental challenges, such as, the destruction of the ozone layer and climate change. Information about risks to health, such as highly infectious diseases or global pandemics, will also be included. This will make clear that these problems have global reach and require global cooperation if they are to be resolved. Some of this material will also maintain that the people of the world are in a state of interdependence and mutual vulnerability; they have to rely on each other if they are to achieve an acceptable level of peace, security, or well-being, both now and in the future.[10]

On the basis of this information, we delegates are charged with determining a fair basic framework for governing the world's inhabitants, understanding that any entitlements selected will generate financial obligations.

Brock determines that we will choose a minimum set of protections and entitlements, calling it imprudent to select policies that might be unbearable for anyone. As people who rationally value the prospects for a decent life, we will deliberate about the content of such a life and reach agreement on two general principles of justice: "that everyone should enjoy some equal basic liberties and that everyone should be protected from certain real . . . risks of serious harms."[11] We will insist on basic liberties, including protection from assault or extreme coercion; freedom of movement, association, speech, conscience, and dissent; the right to exit a society; and guarantees against torture, imprisonment without trial, and other forms of extreme coercion. Mindful of our vulnerability in unregulated markets, we will opt for "certain guaranteed minimal opportunities" that would be "strongly influenced by a certain baseline minimum—namely, what is necessary for us to meet our basic needs for ourselves."[12] These general protections would entail social and political arrangements to deliver these important baseline goods, extensive rules to protect against threats to their realization, and organizations to monitor and enforce these rules. Moreover, we will choose governance structures that will protect our vital interests while retaining as much control for ourselves as possible, consistent with the protection of our basic needs and liberties. So we will stick with states as primary loci of government, given our risk-aversion and our legitimate worries about the potential tyranny of a global state.[13]

I've written the preceding paragraphs in the first-person plural to underscore a jarring shift: Brock initially addresses her readers in the second person, asking "you" to imagine "your" role in the proceedings, but after literally inviting us to the conference, she does all of the deliberating and deciding for us, telling us what we will decide and explaining our thinking and motivations to us along the way. Of course, she has to do so—there is no conference, no deliberation, no randomly selected delegation. It's all purely imagined, a hypothetical scenario modeled to yield the intended principles of justice.

I shall have more to say about those principles and the assumptions that inform them in a moment. For now, however, the point I want to underscore is that there is no *choice* in the initial choice situation, no politics. Though depicted as a site of democratic deliberation, it is in fact a procedure designed to deliver a particular conclusion. The ICS "works" as a heuristic device just insofar as it allows a very broad consensus to emerge—which is to say, allows the theorist to describe her conclusions as a consensus that would or should emerge, since there is no actual dialogue or decision involved. Many constructivists seem to join Brock in thinking that "the thought experiment identifies certain situations as morally desirable because it can be expected that delegates would choose them, when suitably situated"[14] and that the expectation of their being chosen provides them with normative force.[15] But again, there are no actual people and no actual choices: the mechanism clarifies how a theorist reasons about justice, but it demonstrates nothing about the validity or legitimacy of her conclusions.[16]

By disguising the selection of principles of justice as a "choice" made by "delegates," constructivists dress those principles in a pseudodemocratic drag, giving them a veneer of legitimacy through consent while disguising the rather different reality underneath. Worse, the monological reasoning in the ICS assumes either a false uniformity of people's views, values, and ways of thinking or a disconcerting theoretical arrogance. The notion that any individual, however well meaning, could adequately and responsibly speculate about how people whose lives have been shaped by radically different experiences would or should think about justice is itself a kind of injustice, a form of epistemic domination. Despite the illusion of democratic debate, there is no allowance for actual discussion or contestation of the decision on principles. Notably, Brock's list of the equal basic liberties "we" "choose" includes no guarantee of democracy (though association and dissent are protected).

This concern leads us directly to a discussion of the third pathology, distortional thinking. Brock does her best to characterize the ICS in a way that will seem perspicacious and impartial to many readers, but it is nonetheless profoundly and disturbingly marked by positional and ideological distortion. Like most global normative theorists, Brock writes from a position of tremendous privilege in a country whose well-off residents benefit enormously from existing global arrangements. Most of us have never experienced the kind of poverty with which our theories grapple, and our thinking is profoundly, if unconsciously, shaped by that (lack of) experience. From whose vantage point is it "gambling" if delegates know and act on the knowledge that five-sixths of the world's population lives outside of the OECD (which itself includes some pretty vast economic disparities)? From what perspective is it irrational for them to choose massive redistribution and fundamental economic restructuring rather than equal opportunity and minimal guarantees? Who gets to determine that such questions should be treated as philosophical puzzles to be resolved by theorists rather than as questions of power embedded in long histories of domination, oppression, and exploitation, questions to be contested politically?

The point is not to insinuate any indecency or ill intent on the part of Brock or of anyone else; none of us is free of such biases. But IMT amplifies positional distortion because of its dependence upon idealization. To see this, consider the information Brock provides to delegates in her ICS. They receive only minimal data about existing hierarchies of power in our world, how they emerged, and how power operates. The issues they prioritize read like a list of First World concerns: the main threats to peace and security are WMDs, terrorism, and drug trafficking; there is no mention of rape, slavery, grueling poverty, racial oppression, sectarian strife, civil war, or other injustices prevalent in our world. The main environmental challenges are ozone depletion and climate change—significant problems, to be sure—but there is no discussion of preserving indigenous lands from rapacious development, of access to and struggles over water (including its privatization), of threats to biodiversity, of genetic piracy, of monoculture, or of the specific perils facing many poorer countries in connection with climate change, including the mass displacement of populations and the instability it sparks. Challenges to health include infectious disease and global pandemics—the (stereo)typical fears the rich see as emanating from poor, disease-ravaged countries to threaten the safe and sanitary West. There is no mention of infant or maternal mortality, access to clean water, adequate nutrition, sanitation, or basic life-saving medicines and healthcare. The right to exit is, to many millions of displaced people in our world, a cruel joke without a parallel right to enter another country and live a dignified life there, and the notion that states will protect people's basic liberties and provide for their basic needs will surely come as a shock to many of those same people and to millions of others who suffer under oppressive, predatory, or simply incompetent or undercapacitated states or who live at the margins of supposedly "developed" societies.

Such distortion is surely unintentional, but as I have shown, IMT is congenitally prone to it. It is unlikely that principles of justice emanating from thought experiments so poorly calibrated with the experiences of most of the world's people could be helpful in identifying or remediating concrete injustices. The problem is not—as critics of my stance have alleged—that theories or theorists of justice would fail to recognize rape or inadequate nutrition or land theft as injustices; I have no doubt that they would. The problem is rather that the method, through its reliance on a singular theoretical perspective and on monological reasoning, treats everyone in the ICS as in effect facing *the same choice* from *the same position*. The idealizations that shape the ICS, conceived from positions of privilege, erase or obscure historical and ongoing racism, patriarchy, colonialism, and economic exploitation—they obfuscate the structural injustices that produce and perpetuate radically different social positions through a kind of epistemic denial or forgetting that allows the (mis)characterization of the ICS in the first place.

This positional distortion is compounded by the related ideological distortion pervading Brock's account (and most others). Though she is deeply concerned about poverty and critical of social, political, and economic arrangements that generate or perpetuate it, Brock nonetheless adopts a fundamentally neoliberal understanding of the global economy without question or criticism, perhaps without being conscious of doing so. To be clear, and fair: she sharply challenges some of the outcomes generated by neoliberal economic arrangements and some of the rules and institutions that permit or facilitate those outcomes. She does not, however, question core neoliberal assumptions, and as a result her critique is constrained by them. For example, Brock argues that "global justice requires that all persons are adequately positioned to enjoy prospects of a decent life."[17] Notice first that to be "adequately positioned to enjoy prospects" is a far cry from "enjoying." Neoliberal ideology often disguises injustice in the language of opportunity, which Brock firmly embraces, conceiving the neoliberal economic system as a reservoir of opportunities and focusing on ensuring that those opportunities are more widely accessible.[18] Brock also emphasizes the "stress placed on enabling people to help themselves" in her ICS.[19] This focus on individuals and their opportunities deflects critical attention away from structural factors, from relations of domination and exploitation, in global economic arrangements and reinforces the neoliberal narrative of personal responsibility for poverty. It's not surprising, then, that Brock conceives of the challenge of global poverty in terms of "[considering] how modifying some of our institutional arrangements can assist in" its alleviation.[20] She concentrates on the absolute position of the worst off while treating inequality as a secondary and subsidiary issue.[21] In doing so, she tacitly accepts the neoliberal orthodoxy that inequality is the inevitable and appropriate result of differentials in talent and effort.

Her main concern is with the "benefits" of "trade liberalization." After reviewing the weak and mixed empirical evidence on the topic, she endorses the theoretical "presumption" that liberalization will, on average, reduce poverty in the long run[22] and focuses on policies designed to ensure that growth is "pro-poor."[23] These include giving developing countries "more control" over their liberalization programs and, since the benefits of liberalization are "not automatic," ensuring that the poor "should receive special help" to enable them to avail themselves of the "positive opportunities" created by neoliberal reform.[24] This move turns the lack of evidence for this idealized notion of trade liberalization into a kind of support for it via arguments to the effect that "we can do better!"[25] Such reasoning renders poorly substantiated empirical claims impregnable by theoretical presumption, curtailing the consideration of alternatives. Similarly, when Brock worries about people's vulnerability to "unregulated" markets, her reasoning reinforces the neoliberal cant that markets generally protect people and "enable" the poor, when in fact a great deal of systematic exploitation is effected precisely through very well-regulated markets and ancillary policies of social control and economic discipline.[26]

The point is that neoliberal ideology is deeply insinuated into much of Brock's reasoning; she naturalizes the neoliberal global economy, turning it into something like a tornado that leaves destruction in its wake but which arises of its own from conditions beyond our control. On this view, the theorist's job is to assess and clear up the damage, to design better shelters and warning systems, and to suggest ways to fund insurance schemes that aid the victims. Naturalizing neoliberalism in this way turns many of its most fundamental and problematic claims—about "free" trade and "free" markets, competition, comparative advantage, cooperation, and individual responsibility—into idealized background assumptions in the ICS. As such, they cannot be thematized or subjected to critique because they constitute the parameters of reasoning in the ICS. So instead of thinking about fundamental economic restructuring, for instance, (nonexistent) delegates are reduced to (not actually) reasoning about how to make an extensive system of economic domination and exploitation more fair—about how to get a bigger slice of a poisoned cake, as Devaki Jain has said.[27]

Constructivists cannot plead that the information available to delegates in the ICS—their general knowledge of history, economics, and so on—could accommodate alternative viewpoints like the one informing my critique. That's partly because the question of what information they receive is itself ideological and highly charged. Much "textbook knowledge" of economics is unabashedly and uncritically neoliberal; Ha-Joon Chang has shown persuasively that the orthodox economics literature on trade, for example, is both historically inaccurate and economically unsound; it is, however, highly effective in rationalizing an economic hierarchy that benefits and reinforces the rich and powerful states at the expense of developing countries.[28] If genuine disagreement about such basic knowledge were admitted into the ICS, however, the device would lose its heuristic utility: in such a case no determinate reasoning would be possible and no outcome could be presented as rational or impartial. As I've shown elsewhere, constructivism can't resolve disputes about competing values, theories, or principles of justice; it can only help us to distill our thinking about those we agree upon.[29]

The final problem I want to highlight is that by naturalizing neoliberal orthodoxy and relying on idealization, Brock obfuscates the domination and exploitation that structure actually existing economic arrangements. She asserts, for instance, that it's "commonly acknowledged that the Uruguay Round [of trade talks that created the World Trade Organization] could not have been completed successfully without developing countries' approval, and that this would not have been granted in the absence of better access to foreign markets for their goods." The impetus to reach agreement, she continues, "meant that these concessions to developing countries had to be made, which gave them not inconsiderable input into the process and outcome."[30] Bracket the assumption that the Uruguay Round was a "success" (from whose point of view?): contrary to Brock's assertion, it's widely known that the rich countries worked out the deal behind closed doors and offered the developing countries a take-it-or-be-left-out choice.[31] Her idealized reasoning (formal consent gives one power so concessions must have been made) and acceptance of neoliberal understandings render domination of this kind invisible; as a result, her numerous well-meaning and seemingly sensible proposals—such as for new taxes to fund antipoverty programs or for giving greater control over liberalization processes to developing countries—ignore that low taxes on the rich and on corporations and a one-size-fits-all trade regime are policies that protect and advance the interests of powerful states, corporations, and capitalists. They are nonnegotiable features of the neoliberal order. Put differently: much economic injustice is not an accident or an oversight; it is the will of the strong.

THE SCOPE OF JUSTICE

The *scope* of justice "refers to the *range of persons* who have claims upon and responsibility to each other arising from considerations of justice."[32] Despite this rather anodyne description, perhaps no issue is more fiercely disputed among global normative theorists. The stakes are high, both theoretically and politically: the scope of justice dictates who owes what to whom, who can claim justice from whom—and who foots the bill. Early rounds of this debate pitted *statists* (social liberals), who contend that justice obtains solely or primarily within national or "domestic" political societies, against *cosmopolitans* (globalists), who maintain that its strictures apply universally; more recently, *hybrid* and *pluralist* accounts have proliferated. Interestingly, theorists defend each of these positions from within IMT. I shall not take sides in this debate; my aim is again to show how the three pathologies of IMT permeate it.

The primary pathology evident in the debate over the scope of justice is theoretical paralysis. The debate itself instantiates this paralysis: the scope question arose with contemporary global normative theory 45 years ago and remains as intractable as ever—arguably more so with the advent of pluralist accounts. The paralysis reflects that arguments regarding the scope of justice are inherently and unavoidably question-begging. What I mean is that the various grounds (premises or reasons) to which theorists appeal in arguing their respective positions, which are supposed to provide objective or impartial bases for fixing the scope of justice, already presuppose an answer to that question. Each of these grounds—common humanity, mutual respect, basic needs and rights, the bonds of political association, participation in a system of social cooperation, subjection to coercion, mutual entanglement within a shared institutional order, common ownership of the earth, and many more—assumes or implies an answer to the question about scope (and they can be combined in ways that yield different and multifaceted answers). It's doubtful that such arguments can avoid begging the questions they are supposed to resolve.[33] As a result, the debate churns on and on.

Statism

Statist arguments often appeal to ethical grounds like mutual respect or the value of nationalism in restricting the scope of justice primarily to compatriots. Luis Cabrera (a cosmopolitan) points out that in mutual respect arguments

> the distinction between compatriot and foreigner is central, yet there is little consideration of the defensibility of the initial move that establishes the distinction, or of continuing moves to restrict membership. In fact, there is an inherent circularity in a mutual-respect argument. It cannot justify the creation of distinct sets of members

> and non-members, because it justifies restriction of distributions based on the impositions already being made on members. . . . It essentially justifies priority to compatriots by pointing to the fact that individuals are compatriots, thus it cannot speak to whether establishing a system of compatriot priority is defensible.[34]

Similar problems beset arguments premised upon the constitutive role of nations in shaping people's identities and defining their common purposes. David Miller, for instance, argues that state institutions are evidence against cosmopolitan theories.[35] National communities remain the primary sites of identification, loyalty, and lived experience in our world, Miller insists; the state is a "constraining fact" with which political theory must reckon.[36] In treating the existence of states and national ties as constraining facts, however, Miller simply stipulates what he's supposed to show: the ongoing importance of states is certainly a feature of our world, but whether and how far it should constrain normative reasoning is precisely the point at issue. Matthias Risse's recent case for the "normative peculiarity" of the state faces the same problem: there is no way from "normative peculiarity" to "moral priority" that does not assume what it's supposed to demonstrate.[37]

Some statist arguments appeal to their own psychological plausibility and resonance with "common sense" morality.[38] Such arguments are also question begging: that we inhabit and experience an international system of states predisposes and encourages us to view our membership of particular states as natural and significant; the existing system produces a bias in its own favor.[39] Statists cannot cite the recalcitrance or uneasiness of those privileged by existing arrangements as proof of a natural sense of compatriot priority or evidence of a psychological limit to our moral sense or sentiments.[40]

Even so-called relational arguments, which treat the scope of justice as contingent upon the nature and extent of social and economic *relationships*—and which might appear to offer an empirical path out of this circularity—remain question begging. Michael Blake, for instance, maintains that only ongoing systems of intense coercion, like those found in state legal systems, occasion or justify a concern with relative deprivation and give rise to claims of distributive justice. On his view, redistributive justice is the compensation liberal citizens deserve for the restrictions on their autonomy imposed by the coercive state.[41] But notice that these arguments already take for granted the legitimacy and significance of the international states system and the primacy of states within it. As Ryan Pevnick argues, this existing institutional order is itself a result of distributive political conflict and involves intense, ongoing coercion; it already reflects injustice. Even if we accept Blake's claims about coercion, Pevnick points out, policies and institutional arrangements with similarly coercive features already exist outside of states.[42]

There is no way to evaluate the facts in such cases without appealing to the normative positions that the evaluation itself is supposed to establish. If a theorist wants to work out what types of coercion trigger demands of justice, she needs criteria to define the salient types and levels of coercion, and these criteria will already implicitly answer the scope question. Blake maintains that only ongoing, systematic coercion through an established legal system raises questions of justice; contrariwise, Laura Valentini considers any coercion that undermines freedom (democratic autonomy) unjust.[43] The "facts" can't decide the matter because they look different in the light of different normative considerations.

Cosmopolitanism

Cosmopolitan accounts are question begging in most of the same ways as their statist rivals.[‡] Constructivist arguments are perhaps the ones most commonly used to justify cosmopolitan conclusions. Yet as we've seen, the information "delegates" are given in the ICS—in this case about the significance of states, the importance of nationality, the nature and extent of relations among people(s), the threat of global tyranny, and so

‡ I write "most of" because there is little psychological circularity in globalist arguments, for obvious reasons.

on—unavoidably decides precisely the points at issue and determines the "selection" of statist or cosmopolitan principles (constructivists defend both).[44] As Charles Jones has put it, the principles yielded by global constructivist reasoning "are not in fact adequately defended by appeal to hypothetical agreement [because] the correct characterization of the initial choice situation presupposes a substantive view about justice," which makes all constructivist conceptions of justice "potentially question-begging."[45] (I suspect Jones inserts "potentially" here only to soften the blow.)

Cosmopolitans too have relied on relational arguments. Early on in the global justice debates, many cosmopolitans criticized Rawls's restriction of his theory to a "closed system in isolation"[46] and embraced a view that global integration had already given rise to something like a global basic structure (GBS) that warranted the global application of Rawlsian principles of justice.[47] Some rather quickly backed away from such arguments, worrying either about their empirical defensibility or that they "missed the point."[48] Since then, relational arguments have mainly been invoked by statists (as we have seen) to justify a more limited scope of justice. Yet two recent and vigorous cosmopolitan defenses have given new life to the GBS argument.

Arash Abizadeh systematically analyzes the premises of three prevalent anticosmopolitan relational theories, which rely on arguments from social cooperation, from pervasive impact, and from coercion. He maintains that these arguments conflate questions about the *site* and the *scope* of justice and that, once this confusion is remedied, it becomes clear that "regardless of which theory is used to interpret it . . . the Rawlsian idea that the basic structure is the primary subject of justice implies that justice is today global in scope."[49] Andreas Føllesdal similarly argues, against prominent objections to the idea of a GBS, that "the normatively salient features and functions of a domestic BS that give rise to standards of distributive justice among subjects . . . also hold for the GBS."[50] Both are powerful arguments, and the cosmopolitan position on the extent of the impact of global and transnational forces on people's lives is much nearer my own view than the statist position. But rather than take sides in this debate, the point I want to make is that the *debate itself* doesn't admit of closure because the positions on either side inevitably rely on *evaluations* or *interpretations* of facts already informed by a substantive position on the points at issue.

To see this, consider Abizadeh's argument against the "pervasive impact" justification of social liberalism. On this view, "the basic structure is simply defined in terms of the profound or pervasive impact of social institutions on persons' life chances."[51] This is its "fatal flaw," Abizadeh writes, because he thinks it's obvious that there exist some global or "foreign" institutions that have a "profound" impact on people's lives.[52] Surely he's right, but he's missing the key point, which concerns whether the "profound" impact that global and transnational institutions have on people's lives is as "pervasive" as that had by states. I don't pretend to know the answer, but I do know that—as will be apparent in the next section—much depends on which theories one adopts about how the world works. If one adopts an "institutional" thesis about economic growth and development, for example, one is likely to regard the impact of the state as much more pervasive than that of global integration; one's assessment of coercion will likewise depend on whether one regards states and markets, respectively, as liberty-promoting or liberty-inhibiting.

To put the point another way: appeals to the "facts" in such matters are rarely dispositive because they are not innocent. The facts on which theorists rely are already interpretations of the world, already value laden.[53] Miller maintains that it's the job of theorists to "interrogate the facts," to ask why things are the way they are and what reasons we have for condemning particular arrangements as unjust.[54] I don't disagree, but we can't do so independently of our values and our interpretative frameworks—which perhaps explains why it often seems that instead of interrogating the facts theorists are trying to extract confessions from them, to implicate them in our favored normative schemes. The point is not that strong and persuasive arguments cannot be made, but rather that they can usually be made in many directions and that disputes about the interpretive frameworks we adopt can't be resolved analytically. In short, interpretation is inescapable; this inescapability profoundly shapes the approach I develop in the second part of this book.

In an effort to sidestep empirical debates altogether, some cosmopolitans shun relational arguments and appeal instead to abstract principles of justice. Simon Caney's case for global egalitarianism is typical. His argument relies on four analytic claims: first, some valid moral principles exist; second, valid moral principles apply to everyone who is similar in a morally relevant way; third, persons throughout the world are similar in a morally relevant way; fourth, we can conclude that some moral principles exist with universal form and scope.[55] Caney advances parallel arguments for civil and political rights and for global economic justice by relying on these claims, arguing that the same grounds that justify rights and distributive justice at the domestic level also justify them at the global level: "A distributive theory, that ascribes rights and claims on the basis of certain universal attributes of persons, cannot at the same time restrict the grounds for those claims to a person's membership or status within a given society."[56]

Never mind how Caney knows that there are valid moral principles and knows what they are; his argument too is question begging.[57] This is clear in his example of two isolated societies whose inhabitants are morally identical in all relevant ways. Caney maintains that any moral grounds supporting distributive justice domestically would also support it globally, since there could be no justification for limiting the scope of principles based on universal moral attributes.[58] But as Risse rightly objects, the very matter in dispute is whether social or associative relations themselves are morally relevant. Even perfect similarities between the two societies cannot decide the question, which turns on the appropriate balance between these similarities and differences, such as the bonds of political association, shared history and common projects, and so on.

Hybrid and Pluralist Accounts

Recently, some critics working within IMT have concluded that "the discussion of global justice should move past the intellectually and politically limiting debate between cosmopolitanism and its nationalist or statist antithesis."[59] One scholar writes that "finding a philosophically convincing alternative to [this debate] is the most demanding and important challenge contemporary philosophy faces."[60] Some theorists have developed "hybrid" accounts in an attempt to split the difference between the two camps. Lea Ypi argues that defenses of the normative relevance of states are usually coupled with critiques of all cosmopolitan arguments for global egalitarian principles of justice; by separating the two questions, we can see that the normative relevance of the state is consistent with and in fact entails a global egalitarian commitment, at least to the equal distribution of power among states.[61] She advocates a "statist cosmopolitanism" based on an appropriate blend of realism about collective political agency (organized today through states) and idealism about the principles of justice (which are cosmopolitan).[62] Laura Valentini attempts to steer a "middle course between cosmopolitanism and statism," focusing on coercion as a signal of possible injustice. Since coercion manifests in both domestic and global relations, she argues, a theory that locates injustice in unwarranted coercion will speak to both levels.[63] Each of these positions is thoughtfully conceived and carefully argued, and both deserve more attention than I can give them here. Both, however, are question begging.

Valentini's reliance on coercion as a signal of potential injustice is intriguing, but her argument glosses over the question of whether different types or systems of coercion have different normative salience in different contexts—the question central to relational accounts. To assume that similar relations of coercion have similar normative significance in different relational contexts begs the question. Ypi relies heavily on assessing ideal and nonideal considerations at the "fundamentally appropriate" level of analysis; by arguing that political agency is appropriately nonideal and principles of justice appropriately ideal, she generates her statist cosmopolitan account in which cosmopolitan ideals of egalitarian justice are promoted by state-based political agents. Whatever the attractions of this account, Ypi deems statist agency appropriate because states are the dominant political units in world politics today. As we've already seen with statist arguments generally, that's a question-begging inference, because it assumes that a realistic account of agency is more appropriate than an aspirational one. It also ignores significant evidence about the influence of transnational social movement organizations and global civil society.[64] (Ypi never justifies the appropriateness of her cosmopolitan ideals; hers is an exercise not in justification of principles but in thinking through their most likely pathway of realization.)

While hybrid accounts try to combine statist and cosmopolitan elements into cohesive conceptions of global justice, "pluralists" argue that there can be multiple grounds of justice, each of which entails different principles with different scopes and subjects.[65] On this view, "a political morality can be political in a capacious sense, that is, sensitive to the circumstances and associative conditions, to the 'different cases of types of relation' for which it is formulated."[66] Cohen and Sabel argue that different normative principles are appropriate to different types of relations, depending on the normatively salient features of those relations.[67] They call for a theory in which the "spread of new relations and novel forms of association" triggers further exploration of complex questions to do with scope, inclusion, and responsibility.[68] Pluralism tries to take seriously both ongoing political associations and emergent forms of political and economic interaction without conceiving them as mutually exclusive. In acknowledging multiple grounds of justice, it recognizes the diversity of considerations that might apply in different institutional or functional domains of social interaction. It also acknowledges the contingency of moral considerations upon constantly changing empirical facts about our world.

Rather than resolving or dispelling the stalemate on scope, pluralist accounts merely fragment it. This multiplies the trouble by two factors. First, the complexity of the task that pluralism sets itself is staggering: it requires articulating a complete theory of justice for each ground in each distinct domain and practice of justice.[69] Risse's pluralist opus develops several distinct theories of justice, each resting on different grounds and conveying different implications regarding scope and responsibility—all of which is synthesized into a monumental "internationalist" conception of global justice of staggering complexity.[70] Second, there is no reason to think that pluralists can avoid begging the scope question with respect to each of the domains and grounds of justice they consider. Together, these factors risk making paralysis epidemic. Moreover, while both hybrid and pluralist accounts propose innovative answers (or approaches) to the scope question, in doing so they reinforce its salience and reify its centrality in global normative theory, a centrality there is good reason to question.

I won't say much about the second and third pathologies in connection with the scope debates, except to make a few brief but important points. The debate certainly subordinates politics to morality by conceiving questions of scope as philosophical rather than political problems. In fact, questions about the scope of justice and injustice are hotly contested in practice. Whether it's the Palestinian question, the treatment of women in Afghanistan (a Western media favorite), or wages and working conditions in poor countries, questions about the grounds and scope of justice are deeply political and highly politicized, yet IMT treats them as philosophical puzzles. Conflicts over when and where various rules of justice obtain are the stuff of politics; answers get worked out, contingently and imperfectly, through contestation, not through casuistry.[§]

Some versions of pluralism endorse what is frequently called a practice-dependent approach to justice (following Sangiovanni),[71] and this approach might seem to offer an antidote to the contagion I've described here. The idea animating practice dependence is that principles of justice should be justified with reference to the institutions in which they apply; what justice is and requires will vary with the content provided by the aims and functions of particular practices (institutions, systems, etc.) as these are understood by the participants in the practices themselves.[72] Practice-based approaches encounter numerous difficulties of their own. They exhibit an inherent status quo bias because they treat existing institutional arrangements as in some sense settled and worthy of justification.[73] In addition, they idealize practices

[§] That's not to say that arguments don't matter; it's rather to suggest that they don't matter in the way that IMT imagines—a point to which I return in chapter 7.

themselves, which are imagined as products of conscious design possessing clear aims and desirable functions.[74] Historical institutionalism teaches us that institutions originate in complex and contentious political environments that often leave them muddled, incomplete, or riddled with inconsistencies. Institutions evolve (or fail to) in response to opportunities and constraints that can be internal or external to the institutions themselves; they sometimes deviate from or even subvert the original intentions of their creators—assuming those were clear in the first place.[75] Moreover, existing institutional practices are shot through with power relations; institutions are as often instruments of domination as they are implements of justice; despite their attention to "political realities," practice-dependence theorists frequently overlook this point. To reconstruct an institution's operative principles and call this "justice" is to attribute to institutions moral purposes and moral coherence that they might well lack.[76]

The problem of distortion manifests more generally in debates over scope because those debates typically ignore the past. This is especially problematic for nonrelational theories, which provide abstract normative grounds for justice (such as egalitarianism or basic needs), but it also holds for relational views. Social liberals explicitly treat "international" relations as secondary (normatively and conceptually) to "domestic" ones, and they and their globalist counterparts focus almost exclusively on *present* relations.** This is hardly surprising given IMT's assumptions: the scope of justice is supposed to be a question that can be answered *in principle*, not one mired in the messy "nonideal" circumstances of complex histories and their enduring legacies. While the geographic scope of justice is fiercely debated, its temporal scope is barely considered in IMT.

** For an exception see Lea Ypi, Robert E. Goodin, and Christian Barry, "Associative Duties, Global Justice, and the Colonies," *Philosophy and Public Affairs* 37, no. 2 (2009). Of course, many theorists have demonstrated that the invocation of supposedly "nonrelational" ideals and universals has a problematic and oppressive history in practice; my point is that ideal theorists engaged in debates on the scope of justice don't typically regard such histories as relevant to (philosophical) determinations of scope.

THE GLOBAL ORDER AND THE CAUSES OF POVERTY

Global normative theorists have long debated whether and to what extent the global order causes poverty or harms the poor. This ostensibly empirical question might seem an unlikely one for theorists, though different empirical explanations of how the world works have clear and divergent normative implications for who owes what to whom. My primary purpose in this section is, once again, to demonstrate that the debate on this question exhibits all three of the distinctive pathologies of IMT.

I focus here on the two most prominent adversaries in this debate, Matthias Risse and Thomas Pogge.[††] Risse maintains that the global order *does not* harm the poor, attributing most failures of economic and political development to domestic political culture and arrangements rather than to the international system. He bases his claim on what economists refer to as the institutional thesis, the idea that "the quality of domestic institutions . . . primarily explains why a country is rich or poor."[77] More specifically, the institutional thesis holds that institutions function as rules of the game: they structure incentives for social, political, and economic exchange. Institutions can be thought of as constraints that shape human interaction. Such constraints are beneficial when most people follow them; government can implement some of them by fiat, but not all. A legal system, a culture of trust, and shared views of justice can only emerge and persist in a context of broad domestic support. Risse also subscribes to what he calls the authenticity thesis, "the view that especially those institutions requiring broad domestic support matter for prosperity."[78] On this view, there is little that outsiders can do to help improve things in poor countries: intervention can ruin domestic institutions but can't create them.[79] While bad institutions are not necessarily the fault of those living under them, institutions cannot improve without their support.[80] Geography and global integration also play a role in determining levels of poverty and growth, Risse allows; all three factors influence one

[††] Although their dispute occurred a decade ago, both thinkers are still routinely cited and remain the key figures in the debate; this is itself perhaps evidence of paralysis.

another.[81] Yet he maintains that any influences of geography or integration work through institutions, so that the institutional thesis takes them into account by default.[82]

Combining the institutional and authenticity theses, Risse concludes that aiding development is not a question of transferring resources: any transfer of resources that would help alleviate poverty would require better institutions, he argues, since good institutions are necessary for distributing aid.[83] Sustainable measures that might lead to enduring change also require good institutions to work. So, good domestic institutions are critical for reducing poverty, and there is little that outsiders can do to establish them.[84] These considerations lead Risse to advocate a limited duty of assistance in connection with global poverty. This duty is qualified by the institutional and authenticity theses: assistance can only help with analysis, with the identification of internal champions of reform, with training future leaders, bureaucrats, and professionals, and with technical assistance.[85]

Pogge has been the leading proponent of the view that poverty *is* a harm inflicted on the poor by citizens of rich countries, who impose an unjust global order upon them. Wealthy westerners benefit immensely from the global order, thanks both to the legacy of past injustices and to the current rules, which keep the deck stacked in our favor.[86] While acknowledging that local (domestic) factors are important in explaining the persistence of poverty, Pogge finds the prevailing emphasis on them misleading. The huge variation among countries seems to implicate domestic factors as the main culprits in poverty, but Pogge insists that even if local factors explain all of this variation, there is an overall level of performance attributable to global factors. He illustrates the point using the example of a classroom: student-specific factors explain all the variation in grades, yet the quality of teaching determines part of the overall level of achievement.[87] A global political economy explanation is needed to explain "why incompetent, oppressive, and corrupt governments which are unresponsive to the needs and interests of 'their' populations are so very frequent in the developing world," Pogge argues.[88] Such an explanation must take social rules and institutions into account: "the existing world order is itself a crucial causal factor in the prevalence of corruption and oppression in the poor countries."[89]

Three features of the global order contribute directly to the persistence of poverty and the fragility of democracy in poor countries, Pogge maintains. The first is bribery: rich countries only recently made bribery illegal and eliminated corporate tax incentives and other encouragements to bribery. Further, they entice elites in developing countries to buy stuff (from military hardware to development projects) that their countries really don't need; these elites, lured by the prospect of high-level networking opportunities and often encouraged by subsidies or kickbacks, pay little attention to the price, quality, and utility of the stuff they buy. A second feature is what Pogge describes as the resource privilege: the global order essentially permits anyone who gets control of the presidential palace to legally sell a country's resources (or access to them) and to reap the profits. This privilege provides an incentive to coups, Pogge argues, and encourages the mismanagement of national resources. A third, related feature of the global order Pogge calls the borrowing privilege: anyone who gets control of the presidential palace can borrow in the name of the country, and successor governments must make good on those debts or lose access to global credit markets and international assistance. This privilege facilitates the ability of corrupt governments to stay in power and cripples democratic successor governments, again strengthening the incentive to make coups.[90]

When we consider how these global factors contribute to the persistence of poverty and bad government, it becomes apparent that purely local explanations are incomplete in two respects: they don't ask *why* domestic conditions are as they are, and they hold the prevailing global context constant.[91] Once we recognize that that context could be altered, Pogge argues, it becomes clear that the global order is *unjust* because it "foreseeably produces a reasonably avoidable excess of severe poverty and of mortality from poverty-related causes." Further, this unjust order is *imposed* on the poor in the sense that it is reasonably avoidable: there are nearby feasible alternatives that could be (but are not) adopted.[92] Pogge concludes that citizens of rich countries are harming the poor by imposing an unjust global order upon them; the rich have a moral obligation to stop (or to pay compensation for continuing).[93]

I do not intend to join this debate directly; my purpose is once again to show that it exhibits all of the pathologies associated with IMT. Three related factors make a prognosis of paralysis warranted in connection with this debate. First, both sides acknowledge that local and global factors figure significantly into any explanation of poverty. Second, global normative theorists are not typically also political economists, and we are in a poor position to assess, never mind to contribute substantively to, debates about rival explanations for poverty. Finally, it's in any case difficult to separate our assessments of these explanations from their normative implications; the rival political economy explanations invoked in this debate are less grounds than proxies for the normative positions the theorists ultimately endorse. Political theorists can readily avail themselves of credible economic explanations supportive of their preferred normative conclusions, meaning that disagreement about whether the global order harms the poor is less an empirical than a normative or interpretive question after all (again, the inescapability of interpretation). Together, these considerations suggest that the present debate might go on indefinitely.

It's vital to see the fundamentally normative character of this debate to appreciate fully how politics gets subordinated to morality within it. The empirical considerations debated by Risse and Pogge give the conversation a presentist slant, providing a pretext to deny or dismiss history. This charge might seem unfair to Pogge in particular, who—in a widely anthologized 2004 essay—acknowledges the "legacy of great inequalities" left by historical processes of slavery, colonialism, and genocide.[94] Yet in that same essay he explicitly decides to "leave aside the continuing legacies of historical injustice and focus on the empirical view that at least in the post-colonial era . . . the causes of the *persistence* of severe poverty . . . lie within the poor countries themselves."[95] Pogge offers a vigorous challenge to that view, as we have seen, but his case rests entirely on claims about rich westerners' active cooperation in inflicting knowable, foreseeable, and reasonably avoidable human rights violations on the poor, violations enacted through our participation in social institutions.[96] Risse, meanwhile, flatly denies that outsiders can do anything to restore or rebuild weak or damaged institutions—even if they did the damage! In both cases, history becomes irrelevant. Arguments like these, however unintentionally, depoliticize the past, putting questions about acknowledgment, restitution, and reparation off the table.

The debate on whether the global order causes poverty or harms the poor also depoliticizes the present by treating the global order largely as given; in this, it is typical of global normative theory. The idealizations on which this theoretical approach relies (inadvertently?) hypostatize neoliberal capitalism, making real, natural, and permanent what is actually a contingent configuration of power relations justified within a particular ideological framework. In this way, the debate limits the political imagination; its reliance on idealization of existing conditions encourages theorists to accept that there is no alternative to the extant neoliberal economic order. Neoliberal capitalism becomes a kind of background condition, insulated from thoroughgoing critique. Active global resistance to neoliberal economic policies finds no place in these debates.

Again, this charge might seem unfair to Pogge, whose criticisms of bribery and of the borrowing and resource privileges challenge how existing social institutions and arrangements contribute to the persistence of severe poverty. As with my criticism of Brock, I want to insist here on the difference between criticizing specific arrangements and their effects and criticizing their underlying assumptions and ideology. I don't mean to denigrate Pogge's monumental contributions to the field, but it's noteworthy that his conjectures about the persistence of severe poverty never question the existing trade regime, structural adjustment programs, or any other basic aspect of the neoliberal economic order, never mind the overt militarism and informal imperialism through which it is maintained. Indeed, he explicitly embraces the possibilities offered by *nearby feasible alternatives* to our existing social arrangements, in effect an embrace of incrementalism that rules out deeper transformation as *distant* and *infeasible*. (Feasibility has become something of a cottage industry within IMT, and I worry that theorists working in it have paid insufficient attention to the ways in which the very discussion about feasibility helps to reinforce the logic of "no alternative.")[97] Pogge's own proposals for incentivizing large pharmaceutical companies to develop drugs to treat diseases afflicting poorer countries embrace and seek to leverage the logic of neoliberal capitalism. (If this seems unclear, ask yourself: why publicly subsidize corporations rather than universities to do this research? Why permit patents on publicly funded discoveries and inventions?)[98]

Finally, distortion pervades this debate as well, much of it resulting from the extreme simplification and idealization already mentioned. Theorists on all sides of the debate, for instance, typically assume that the global order affects rich and poor *countries* in uniform ways, masking the profoundly divergent effects that neoliberal capitalism has within countries. Firms and their employees will be affected differently depending on their exposure to global competition and their dependence on international capital, currency, and commodity markets; differently skilled and educated workers will be affected differently in different local and national economies.[99] Further, the focus on rich and poor countries easily distracts attention from the rapid growth of inequality *within* rich and poor countries alike. (Inequality *among* countries is actually narrowing slightly, driven by trends in China and, to a lesser extent, India.)[100] Moreover, if we think of poverty as resulting from a global order "imposed" by the rich (countries) on the poor (countries), it is almost impossible to theorize increasing poverty and growing inequality in Europe or the United States as problems of global injustice or to think about how they might be related—economically or politically—to poverty and underdevelopment elsewhere. Such simplifications distort our understanding of crucial economic processes, and they are also deeply depoliticizing, reinforcing a kind of nationalistic thinking about the global economic order that obscures potential bases of transnational solidarity.

Treating economic injustice as a problem between countries also deflects attention away from a more complex and nefarious web of power relations among elites in rich and poor countries who collude in the maintenance of the existing order.[101] Local elites often embrace structural adjustment programs, for example, regardless of their general effects on growth, poverty, and inequality, because they and their cronies—including local and international bankers, businessmen, and financiers—benefit from increased foreign direct investment, revamped tax and regulatory schemes, and relaxed restrictions on capital flows that such policies portend—never mind rigged privatizations, outright repression of labor, and worse.[102] The same applies, it should be emphasized, in richer countries undergoing "austerity." This enthusiasm cannot simply be attributed to corruption or to authoritarian rule, since these very policies are actively promoted by international financial institutions as important ingredients in the recipe for "good governance" or required as conditions of aid or loans (which themselves mainly benefit the elite).

The last point indicates that distortion also results from the naturalization of neoliberal capitalism discussed earlier. The pervasive focus on inequality in global normative theory provides a telling example. Because the basic parameters of the neoliberal capitalist economy are accepted as constraints on our theorizing, global economic injustice gets conceived mainly in terms of inequitable distribution—of wealth, income, opportunity, whatever—among states and individuals. These assessments are often linked to the "unfairness" of global trade, financial, and institutional arrangements. Notice that this way of thinking assumes that inequality and unfairness are deviations from an ideal in which economic arrangements function fairly to promote equality.

For those who see the global order as at least partly implicated in harming the poor, redistribution seems like the obvious solution. Indeed, many global normative theorists recommend transfers to bring us closer to their egalitarian ideal, focusing on justifying the form and degree of redistribution required and changes to the rules of the game needed to create a fairer global economy. I am not necessarily opposed to transfers—although it's important to note that what's typically proposed within IMT is the redistribution of the *surpluses* generated by an exploitative economic system. My objection is to the way in which IMT focuses on the symptom of injustice—inequality—rather than on the underlying disease: a global economy constructed and maintained by powerful actors precisely to ensure the very inequalities to which ideal theorists object.[103] Idealizing economic relations in terms of fair institutions and a level playing field is not a harmless, aspirational misdescription of reality.[104] Rainer Forst complains that it's euphemistic to characterize the global economy in terms of "cooperation" or "interdependence" when it is really "a context of force and domination."[105] I would go further: such idealizations fundamentally distort and obscure the power relations that uphold and enforce the existing global order.

In sharp contrast to the idealized view, very many people experience the global economy as a system of power relations that comprehensively subjugates them to domination by rich countries and individuals, by corrupt governments, by banks, criminal networks, transnational corporations, and international financial institutions that often ally with and support those governments—all backed by the military might of the "developed countries." Many people also experience this subjugation as continuous with prior systems of domination, oppression, and exploitation that have ravaged their communities, societies, and economies for centuries. For them, the global economy functions as a system of exploitation; a system that functioned fairly to promote equality and improve their lives would represent a deviation, not the norm.

As a result of these distortions, the theories generated by IMT are neither informed by nor informative about actually existing injustices—the former by design, the latter as a consequence. Part of what's missing is an explicit critique of the broader ideological context in which these various economic processes and institutions are embedded. The focus on institutions and on the distribution of wealth and income diverts critical attention from the relationships of power at work in the global economic domain. In fact, proposals to curb inequality through redistribution may inadvertently serve the interests of the powerful and privileged by normalizing and legitimating the structures that generate egregious inequalities in the first place. Likewise, calls for fairer rules and more level playing fields in global trade relations actually discourage thoroughgoing critique of the trade regime itself and render possibilities like the democratization of economic governance almost literally *inconceivable* within the parameters of IMT.

As the larger discussion makes clear, however, IMT lacks the resources to generate a critique of its own idealization of the existing neoliberal global economy because it cannot see itself as ideological. It similarly is unable or neglects to problematize the ideological framework in which its ideals "make sense" in our world. Without both kinds of critique, it will be impossible to imagine pathways of social transformation likely to have a significant impact on the profound economic injustices in our world.

CONCLUSION

In this chapter, I've shown that some of the central debates in global normative theory are severely afflicted by the pathologies of paralysis, depoliticization, and distortion that plague IMT. While the various pathologies may be more or less pronounced in each case, their overall effect on our thinking is, I believe, crippling. This conclusion, or my specific criticisms, might appear harsh to some readers. I think that's because I'm not challenging specific conclusions but rather the familiar ways of thinking that lead to them. The exercise of defamiliarization is inherently unsettling—by design. The whole point is to make IMT seem strange, bewildering, and inherently problematic.

It's not just that IMT generates flawed answers to the questions it asks; those questions themselves are largely specious, artifacts of the approach itself. It's only because IMT assumes that moral principles of justice are the necessary conceptual and procedural starting point for thinking about (in)justice that debates about the selection of such principles and their scope appear so momentous. Obviously, a normative argument needs an account of the values and ideas that animate it; the point is that this needn't be an ideal moral account. Likewise, we need to address questions about responsibility for injustice, but treating them as part of a philosophical puzzle about the scope of ideal moral principles of justice is not the only or even a very helpful way of tackling them. In short, questions about the selection of principles and their scope only appear urgent if one subscribes to an approach that makes them urgent. From the outside, it appears that ideal moral theorists are barking up the wrong trees in pursuing these questions. The pathologies I identified in chapter 1 and illustrated here are easily avoided if we give up on the approach that engenders them. Admittedly, questions about the functioning and effects of the global economy are important ones to answer; here it's a case of "right tree, wrong bark." IMT poses these questions in a way that requires abstract and idealized answers to them, answers that unavoidably distort the complexities of the global economy and the operation of power and ideology within it. As a result, we've seen, the answers it generates prove unhelpful and deeply problematic.

Critics might object that while I have identified serious problems with the approach, the appropriate response is not to abandon but rather to do better with it. With more cautious idealizations, more carefully specified choice situations, more nuanced understandings of the global economy, more pluralistic reasoning, and so on, we can specify the conceptions of justice we need to take on problems of justice in the nonideal (real?) world. This objection misses my two main points, which are that the pathologies I've diagnosed are congenital to IMT and so can't be avoided and that we anyway *don't* need ideal moral principles to theorize justice and injustice. I'm suggesting—so far indirectly—that a more realistic approach to these matters is called for, one that pays greater attention to the knowledge and experience of people who endure and struggle against injustice and to the politics in and through which those struggles play out. IMT ignores the concrete power relations that create and sustain injustice and the wider ideological context in which they operate.

In the next chapter I being to reconceptualize the problem by engaging with IMT's realist critics, who share many of my concerns and propose an alternative approach. While I endorse their rejection of IMT's moralization of politics, I believe it goes too far, becoming a sort of blanket rejection of normativity in political theory. Through this engagement, the key challenge for an alternative approach becomes clear: to integrate a realistic analysis of conflict, power, and politics with an account of normativity that avoids moralization but enables substantive critique and orients practical action.

PART II

Reconceptualizing the Problem

3

Getting Real?

In this chapter I begin to reconceptualize the problem of theorizing justice and injustice in political theory, as a first step in developing an alternative to IMT that helps theorists to do better in addressing concrete injustices. One of the key lessons of the first two chapters is that such an alternative must adopt a more realistic approach to politics, paying greater attention to people's actual experiences of injustice and to the conflicts, power relations, and ideologies that shape the politics of injustice. It's thus appropriate to begin by engaging with IMT's realist critics, who share many of these concerns.

Realist political theory is an expression of frustration with, and a reaction against, the "colonization of political theory by ethics over the past 40 years."[1] In its contemporary incarnation, realism is more a genre of criticism than a school of thought[2]—a "bricolage."[3] Realists worry that ideals too distant from our actual political experience will lack relevance outside the closed systems of thought in which they are worked out.[4] They complain that IMT's obsessive search for the idealized grounds of the legitimate exercise of political power erases key aspects of political life and encourages the "fairly spectacular neglect" of the most typical and fundamental features of politics, a shortcoming that contributes to—and also reflects—processes of idealization that render IMT's prescriptions irrelevant or inert.[5] The solution to the problem, realists typically agree, is greater descriptive accuracy, greater attention to power and politics, and the strict avoidance of moralism.

The rejection of moralism is the unifying and distinguishing feature of contemporary realism, the "anti-Kantian gesture" that promises to redeem political theory through greater attention to real politics.[6] While some realists equate moralism with a utopianism that they believe makes IMT "largely *practically* irrelevant," others locate the problem with moralism in absolutism, the insistence on resolving all contextual judgments into categorical ones.[7] Moralism, in whatever form, distracts political theorists from questions arising *within* politics, which realists conceive of as a distinctive and perhaps autonomous domain of human activity.[8] Hence their call for more attention to the "circumstances of politics," or what Williams called "the first political question": the supposed imperative that people reach a binding and legitimate social agreement backed by state power.[9]

Realist approaches direct theoretical attention to *political* questions, and they also transform our understanding of political institutions. Realists see institutions not as embodiments of or vehicles for moral ideals but rather as arenas for taming and constraining clashing values and interests and allowing for productive conflict. There is no guarantee that institutions will remain fixed in their purpose or function or retain their relation to their founding purposes, on this view, making it all the more urgent to resist the temptation to understand them in moral(ized) terms.[10] Similarly, for realists the crucial decisions facing politicians and citizens are those to do with the exercise of public power in empirically and ethically messy situations and with the legitimacy and maintenance of the political order.[11] If political theory is to be relevant, it must concern itself with understanding how institutions work and evolve and what possibilities and constraints they present, not with principles that—even if implemented—would quickly be distorted or discarded.[12] Given this antimoralist stance, it's hardly surprising that many ideal theorists perceive realism as a complete rejection of normative judgment, "a pernicious foe that needs vanquishing" on the march toward justice.[13]

My own thinking about IMT and its debilities has been profoundly shaped by realist criticisms, as have my views on taking power, conflict, and politics into account in theorizing justice and injustice. I worry, however, that in their rush to "get real," many theorists have ignored or dismissed questions of normativity, leading them to endorse deeply conservative accounts of justice and political possibility or to abandon substantive critique and prescription altogether. So while realism is a good place to begin reconceptualizing the problem, it's only a first step: by working through its assumptions, errors, and omissions, I'll argue that while an attractive alternative to the moralism of IMT must be *realistic* in making power and conflict central to its conceptualization and analysis of politics, it must also include a conception of *normativity* that enables the analysis and critique of injustice and enables a transformative politics.[14]

SEN'S COMPARATIVE APPROACH: REALISM "LITE"?

There are (at least) two distinct—and incompatible—understandings of realism in play among contemporary political theorists. One treats realism as a subset of nonideal theory, emphasizing the search for effective principles of justice that can address immediate and pressing concerns; the other breaks with "contemporary Anglophone political theory's moralistic tendency to proceed as a branch of applied ethics."[15] The recent work of liberal social theorist and philosopher Amartya Sen qualifies as realist only on the first understanding, even though he eschews appeals to ideal or transcendental justice.[16]

Sen has argued quite forcefully that it's both logically and practically possible to progress toward a better society, one that has less injustice and less suffering, without reference to spotless justice. Making comparative assessments, which involves "ranking alternative societal arrangements" as more or less just, does not require ideals at all; in fact, identifying "fully just social arrangements is neither necessary nor sufficient" when undertaking such assessments.[17] It is "entirely incorrect," Sen insists, to think that either rigorous comparison or effective reform requires ideals of justice of the type sought by the transcendental approach.[18] In Sen's view, IMT simply isn't asking the right questions about justice and injustice and, as a result,

> the answers that . . . [it] gives—or can give—are quite distinct and distant from the type of concerns that engage people in discussions of justice and injustice in the world—for example, iniquities of hunger, illiteracy, torture, arbitrary incarceration, or medical exclusion as particular social features that need remedying.[19]

His conclusion is unequivocal: "The question 'What is a just society?' is . . . not a good starting point for a useful theory of justice. To that has to be added the further conclusion that it may not be a plausible end point either."[20]

As we have seen, IMT presumes that determining and justifying ideals is a necessary first step in evaluating proposed reforms, but Sen disagrees, noting that "the characterization of spotless justice, even if such a characterization were to emerge clearly, would not entail any delineation whatever of how departures from spotlessness would be compared and ranked."[21] Sen utilizes three vivid metaphors—involving Mount Everest, a flute, and the Mona Lisa—in arguing that IMT is unnecessary, infeasible, and unhelpful (respectively) in what he regards as the most important task of a theory of justice: making comparisons and facilitating choices among alternative social arrangements.

First, Sen claims that ideals of justice are unnecessary, a point he illustrates through an example involving Mount Everest. One does not need to know that Everest is the world's tallest mountain to assess which of two less lofty peaks stands higher than the other.[22] Sen thinks that we can rank and choose among different policy options by comparing the different social realizations available under each option, using capabilities as a metric of evaluation. The capabilities approach identifies the basic human capabilities needed to live a minimally good or decent human life and uses this information to evaluate social development and human freedom under different social arrangements. Development is conceived of as a process that expands the range of different "functionings" that a person might fulfill by making full use of her capabilities (regardless of whether she chooses any of those functionings). These functionings are closely tied up with human freedom.[23]

Sen seeks to embed these evaluations, and the social choices that flow from them, in a process of "open impartiality" designed to ensure that all policy proposals undergo and survive public scrutiny, accommodate the perspectives of outsiders, and recognize a plurality of reasons.[24] He invokes Adam Smith's "impartial spectator" in explaining how open impartiality might work: unlike Rawlsian impartiality, which requires a "common standpoint" or agreement in the original position, the impartial spectator heeds "voices from a distance." The spectator is not an outside arbitrator but rather represents a thought experiment through which other perspectives and experiences can be introduced into deliberations about justice. Sen sees three distinct advantages in "consulting" impartial spectators. First, doing so allows a theory to take into account the interests of others affected by a choice; second, it helps to avoid local parochialism, enabling a society to challenge its own norms and understandings. Finally, it provides greater insight into what is feasible.[25] These advantages should, Sen believes, improve the quality of public deliberation, which he sees as essential to democracy and to informed social choice.

The capabilities approach can certainly facilitate comparative assessments, providing a useful, multidimensional metric that can (partially) overcome the incommensurability of values. Gerald Gaus has recently claimed, however, that it can lead to suboptimal social outcomes. Sticking with the Everest motif, Gaus characterizes Sen's view as a "climbing" or "continual improvement" account of the realization of justice.[26] When faced with any (social) choice, we elect the path that takes us higher, confident that we'll be moving closer to the summit, even if we don't know what or where it is. The climbing view presumes what's known as a Mount Fuji distribution, essentially one in which the terrain of justice looks something like this:

In mountaineering terms, choosing the higher path always takes us closer to the summit; in theoretical terms, the preferable choice in any pairwise comparison of alternative social realizations takes us closer to the optimum.[27]

Gaus, with Simmons and others, worries that the climbing view is misleading and dangerous because it assumes a Mount Fuji distribution; they recommend an "orienting" view, in which choices about what path to follow are made with reference to the ultimate goal, the summit or social optimum we are trying to reach.[28] They do so because they worry that the terrain of justice may be much more uneven than the climbing view assumes. Imagine a case of what Gaus calls "rugged terrain," in which the distribution of social realizations looks more like this:

The climbing view won't do in such cases. In mountaineering terms, choosing the higher path in every instance might lead us to a lesser summit than we could otherwise obtain; in theoretical terms, the preferable choice in any pairwise comparison of alternative social realizations might leave us stuck at a local optimum significantly inferior to the overall optimum. To choose well in such cases requires that we orient ourselves to the highest summit.[29*]

Climbing and orientation represent two different ways of organizing the pursuit of justice. Sen's climbing view assumes that we don't need to identify the summit in advance, while Gaus's orienting approach assumes that we do need to know, despite the difficulty and uncertainty involved. Interestingly, both thinkers, while critical of the notion that ideal theory can or should determine what spotless justice requires, nonetheless conceive of justice as an Everest problem. Both take for granted that achieving a more just society requires evaluations of alternative social realizations measured by a single metric of justice. They differ not in their confidence that such a metric can be identified but rather in their views about whether "climbing higher" at each opportunity is an effective optimizing strategy.

Justice, however, is not like height. The Everest example is misleading because it invites us to conceive of justice as unidimensional and thus scalar, when it may well be variable along numerous vectors. Broad reliance on a mountaineering metaphor obscures this because when measuring mountains, height is (always) the appropriate and uncontroversial metric. When it comes to justice, disagreement about metrics of evaluation is profound, reflecting differing and often conflicting ideals.[†] Sen ought to recognize this, given his awareness of what he calls "the plurality of reasons," which he illustrates through the example of a debate about which of three children should be given a flute. A utilitarian will deem the

[*] Gaus is particularly concerned about what he calls "the problem of neighborhoods," which is that we are often more familiar with what's nearby than with what's far away. This problem generates "The Choice" between a local optimum, one located in "our neighborhood" whose contours are familiar to us, and an overall optimum, located in a distant neighborhood about which we are much less certain. He ultimately advocates the simultaneous pursuit of multiple optima. This is an alternative approach to ideal theory rather than *an* ideal theory. To stick with the theme, Gaus describes what kind of expedition is likely to find the summit rather than describing the summit itself. I shall have more to say about his proposal in chapter 6.

[†] Sometimes Gaus seems to acknowledge this, arguing that diversity among evaluative frameworks justifies the accommodation of various conceptions of justice. Yet his constant reliance on the "rugged terrain" metaphor—which motivates "The Choice"—indicates that he regards the various optima as comparable on a single metric.

child who knows how to play the flute most deserving; an egalitarian will award it to the child who has no other toys; a libertarian will think that the child who worked hard to earn or own the flute should receive it. There is nothing unreasonable or unseemly about this disagreement, in Sen's view; it simply reflects different value systems. "The general point here," he writes, "is that it is not easy to brush aside as foundationless any of the claims based respectively on human fulfillment, or removal of poverty, or entitlement to enjoy the products of one's own labor."[30] All three proposals have justificatory arguments that can't be reasonably dismissed.[31]

Sen relies on the flute example in arguing that IMT is *infeasible* because it hopes for agreement on a single set of ideals, a hope that ignores or erases the plurality of reasons. Such agreement is often unnecessary, Sen maintains, since for many "substantive issues of rights and duties (and also of rights and wrongs), there is no need to insist on" complete agreement on ideals, or on complete rankings of alternatives.[32] We can often choose among alternatives on offer without such agreement. Similarly, determining that some state of affairs is unjust doesn't require agreement on the grounds or reasons for that determination; what matters is that reasonable approaches all yield the same conclusion.[33] While Sen is well aware that the difficulties arising from divergent perspectives won't always resolve themselves easily, he hopes nonetheless that by bringing together many different unprejudiced perspectives through a process of open impartiality, some common understanding might emerge forcefully to guide social choice.

But it can do so only if those reasons (conceptions of justice) agree or converge upon the capabilities metric itself. Sen doesn't worry much about this because he treats capabilities as a purely informational and analytic metric; that is, instead of seeing the capabilities approach as representative of a substantive conception of justice, Sen treats it as a sort of freestanding, all-purpose metric for social choice. Put differently, he never tackles the flute problem head-on because he thinks he's evaded it. That he thinks so is clear in his discussion of the Mona Lisa example, which he introduces to demonstrate the insufficiency or unhelpfulness of ideals of justice. Knowing that a particular critic regards that painting as the world's most beautiful tells us nothing, Sen argues, about how she would rank a Picasso and a Van Gogh.[34]

The Mona Lisa example has received much less critical attention than Mount Everest, perhaps because critics share Chris Brown's view that it's a poor analogy, "since what constitutes a 'better painting' is unclear."[35] Several commentators have noted that it's not necessarily correct to say that knowing a critic prefers the Mona Lisa won't tell us anything about whether she's likely to prefer *La Femme aux Bras Croisés* to the *Starry Night*.[36] If the critic's preference for the smiling lady is not merely idiosyncratic but rather reflects a considered application of carefully reasoned criteria, those criteria (though not mere knowledge of her rankings) might well be sufficient for determining her lower-order preferences in many instances. Sen's critics appear content to leave it at that, satisfied that the Mona Lisa example actually demonstrates that ideals *can* be relevant after all.

But Sen and his critics alike are missing what I take to be the most important aspect of the Mona Lisa problem: that it's really a kind of flute problem—that is, a problem arising from the plurality of reasons. Brown was right to observe that "what constitutes a 'better painting' is unclear"—but that's what makes the example so useful. Unlike Everest problems, in which we assume or stipulate the relevant metric, Mona Lisa problems confront us with choices set amid competing and potentially irreconcilable values and evaluative frameworks. If critic A prefers technical mastery as the supreme painterly virtue while critic B is moved by bold colors and textured brushstrokes, there is no reason to assume that their assessments will converge and no objective or impartial way to adjudicate the disagreement. Critic A can rely on her values to inform comparative assessments, contrary to Sen; what she can't do is appeal to them in justifying her choice to Critic B, who holds different values and reaches different judgments.

Think of it this way: what could Sen say to a critic who rejected the capabilities approach—and the substantive conception of justice on which it relies? If Sen were to articulate a robust normative justification of capabilities—as Martha Nussbaum has long urged him to do and has done herself—his capabilities account would lose the luster of impartiality and objectivity.[37] Only by treating capabilities as a purely informational conception can Sen deny that at bottom it is just another controversial substantive ideal. Capabilities might give an answer to the question of which of two alternative social realizations will better address poverty, but that answer already assumes that poverty is a lack of freedom. Neoliberals regard poverty as a problem of personal responsibility and argue that society should cut welfare benefits and impose strict work requirements to encourage effort and self-reliance; implementing welfare schemes to increase people's functionings only contributes to the problem of a "culture of dependency."

Put differently, Sen's comparative approach relies, much more than he recognizes, on overcoming or ignoring the plurality of reasons (the flute problem); once we recognize capabilities as a substantive ideal (or at least as incompatible with some substantive ideals), the problem of infeasibility returns. This is not to take a position on whether a substantive, normative account of capabilities is appealing; the point is that it doesn't provide an uncontroversial metric like height, as Sen needs it to do. I don't see a neat way out of this difficulty for him but I think the problem itself is tremendously important and productive because of what it suggests about the challenge facing theorists concerned with injustice. Injustice is a Mona Lisa problem; critics need substantive normative arguments to inform our evaluations of social arrangements, but we have to make sense—theoretically and politically—of the fact that those arguments will themselves be controversial and contested.

Sen's blind spot regarding capabilities is of a piece with his highly idealized understanding of social choice. He imagines politics and policymaking—in which a "society" straightforwardly selects optimal or preferred outcomes from a list of rational and purportedly impartial options—in a way that completely ignores power, interests, and conflict. This account is so distant from the reality of how social policy and priorities are determined as to severely distort our understanding of how and why existing arrangements come into being and what might be required to alter them. The account is not only unrealistic but also unjust, insofar as it obscures the sources of injustice.[38] Further, Sen's assumption that societies are distinct and discrete units of social choice, containers of politics and policy that are neatly coterminous with the injustices they seek to address, is implausible today, probably always has been,[39] and potentially another source of injustice. Moreover, his confidence in people's ability to make good choices for themselves notwithstanding, a voluminous literature shows that many public deliberative forums mask and often replicate power dynamics and reproduce marginalization and exclusion, raising serious doubts about the process of "open public scrutiny" itself.

Worse, Sen admits (in answering a concern about the pervasiveness of unreason) that open scrutiny is merely a hypothetical exercise, a thought experiment that doesn't assume people are actually engaged in discussion.[40] As in IMT, a seemingly deliberative procedure turns out to be purely imaginary, a hypothetical exercise rather than an actual forum for contestation, making it susceptible of the same biases and distortions that hamper IMT and raising the same questions about the relevance of the "decisions" taken in the hypothetical mode to actual decision-making and real politics.[41] Sen "invites us to trust our capacity to identify injustice, if we can but project ourselves out of our natural partiality for our own interests."[42] Such a projection, especially in the absence of meaningful engagement with others, seems implausible at best.

Moreover, Sen never delivers on his promise to build on the visceral experience of injustice and the ways in which it motivates people to demand and work for change. Recall that he motivates his search for an alternative to IMT by arguing that in the real world people are moved by their recognition and experience of injustice much more than by departures from theoretical ideals.[43] Although he acknowledges that "the diagnosis of injustice will figure often enough as the starting point for critical discussion," Sen's interest lies in developing an impartial framework in which policy alternatives can be compared. So while he treats the sense of injustice as a signal, it's not a signal to be trusted; rather, it must be scrutinized, its soundness tested through rational, objective, and impartial reasoning.[44] In the end, Sen may eschew transcendental theories, but his approach relies on procedures very like those of IMT.

OBVIOUS INJUSTICE?

Sen began with the insight that people in the real world are mainly concerned with egregious injustices like poverty, hunger, and torture. For him, these injustices and the indignation they beget are a kind of signal that prompts analysis; for another group of realist thinkers, however, they constitute a normative starting point for political theory. As we have seen, this is Shklar's view, and while she is lonely in it she is not altogether alone.[45] Other thinkers have also seen obvious injustice as the basis for an account of political normativity that avoids moralism. Stuart Hampshire, for instance, maintains that the great injustices in the world "are felt as evils directly and without recourse to the norms of any particular way of life or to any specific set of moral ideas."[46] Barrington Moore argued that while it is difficult for people to agree on the meaning and causes of happiness, it is easier for them to know when they are miserable.[47] He attempted to construct a "unitary conception of misery" grounded in what he regarded as "good evidence for a common substratum of universal human feelings that one can call the sense of injustice."[48] Bernard Williams, whose work I shall consider in a moment, also insisted that "there are indeed universal paradigms of injustice and unreason"; the most egregious injustices, he believed, are so clear, so obvious, that no proof or demonstration of their injustice seems necessary or helpful.[49]

Appeals to the obviousness of injustice or to the "sense of injustice" resonate powerfully, I think, because many injustices are so awful, so brutal and unbearable, that they seem impossible to deny or ignore. It is tempting—and not altogether wrong—to think that a great deal could be gained simply by training our attention on these injustices and finding ways to avert or ameliorate them; the world would be a much better place if only the most egregious injustices could be eradicated. Still, there are profound inadequacies in these bare accounts of injustice and therefore good reasons to resist the temptation to bootstrap our way to obvious or self-evident injustice.

My reservations begin with the narrow and often quite conservative politics upon which many of these theorists settle.[50] For all of them, the prioritization of injustice straightforwardly recommends liberalism of one variety or another: for Hampshire, this is a procedural liberalism anchored in something like discourse ethics; for Shklar and Williams, it is what they evocatively call "the liberalism of fear." Shklar describes this as a politics grounded in the memory of past injustice rather than in hope for a better future. For her, putting cruelty first invigorates liberalism with a sense of purpose: to prevent cruelty and the fear that it engenders is essential for human freedom and dignity.[51]

There is certainly a compelling argument from the recognition of the cruelty and misery that human beings suffer to a politics that seeks to protect people both from that suffering and from the corrosive fear of it. Yet accounts that focus on obvious cruelty and clear-cut violations can provide only a partial and ultimately distorted reckoning of injustice. That's because such accounts can't register *contested* claims about injustice. In prioritizing those wrongs that *everyone* agrees are obvious, these approaches systematically incorporate the interests and perspectives of the powerful and privileged while ignoring claims made by the most vulnerable people in society or rejecting them as "controversial" or "aspirational." This cognitive or epistemic bias makes it difficult to identify structural or systemic injustice[52] but easy to dismiss economic injustice as natural or as a kind of misfortune.[‡] Liberalism's concern with autonomy, civil liberties, physical integrity, and formal due process is neither misplaced nor malign,

[‡] Shklar had more complex—and more muddled—views on economic injustice than other realistic liberals, who mainly cling to the easy but problematic distinction between negative and positive rights/liberty. She was keenly aware of the foundation of economic inequality on which "normal justice" rests (*The Faces of Injustice*, 23). Unlike Berlin (and Williams), she insisted that at least some attention must be paid to the social preconditions of negative liberty, including attention to "such forms and degrees of social inequality as expose people to oppressive practices" ("The Liberalism of Fear," 10). Yet in chiding Hayek for his indifference to economic suffering, she did not rebut his characterization of the market as natural and impersonal, a depiction that allows him to portray the misery it causes as misfortune rather than injustice; she instead argues that the source of misery is irrelevant to the question of whether we can do something to alleviate it (*The Faces of Injustice*, 80ff.). This stance contradicts her insistence elsewhere on the political significance of the distinction between injustice and misfortune, a distinction about which she never seemed clear or comfortable.

but it is—as critics of various stripes have long argued—distorted, significantly incomplete, and wholly inadequate as a basis for an emancipatory politics.

These difficulties become vivid in the influential realist liberalism of Williams, who casts legitimacy as the key problem for political theory. He calls it "the first political question . . . the securing of order, protection, safety, trust, and the conditions of cooperation."[53] This question arises *within* politics, Williams argues; it is the original exigency of political life, and an answer to it is a necessary condition of political legitimacy. (It may be that an *acceptable* answer to it is a sufficient condition of legitimacy, though Williams is cagey about this.)[54] He approaches political legitimacy as a response to what he calls the Basic Legitimation Demand, or BLD. The BLD requires the state "to offer a justification of its power *to each subject*."[55] This justification must clarify how the solution to the first question—which is state power itself—differs from the problem; that is, the answer must be more than "simply . . . an account of successful domination."[56] Otherwise, those subjects who are merely dominated by the state will have no reason not to rebel, meaning that such a justification would not constitute a satisfactory answer to the question after all.

For Williams, an acceptable justification of power must be roughly equally acceptable to each subject.[57] Such justifications must also satisfy what he calls the *critical theory principle*, the proviso that "the acceptance of a justification does not count if the acceptance itself is produced by the coercive power which is supposedly being justified."[58] Liberalism, Williams argues, is one answer to this first question, one rooted in history and politics; it provides a contextually specific answer to the BLD that rules out disadvantages based on race and gender and denies that hierarchical structures can be self-legitimating.[59] As such, liberalism "makes sense" to us, in our particular circumstances, as an acceptable solution to the BLD, a successful justification of political power. Williams is reluctant to call the BLD a moral principle, though he asserts that "if it is, it does not represent a morality which is prior to politics. It is a claim that is inherent in there being such a thing as politics."[60]

Because Williams sees politics as normative in its inception, he argues that a nonfoundational approach can help us to understand our ethical life as a genuinely local and historicized structure, lessening the temptation to regard it as a "satisfactorily functioning whole"; as a result, "we shall be more likely to recognize that some widely accepted parts of it may stand condemned in the light of perfectly plausible extrapolations of other parts."[61] This historical specificity does not mean that other societies elsewhere or in the past lack(ed) valid justifications. "Making sense" is itself "a category of historical understanding"; it is an evaluative concept, not simply a fact or description of the facts. It is not, however, a normative principle—except in our own case. For us, what makes sense has a bearing on how we should act and react toward our own political arrangements, but this does not mean that we can or should view other solutions to the BLD as wrong or false; at most we can say that while those solutions might have made sense to others, they do not make sense to us.[62] For Williams, then, there is little risk that a historicized nonfoundationalism will degenerate into an inactive or functionalist conservatism; rather, it enables criticism through the possibility of deploying some parts of our ethical framework against others.[63]

Williams may be correct in thinking that realist liberalism of this type can generate useful internal critique. He is mistaken, however, in thinking that this inoculates it against conservatism. To see this, consider his views on human rights, which he regards as closely related to the problem posed by the first question of politics, necessary protections against the threat of power.[64] Human rights violations "are abuses of power that almost everyone everywhere has been in a position to recognize as such."[65] Thus "in their most basic form, violations of human rights are very obvious, and so is what is wrong with them: unmediated coercion, might rather than right."[66] Williams refers frequently to the "self-evidence" of fundamental human rights and argues that because "we have a pretty good idea of what human rights are" the most important problem is "that of getting them enforced."[67]

This "pretty good idea" of what rights are follows from the requirements of the BLD. Williams conceives human rights as protections against torture, assault, censorship, unwarranted detention, and the arbitrary use of power.[68] As this list makes clear, he sees human rights as protections against threats posed by states to citizens. He is quite explicit about what he sees as the dangers of going beyond these "self-evident" rights: recognizing social, economic, or other rights that states might find difficult to deliver risks making rights seem merely aspirational.[69] Besides, the obviousness of rights is jeopardized, in his view, when we allow the convictions of advocates to determine what rights are or should be.[70] Williams allows that fears like those related to subsistence might be addressed politically, but he denies that they are fundamental and insists that the failure to address them does not make a state despotic.[71]

This treatment of human rights reveals several problems with Williams's approach. Although he recognizes the normativity of human rights claims and locates it in political exigencies, his conceptualization of these exigencies accepts and reifies the dominant ideological position in society. Williams's list of "obvious" or "self-evident" rights reproduces a masculinist idealization of the autonomous (economically independent) citizen acting in a public sphere where the state poses the primary threat to liberty and security. As feminists have been arguing since at least the 19th century, such idealizations ignore the fact that for women, it is men in the so-called private sphere who pose the greatest threat to liberty and security, with the state abetting and frequently enforcing female subjugation in myriad ways. Similarly, Williams's dismissal of social and economic rights as aspirational rather than fundamental rights ignores the widespread societal violence engendered by an economic system in which many people lack adequate food, income, and shelter and are frequently humiliated or degraded—a system, once again, upheld with the complicity and through the exercise of state power. No *realistic* account of legitimation—no empirically grounded, sociologically informed account—could seriously regard a reply to the "first question" that overlooked the structural subordination of women (or systemic racism) and that excluded questions of basic subsistence and social reproduction from politics as one that "each citizen" would find an "acceptable justification of power."

Williams's liberalism informs his account of politics, rather than the other way around. That is, his liberal beliefs about order, stability, limited rights, and limited state power infuse his understanding of politics and shape his framing of its "first question" as well as his answer to it.[72] That's why demands for food or income or shelter are "aspirational" and why Williams sees them as threats to hard-won social stability. His protests notwithstanding, he offers us a static account that ignores historical and ongoing struggles over precisely what counts as an acceptable justification of power to whom by placing whole categories of rights and protections outside the boundaries of what makes sense to "us." The critical theory principle can't help us here, because what counts as an instance of dominant power "illegitimately" producing acceptance is itself a matter of interpretation. When a particular social and political configuration is valorized as a successful solution to the problem of legitimacy, challenges to that solution can easily appear as deviations from good political sense; ideology and good political sense become indistinguishable.

I want to return to the claim that realism is somehow automatically historical and historicized because of its attention to context. Williams's account actually erases the centuries of struggle that made it even plausible to describe liberalism as a creed that "rules out disadvantages based on race and gender and denies that hierarchical structures can be self-legitimating." Indeed, throughout its career liberalism has not only condoned but actively promoted and supported class, racial, and sexual inequalities and hierarchies. Moreover, by framing the first question as one of *state* power, Williams deftly deflects attention away from the role that empire has played—conceptually, rhetorically, economically, and politically—in liberal theory and practice.[73] This deflection makes it impossible adequately to conceptualize questions about the legitimacy of transnational arrangements and exercises of power. Williams's dual insistence that only members of the state are entitled to a justification of power and that there is no right to be a member of a state to which one does not already belong[74] denies the history of empire and colonialism and arbitrarily imposes a statist morality and analytic framework onto real politics—which is rife with contestation about boundaries, movement, membership, and accountability.

Again, Williams's liberalism seems to shape his understanding of what counts as power and politics, rather than the other way around. As a result, he ends up providing an account of the dominant values and power structures of liberal society, one lacking in critical reflection on the relations and structures of power in that society. Such an account is not, in the end, realistic.[75] The problem is not that Williams provides us with a normative account of politics; as I shall argue in the next chapter, we *need* normative political accounts and anyway can't avoid them. The problem is rather that he depicts the substantive normative claims of this account as obvious, as found or arising within politics rather than within the value system and epistemological framework of the author.

Realism as Radical Critique?

If realism for Williams and his followers is a way of answering the inescapable first question of politics, for Raymond Geuss and his followers, it is a vehicle for radical critique. On this view, realism should be concerned primarily with "the way the social, economic, political, etc., institutions actually operate in some society at some given time." This means not that people have no ideals or aspirations, but that "tautologically . . . these ideals and aspirations influence their behavior and hence are politically relevant, only to the extent to which they do actually influence behavior in some way."[76] Beliefs can be important in understanding politics, but only insofar as they influence actions.[77] The focus on power, interests, and institutions means that "politics is historically located." This implies that "as a matter of fact . . . excessive generalizing ends up not being informative. There are no interesting 'eternal questions' of political philosophy"; at most, such questions are really just schemata to be filled in with relevant facts.[78] Observing, for example, that all humans must eat to survive is not, in itself, enlightening; it only becomes enlightening when we supply details about the system of food production in a given society, who controls it, and what form it takes.[79]

An explicitly descriptive political theory that adhered to these guidelines would, according to Geuss, allow theorists to understand systematically how the world works; to evaluate our surroundings, including others (and ourselves); to orient ourselves in the world, perhaps within a larger imaginative structure that helps to make sense of things and to guide our actions; and to undertake conceptual innovation, providing new "thought-instruments" or conceptual tools to help us deal with certain problems.[80] (Geuss mentions almost in passing that another controversial function of political theory is to analyze or propound ideologies; I run with this suggestion in the next chapter.) He is skeptical, however, that political theory can separate its methods from its substantive commitments and from politics itself; theory is embedded in power relations and is itself a kind of political action. As a result, the theorist must constantly beware of partisanship and of ideology—especially since all description is normatively laden.[81] This is partly why Geuss has dropped the term "description" and instead emphasized "diagnosis." Diagnosis is a kind of negative criticism that interrogates and problematizes the present and its essential concepts; it "combines phenomenological and genealogical elements in order to produce local, practical knowledge about and for a specific context."[82] The point is not to bring norms to our analysis but to analyze the norms that animate our institutions and our social practices.[83]

For Geuss, the opposite of realism is not utopianism but rather moralism, by which he means a view about "the *importance*, centrality, and efficacy of expressing judgments of morality."[84] Moralism reflects or embodies an absolutism about moral or value judgments; it tries to eliminate the contingency and indeterminacy that surrounds such judgments (in politics) by locating them within a closed, encompassing framework of analysis. To illustrate this point, Geuss uses the example of an inherently contextual judgment, the decision whether to carry an umbrella when leaving the house: it's a judgment informed by the weather forecast and one's own assessment of conditions. Moralism is the equivalent of subordinating those judgments to a general rule that one should always carry an umbrella when there is a chance of rain. Obviously, rain protection is not a moral judgment; the point here is to illustrate the moralist urge to resolve contingency through the appeal to higher-order rules.[85]

There's a lot to like in Geuss's approach, much on which I shall build, but there is also a disturbing conservatism in it—one again revealed in a discussion of human rights. To Geuss, the ideal-theoretical discussion of human rights illustrates what he views as one of IMT's worst tendencies: the desire to create an idealized legal system structured around a set of moral claims.[86] This "idealist" approach imagines human rights as prior moral constraints on politics and treats rights as somehow attached to human beings as such. Human rights substitute wishful thinking for careful descriptive analysis, Geuss complains. When ideal theorists call something a human right, they are effectively saying that they think it is a good idea. But the very notion of human rights is vacuous, he argues, "puffery" or "magical thinking"; the politics of human rights for him boils down to the hope if that something is repeated often enough it will become true. This is, he reminds us, unlikely if those in power hold different views.[87]

Instead, Geuss recommends a positivist account that is limited to describing those rights specified and enforced by existing legal structures.[88] He does not deny that a rights-based society is possible or that it might be desirable; he only insists that until such a society exists, some other society exists and that political theory is best suited to describing and understanding that other—actually existing—society. Idealism about human rights is an attempt to provide normative grounding for rights or to provide a basis for criticizing existing legal systems. But human rights (and other ideals) cannot do this, Geuss argues, because they are merely the flickering of our own weak moral lights; they can only dimly and haphazardly illuminate real politics. If human rights are achieved, it is because someone has enough power to impose them upon others—and once again, in such cases, the realist approach is best suited to understanding such developments.[89]

I agree with many of Geuss's adjurations regarding the need to focus on existing social arrangements and to be attentive to structures of power, and I share some of his misgivings about idealist conceptions of human rights.[90] Nonetheless, I find his account of rights to be profoundly *unrealistic*. His discussion reveals an almost crude empiricism about human rights that distorts our understanding of politics every bit as much as an idealized, moralistic account does. For one thing, Geuss focuses almost exclusively on legal arrangements, ignoring broad swaths of human rights practice. For another, despite what philosophers writing on the subject might think, most people involved in human rights movements do not imagine that they are working to build a perfectly just society from the ground up or that the rights they advocate reflect timeless philosophical truths or self-enacting moral principles. They view human rights as tools for challenging unjust laws, norms, and institutions. People hope, in claiming rights, to advance the struggle for their legalization and institutionalization and ultimately thereby to improve their own lives and their communities. To claim human rights is to express political demands in a normatively potent language (one might equally say that doing so expresses normative demands in a politically potent language), an expression usually directed against systems of power that deny or repudiate rights or dignity.[91] In the process, claimants constitute themselves as groups and as individuals and work to shape the meaning of rights.[92]

In rejecting idealized and moralized accounts of human rights, Geuss dismisses the normative salience of rights altogether and, in so doing, he gets the politics of human rights descriptively and theoretically wrong. We misunderstand that politics if we treat rights as emblematic of delusional thinking rather than as practical political demands—though admittedly, demands laden with normative aspirations.[93] It is difficult to comprehend the *appeal* of human rights for political activists if we think of rights as puffery rather than as claims meant to challenge power and to rally support for that challenge. It's true that human rights politics is prescriptive: it calls for a different and better (in the view of advocates) society, but does so without imagining that that society is ideal and without recourse to any starting point or perspective outside of politics. That is, it does so without engaging in idealization or relying on inaccurate empirical description. Normative arguments can energize and motivate people; they can also provide guidance about how to act, what policies to oppose and pursue, and how to assess our existing social arrangements. Recognizing these facts is essential for any realistic account of people's motivations and psychology.[94] To ridicule human rights for their normative and aspirational character and to limit the remit of political theory to a description of existing power relations is to embrace not merely political but also methodological conservativism. Although his conceptualization of realist political theory leaves room for ideals and beliefs to influence people's behavior, Geuss's account of human rights misses their crucial aspirational character and thus misleads us about what people are doing in claiming rights.

Again, Geuss seems recently to have moderated his approach—or at least his rhetoric. He now insists that being realistic does not mean refraining from demanding what's impossible. What's possible or not reflects the distribution of power and interests in society; it's context dependent.[95] One can demand, say, healthcare for everyone without being committed to the idea that this demand reflects some absolute, categorical, or transcendental value. One might simply think that universal healthcare is more important than the alignment of power and interests that presently makes it impossible. It's possible, Geuss acknowledges, to make evaluative judgments of this kind without committing moralism.[96]

Still, it seems doubtful that this shift makes meaningful room for normativity within a realist political theory and thus that realism can generate radical or transformative critique of the kind needed to combat injustice. I am skeptical in part because realist theorists often equate realistic attention to power and politics with treating existing power structures and political ideologies as constraints on political values.[97] So for Matt Sleat, we must distinguish between all political values and those that can be "values for us," those whose "preconditions" of realization are present in our society.[98] On his list of the values not "for us" because they "simply do not represent values that can be integrated into a life [a people] can coherently lead," Sleat includes "basic rights" and "equality." Both are disqualified because at present we lack the institutions to realize them and the solidarity to uphold them.[99] In his view, "a theory of the values appropriate for any practice is going to depend upon a viable account of the practice in which those values are to function as ideals to be realized, normative standards of assessment, or categories of understanding."[100] Treating normative aspirations as constrained by "political reality" in this way lets realists deny that their position is antiethical while sharply constraining the range of ethical positions they recognize as "realistic." Sleat denies that this makes realism conservative, insisting that realism is "compatible" with utopian or radical speculation about values that cannot be "for us." But by questioning the "sensibility" of and the "intellectual motivations" for studying politics this way, he shows his (and realism's?) true stripes; conceding that "there is a significant difference between an enterprise being mistaken and its being unwise"[101] probably helps less than he imagines.

Janosch Prinz, another of Geuss's followers, insists that realism is not only compatible with radical/subversive/transformative normative critique but that it offers a distinctive and useful modality for such critique. What Prinz means by normative critique, however, is the critique of existing norms. This is clear in his discussion of the "detoxification of power," which he regards as a model. Following Foucault and Geuss, Prinz stresses that theorists can and should ask about the operation of power and its effects in a particular context, but not about whether power is good or bad.[102] For him, the point is to show how power operates and to reveal tensions and contradictions with how it's explained and justified. This kind of realist critique is compatible with—it constitutes a kind of—normative critique, in his view, because it focuses on existing norms and understandings, on the normative orientation that is always embedded and revealed within a particular context.[103] By focusing on the epistemic flaws and contradictions in justifications of power (or private property, or whatever), we expose the "hegemonic normalizations" that necessarily shape the ideological "common ground" of our social world.[104]

In scrutinizing and debunking these prevailing public understandings—diagnosing our condition—our goal is not to peel away false consciousness and achieve emancipation but rather to attain a "high level of self-reflection" about those understandings. Our alternatives, however, are limited by public understandings of the purpose of the social order.[105]

Hall and Sleat likewise hold that identifying the "epistemological errors" that plague our present beliefs helps us to recognize "where our values and commitments might be the result of self-deception, metaphysical illusions, or social deceit."[106] The aim is to develop "a more realistic world-view" through "truthful, realistic reflection on our existing practices." This "ethics of truthfulness" represents "a willingness to see our political reality as it really is."[107]

Again, I share the impulse to begin with a realistic assessment of power relations and of the ideological common ground that shapes prevailing understandings of our social arrangements and the norms that govern them. I reject, however, the notion that we can get to some "truthful" account of how things really are. Faith in "truthfulness" or "realistic description" verges on naive empiricism—something realists should be wary of, given their recognition that all description is normatively laden and that our political methods and theories are themselves deeply entangled in politics.

I also reject the idea that a realistic account must forgo normative evaluation. I want to know not merely how power operates but whether it is operating in good ways or bad in society. I want to know this because I am interested in emancipatory social transformation, in the eradication of injustice. While a realistic critique of prevailing ideologies and institutions can be subversive, and even radical, it isn't *therefore* transformative, let alone emancipatory. It's one thing to understand how power operates, to understand a relationship of subordination, even to call it an instance of domination according to some analytic definition of that term. All of that fits within the "critique of norms" that realist diagnosis enables. To actually make a substantive (normative) critique of power—to call domination wrong, to demand changes in our social arrangements to end it—requires a critical normative perspective on power and power relations that "truthfulness" and "self-reflection" can't, on their own, provide. Prinz and Rossi invoke immanent critique in explaining their own normative orientations,[108] but this poses a dilemma: the normativity of immanent critique is either "immanent" in the sense of being derived from practice, in which case it is inherently conservative; or, it is "immanent" in the sense of being somehow implicit within human nature or interactions or discourse (or whatever), in which case it becomes the kind of moralism that realists rightly ought to reject.[§]

A REALISTIC, NOT REALIST, ALTERNATIVE

Political theory needs a realistic analysis of power, conflict, and ideology, and (some forms of) realism can provide it. Realists' attention to the history, contingency, and particularity of politics and to the dynamic, constructed character of power relations and social arrangements provides a welcome antidote to the static idealism and moralism of IMT. But if political theory is to combat injustice, it also needs a conception of normativity that avoids moralism while enabling transformational critique and guiding emancipatory political struggle. Here I find contemporary realism wanting. Sen's retreat into the old liberal redoubt of impartiality leaves him with insufficient critical perspective on real politics. The liberal realism of Shklar, Moore, and Williams appeals to obvious injustice and a minimal conception of legitimacy in ways that render it inherently conservative and ideologically distortional while disguising its normativity. The critical realism of Geuss and his followers promises radical and subversive critique through the scrutiny and debunking of prevailing social understandings and justifications of power, but it only partly delivers.

It falls short in leaving theorists without a substantive normative orientation to the real politics they interrogate and to the operations of ideology that they unmask. Critical realism confuses—or misses the distinction between—two kinds of normative critique: critical *analysis* of political norms, the aim of which is understanding and unmasking norms and their function in society, and the critical-normative *evaluation* of social arrangements and alternatives and of norms themselves, the aim of which is to offer substantive critique that can guide transformative social change. Geuss's critical realism can support critical analysis of political

[§] I return to the normativity of immanent critique in chapter 5.

norms and their functioning in society, and it's on this basis that he rejects the charge of being antiethical, but it cannot support—it openly rejects—the normative evaluation of social norms and arrangements, because such critique must be animated and oriented by substantive normative values. Like ideal theorists, realists seem to assume that such values must be understood as ideal moral principles and entail moralism. This is why Horton believes that political theorists must give up on the aim of providing practical guidance: he believes that this normative ambition invariably corrupts our analysis of politics. It also explains Freeden's evident contempt for "prescriptive realists" whose "ethical mission" makes them "strangely blind" to political realities.[109]

Realists are right to insist that idealization and moralization can and often do distort our analysis of the real world. But that only rules out transformative social critique if such critique entails idealism and moralism. I shall argue in the next chapter that it does not, that it's possible for political theory to provide guidance and be prescriptive without idealizing or moralizing the values on which substantive normative critique relies. If this argument is correct, it suggests that it should be possible to integrate realistic analysis of politics with transformative (prescriptive) social critique in a single theoretical framework—not only possible, but vital because, as my argument has shown, realism without substantive normative critique is prone to naive empiricism and to political and methodological conservativism. Realism is less an alternative to IMT than its alter ego, a mirror image reflecting many of the same assumptions about the ideal, moral nature of claims about justice but reversing the conclusions it draws from them.

4

The Bifocal Approach

We have seen repeatedly that justice claims function ideologically: recall Shklar's observation that "normal justice" is perfectly compatible with and often tolerant of injustice, or Shelby's worry that "the prevailing conception of justice in the society or the political views of the ruling elite" might in fact be unjust.[1] Ideal moral accounts of justice can also, if inadvertently, function ideologically by naturalizing and normalizing dominant viewpoints and interpretations through idealizations of the world and of the positions and experiences of theorists within it. Even realism, despite its explicit concern with power and ideology, can function ideologically—especially in its liberal modality, which turns "obvious" injustice into a conservative regime of legitimacy and stability.

A realistic response to the ideological character of justice is to accept and try to make sense of it. Justice functions ideologically not because it is improperly defined or inadequately realized but rather because its meaning is essentially contested. To make sense of claims about justice and injustice thus requires that we treat them as ideological claims. Doing so requires a theoretical framework that accommodates an understanding of justice as a contentious, partisan concept and enables a realistic assessment of the power relations in which justice claims are enmeshed and contested. In short, it requires a political, not a philosophical approach.

GLOBAL POLITICAL JUSTICE

One group of scholars working to develop such an approach identifies its subject or focus as *global political justice* (GPJ). Adherents of GPJ share several core interests and concerns, including frustration with the theoretical approach and the distributive focus of IMT, an appreciation of republican arguments stressing nondomination as a central component of freedom, and a concern with global public power. If there is a unifying premise underlying theories of GPJ, it is that complex new forms of arbitrary and unchecked power are being exercised across borders, making people increasingly vulnerable or subject to decisions they cannot control.[2] These (new?) global circumstances of justice have sparked growing interest in the global political sphere, which these theorists regard as *political* in two respects. First, many problematic forms of power are already being exercised transnationally and globally, and these are in need of justification and control.[3] Second, "the kinds of social conflicts typically in need of institutional 'taming,' and the kinds of shared social problems typically solved through collective political decision-making institutions, now occur beyond sovereign territorial boundaries," indicating the need "to overcome these social conflicts and challenges through the development of new political institutions at the transnational and at the global level."[4]

If we live in global circumstances of justice, theorists of GPJ argue, and if there exists a global political sphere in need of theorization and justification, we would do well to

> investigate the normative credentials of this underlying political order directly. . . . [T]here is a need to investigate more directly and systematically which features of the global order call for distinctively political forms of normative critique and institutional response, and to consider what should follow from this for our practical attitudes and decision-making in relation to these.[5]

Theorists of GPJ see it as a complement to global distributive justice rather than as a replacement—though some perhaps also regard these political questions as analytically and morally prior to distributive questions—the idea being that determinations of the just allocation of the benefits and burdens of a basic structure should *follow* assessments of that structure's legitimacy or justifiability.[6]

Accordingly, GPJ takes up questions about the basic structure of global society that global normative theorists working within IMT don't and can't raise, questions concerning the creation and reform of institutions, the fairness of background contexts in which political decisions get made globally, and the determination of who has standing to make or participate in making political decisions globally.[7] These questions raise concerns about domination at both the individual and the institutional levels. Many theorists conceptualize these problems in terms of *global public power*, political or decision-making power exercised by international, transnational, or global actors and institutions (including states, when they act as particularistic agents in a global context). For Buckinx, the challenge is to determine which actors should be assigned and entrusted with governance roles. In republican theory, she argues, public actors (the state) are tasked with reducing citizens' vulnerability to domination, a task they approach mainly through creating and upholding a regime of law.[8] She seeks to identify global actors who can be "properly public in the global sense," which is to say, who both function and conceive of themselves as public actors and who advance the good of all (roughly, the public interest). Institutions like those of the UN system most closely approximate global public actors, she argues, and are the best candidates for the just exercise of global public power. Buckinx is optimistic that agreement can be reached on the public interest: she lifts up the prevention of disastrous climate change and the settlement of trade disputes as examples.[9]

For others, the problem of global public power raises questions about democratic institutions and decision-making as well as more fundamental questions of legitimacy and justification.[10] According to Hurrell and Macdonald,

> political justice seeks to determine not only the principles by which agents and institutions within political societies should politically *regulate* one another, but also how these fundamental sociological entities should be politically *constituted* in the first place—that is, what their basic institutional structures and social identities ought to be.[11]

Political legitimacy is preoccupied with "solving *the problem of political order*, and building political institutions that can achieve *real political acceptability* among their participants as a central instrument for doing so."[12] Hurrell and Macdonald regard legitimacy as different from other moral principles in part because of its political character; they also contend that the justification of legitimacy is different from that of moral justification because it takes account of strategic goals that "can be pursued only with the right kind of responsiveness to a very full range of empirical facts."[13] Indeed, they view legitimacy and its distinctive model of justification as the basis of a new political normativity that they believe can grapple effectively with empirical realities. Likening their approach to the realism of Williams, they maintain that restraining political power is the paramount goal of legitimacy and that this restraint must be conceptualized with pervasive noncompliance in mind.[14]

There is much I admire in the work of theorists of GPJ, including their focus on power and domination. I also applaud their effort to think outside the distributive frame of global normative theory—even though I wonder if some of them aren't really calling for the expansion of that frame to encompass the redistribution of political power.[15] That said, I'm skeptical whether GPJ represents a significant new departure from IMT; indeed,

I worry that while theorists of global political justice want to shift the *subject* of justice from distribution to global political power, their approach to *theorizing* justice remains essentially unchanged. Their key objectives are to define and justify—primarily analytically—criteria of legitimacy, principles to regulate the global basic structure, and so on. These problems are theorized and addressed through reliance on notions like the global circumstances of justice and global political power, which resemble the extreme abstractions and distortional idealizations familiar in IMT. The circumstances, for instance, are not subjected to analysis or critique in themselves but are assumptions employed in theorizing principles of political legitimacy, assumptions far too abstract and idealized to provide much leverage on concrete problems of injustice.

Likewise, the notion of global public power, which is presented as a necessary solution to problems of domination arising from the circumstances, is highly idealized, raising concerns about distortion. Is there such a thing as power that pursues the good of all? If so, who wields it, and to what ends? And who defines the good of all? Theorists of GPJ often conceptualize global public power with reference to UN-related agencies like the International Monetary Fund and the World Trade Organization, but in doing so they uncritically endorse a particular understanding of the good of all. That's not to say they uncritically approve of how these institutions wield power; it's possible to generate an internal critique of the gap between the stated goals of these agencies and their practices. It's rather to say that idealizing global public power in this way makes a trenchant critique of those goals and their underlying ideology impossible. As a result, the "laws" of the market, the "benefits" of trade, the "necessity" of structural adjustment—not to mention the supposed "need" for regimes of trade and finance that in practice promote debt, surplus accumulation, and the uninhibited movement of capital—get normalized, baked into the global circumstances of justice and shielded from critique. The resulting complacency in—and complicity with—neoliberalism is evident in Valentini's remarkable claim that when institutions satisfy the minimal requirements of political justice, "they are *as just as they can be*."[16] A critical, realistic analysis of politics needs to do better.

I'm also not persuaded that the turn to legitimacy represents much of a break with the assumptions and procedures of IMT. With respect to the claim that it entails a different mode of justification, I find it troubling that Hurrell and Macdonald's discussion of legitimacy remains concerned with validity, moral principles, and the like. In addition, their analytic approach to defining the criteria of legitimacy for global public power renders the problem rather abstract and comes close to idealizing it (though this is surely not their intention). With respect to legitimacy itself, I'm not convinced that it isn't simply functioning as a moral principle regulating a different domain of justice, rather than as a different *kind* of principle. I also worry that they have been seduced by the seeming minimalism of legitimacy into treating it as lower-hanging normative and conceptual fruit. It is fruit different from justice, to be sure, but I don't see any compelling reason to treat it as riper for agreement or consensus than other moral principles or as easier to pluck than justice in any normative or epistemological sense.

So while I share the view that global normative theorists need to focus more on power, to expand IMT's narrow, ideal, moral conceptualization of justice, and to develop a new conception of normativity and new modes of justification, I think GPJ doesn't go nearly far enough. We need a realistic analysis of power and its operation, not merely an idealized conception of power with attention to noncompliance. We need not just to change the subject of global normative theory, but to change our approach to theorizing it. We need an account of normativity that comprehends its plurality and contentiousness, one that helps us recognize and reckon with conflicts about the meaning of justice itself.

RECONCEPTUALIZING THE PROBLEM

What would it mean to take the disagreement and conflict over the meaning of justice as the starting point for our theoretical approach to it? What if, instead of treating that conflict as a philosophical puzzle to be solved, we took it as the subject of our theorizing? Could we do so in a way that nonetheless enabled political theory to offer substantive normative critique of existing social arrangements and prevailing social understandings and to orient transformative social change? These are the questions I shall wrestle with in the rest of this book.

Let's dive right in. I propose that we conceptualize justice claims as *ideological*. Instead of treating the contentious nature and ideological function of justice as problems or shortcomings, I want to make them the starting point of my approach. Ideologies are inherently normative; they provide interpretive frameworks as well as value orientations that guide action and inform critique. In a sense, they allow people to impose meaning(s) on the world. "Ideologies are powerful systems of widely shared ideas and patterned beliefs that are accepted as truth by significant groups in society. Serving as political mental maps, they offer people a more or less coherent picture of the world not only as it is, but also as it ought to be."[17] Crucially, ideologies are also constructed through intersubjective processes of meaning- and identity-formation.[18] The term *ideology* and its cognates are frequently deployed as epithets in public and scholarly discourse alike to insinuate that an opponent's thinking is rigid, unreflective, distorted, or manipulative.[19] Here, I use the term without prejudice to refer to the systems of values and ideas through which people "posit, explain and *justify* ends and means of organized social action, and specifically political action, irrespective of whether such action aims to preserve, amend, uproot or rebuild a given social order."[20]

This emphasis on action and behavior indicates that power is deeply implicated in the operation of ideology, in at least three related ways. First, part of how ideologies function is by "decontesting" disputed concepts like liberty or property through clear definitions and supportive interpretations that stabilize them. To (try to) fix meaning in this way is an exercise of power. Second, power is involved in more direct attempts to influence people's thinking and behavior as well.[21] Finally, power plays a key role in constructing ideologies, in creating and promulgating systems of belief and persuading people to adopt them. According to Freeden, ideologies are constructed through the (not necessarily coordinated or even conscious) efforts of professional political thinkers, political organizations like parties or interest groups, and the mass populations who subscribe to them (again, consciously or not).[22] I would add—or emphasize, depending on how broadly Freeden understands "political organizations"—that social movements (also) contribute significantly to the formulation, proliferation, and consolidation of ideologies.

Freeden asserts that "we almost always encounter political thought in the form of ideological discourses."[23] On this view, political theory or philosophy, when it presents a case for one particular configuration of concepts and interpretations, is ideological. Put differently, political theory in its prescriptive mode is ideological thinking, and it can be profitably studied as such (though not only as such).[24] Many political theorists and philosophers might object strongly to this characterization on the grounds that their rigor, their methods, or their subject matter differentiate theirs from the efforts of (other) ideologists. Freeden argues persuasively that they do not, and I concur.[25] Theories of justice—for example—fit perfectly the broad definition of ideology with which I am working.

To conceptualize justice claims (or any other normative propositions) as ideological claims can help us to make better sense of their disputed status and of the conflict that surrounds them. Studying justice claims ideologically, Freeden argues,

> involves asking a new set of questions of existing texts, utterances, discourses, and practices, reassessing the relative importance of their diverse messages, and preparing different methodologies through which to interpret them. . . . It is not a specialized study of certain doctrines, but a particular approach to the study of political thinking as such.[26]

This approach, he insists, injects a strong dose of realism into our analysis—I'd say two doses. First, it reminds us that there's "no escaping that politics is about power and there is consequently no escaping that good political theory needs to give plausible accounts of what is entailed, in the broadest sense, by political thinking relevant to power."[27] Second, an analysis of ideology helps us to grapple with the indeterminacy and pluralism characteristic of politics, both of which originate in the complexity and contingency of political meaning, its essentially contested character.[28]

Treating justice claims as ideological claims acknowledges their contentiousness and contestedness in a way that helps us to view indeterminacy and pluralism as resources for understanding politics. It's perhaps the single greatest weakness of IMT, the ur-mistake from which its other problems flow, that it *denies* the essentially contested nature of justice and the pluralism it engenders, regarding them as errors or obstacles to be rectified or overcome through better philosophizing. All three of IMT's congenital disabilities are consequences of this denial. This is, from my point of view at least, a momentous ontological mistake, one with profound epistemological repercussions. Any realistic analysis of the politics of justice and injustice must reckon with the contingency of meaning and its political consequences.

A BIFOCAL APPROACH

So far, in developing my position, I've relied heavily on the insights of Freeden, the leading scholar of ideology in the field. His work has—as must be apparent—profoundly shaped my thinking. One way it has done so is to reinforce my sense that a realist approach to ideology, while indispensable, is also inadequate. Over the years, Freeden has been careful and insistent in distinguishing what he calls the analysis of ideology from ideological theorizing, which attempts to direct or recommend political action.[29] In comparing his "interpretive" realism with what he denigrates as "prescriptive" realism, Freeden contrasts the "scholar," who adopts an analytic perspective on ideology and whom he characterizes as careful, responsible, and self-reflexive, with the "missionary," who practices prescriptive realism and whom he regards as a "politically and ethically fashionable" zealot.[30]

While Freeden maintains that the study of ideology must "demonstrate that . . . [it] can provide tools to the ethico-political philosophers,"[31] these tools consist mainly of reminders that the work of normative theorizing as it is conventionally understood in the discipline is risky and misguided. Like other critical realists, Freeden maintains that his approach enables normative critique—in the form of conceptual clarification, ideological unmasking, identifying epistemological errors, and so on.[32] But as I argued in the previous chapter, these critical tasks, while essential, are not equivalent with or substitutes for substantive critique and transformational prescription, both of which require an explicit value orientation. In short, I find Freeden's approach unnecessarily and unhelpfully narrow. It cannot accommodate the important orienting and prescriptive work that's elemental to political theory, and he's quite insistent that it *shouldn't* do so.

I want an approach that can support substantive normative critique of existing social arrangements and provide guidance for social transformation without sacrificing realistic political analysis. I shall call mine a *bifocal* approach to indicate that it differentiates between but integrates two distinct tasks or functions of political theory: explanation and critique/prescription. Calling this a bifocal approach highlights that we need multiple lenses to focus clearly on these distinct tasks, while also indicating that, as with bifocal eyeglasses, the integration of the two lenses within a single apparatus or framework affords more comprehensive vision. This label also makes clear that while both lenses contribute to this comprehensive view, one must switch back and forth between them, always conscious of the distinct tasks for which each is appropriate, the unique focus each provides.

Let's call one of these lenses the analytical lens, to honor my debts to Freeden. This is the lens or perspective through which we focus on how ideologies work—on their conceptual structure, their morphology, and their operation within a political field itself saturated with power and interests. This lens comes in different refractions—those ground by Freeden, by the Cambridge School (maybe that's several in itself), by poststructuralists, and others. I'll refer to the other lens as the partisan lens. It is the perspective theorists adopt when we work on or with a particular substantive normative view, consciously *as ideologists*, to organize and clarify concepts, articulate their meaning and relation to one another, formulate critiques animated by those conceptual frameworks, and recommend political action.

I insist on a bifocal approach because it accommodates normative and prescriptive theorizing from inside an ideological perspective without confusing that work with an exercise in ideal moral theory—a confusion that leads ideal theorists to deny the ideological character of their work and realists to reject normative theorizing outright. A bifocal approach improves our overall vision by allowing us to focus on two distinct (though closely related) objects of theoretical interest while acknowledging that we can't look through both lenses simultaneously—that political analysis and moral prescription are not the same thing. Instead, we move back and forth, depending on our tasks and needs, to focus appropriately. Each perspective complements the other: our analytical understanding of power and of how ideologies work orients and enriches our partisan thinking about how best to articulate arguments, critiques, and prescriptions in ways likely to influence people's behavior, to win their hearts and minds. Our partisan understanding of ideology helps us to recognize people's multiple and diverse political commitments as a central component of real politics and a manifestation of the complexity and contingency of political meaning. Different ideologies offer differing meanings and interpretations of the world, reflecting the pluralism and indeterminacy of politics. People are deeply invested in these meanings and interpretations, reminding us that it is not just power and interest but also sincere conviction that drives political behavior and conflict.

These two perspectives illuminate two complementary dimensions of what I shall refer to as *the politics of injustice*. One dimension refers to conflicts over justice claims, over the meaning of justice and injustice themselves; these conflicts originate in the divergent values and ideas animating rival ideologies. We view these conflicts analytically, using an approach like the one Freeden recommends. The second dimension of the politics of injustice refers to a particular modality of political contestation and political struggle—to the theory, strategy, and tactics of transformational politics. By transformational politics, I mean politics that seeks to eradicate injustice by challenging and changing existing social arrangements and the ideologies that justify and normalize them. We view these struggles through the partisan lens, because the conception of injustice, the strategy, and the tactics of any transformational political movement will be determined by its values and ideas, its ideology. Any political theory for the real world must make sense of both dimensions of the politics of injustice.

To make the contrast and the complementarity between the two lenses of my approach more vivid, consider briefly how each might focus on a concept like freedom. The analytical perspective would help us to clarify the genealogy of the term, its core concepts, key permutations, and place within various ideological formations, helping the theorist to make sense of disagreements and conflicts about freedom in our contemporary discourse and practice and to isolate and criticize its specific uses in different discursive and institutional domains. The partisan perspective would advocate a particular (substantive) conception of freedom, showing its strengths and appeal, and using it critically to evaluate rival conceptions as well as existing institutional arrangements. Notice that each dimension informs the other, so that the two perspectives of the bifocal approach together provide a more comprehensive picture of the politics of injustice than either could alone.

If we ask of realism and of IMT, "what's the politics being theorized?" the answers reveal that each of these approaches sees only half—different halves—of the picture. Each winds up with a distorted view as a result. Realists theorize the politics of the real world, shot through with power, conflict, and complexity, but in their focus on the first dimension of the politics of injustice they overlook the second, which they dismiss as moralizing, delusional. IMT theorizes substantive (ideological) accounts of justice, paying attention to the meaning and implications of particular normative claims, but in focusing on the second dimension of the politics of injustice it ignores the first—though it doesn't realize that this is what it's doing because it doesn't recognize justice as an indeterminate and therefore contentious notion (as ideological).

We might push the extended metaphor of bifocality to its limit by using it to summarize and contrast these respective blind spots of IMT and of realism. In a sense, IMT sees everything close up, always working within one particular ideological account of justice (though not always the same one) to develop idealized and moralized conceptions of justice. Like reading glasses, it provides a lens good for only one focal distance, and as a result, it doesn't and can't focus on other ideological perspectives or on the broader contentious politics in which claims about justice are inevitably situated. Realists, by contrast, see ideology only from a distance; they discern power, conflict, and politics quite clearly, but again, only through one lens, which can't correct their myopia about the normative tasks of political theory.

To be clear, I don't imagine that the analytical lens affords theorists some "objective" or "impartial" perspective from which to adjudicate among rival substantive claims about justice. Rather, it is a perspective from which *all* substantive conceptions of justice appear essentially alike, as ideological accounts. One reason for calling this an analytical perspective is that it enables theorists to pose questions about justice and injustice that are not (immediately) normative—such as how to make sense of ongoing disagreements over injustice. Questions like this do not turn on which if any substantive account of injustice might be true or correct; from this standpoint *it doesn't matter* whether any or none of the particular ideological accounts of injustice is true or correct, or even whether its partisans regard it as such. At the same time, I don't imagine that the normative lens affords theorists some privileged access to the truth. Rather, it's a perspective from which to carry out the partisan work of critique and prescription in full awareness of the ideological character of that work.*

While these two perspectives are distinct, they are not and cannot be wholly separate. That's because, on an ideological understanding, both political thought and political knowledge have to be understood in connection with their social origins and with the concrete setting

* I regard IMT as an example of partisan theorizing of this kind, but most ideal theorists would reject this characterization. It seems natural to treat republican, liberal, consequentialist, and other accounts of global justice as ideological, especially when we consider them together, but most practitioners simply regard themselves as getting at the truth.

of particular social-historical situations.[33] Put differently, values and commitments are implicated in the production of knowledge. The bifocal approach thus offers a powerful and productive way to make sense of the otherwise "alarming fact that the same world can appear differently to different observers."[34] This approach also reminds us that all description and analysis are normatively laden; interpretation is an inescapable predicament for political theorists, who are always enmeshed in politics. Neither the analyst of ideology nor the ideologist can pretend to a view not colored by her ideological commitments. IMT tries to avoid this predicament by stepping outside of politics, imagining a view from nowhere (or a view from everywhere). However appealing this step might appear, it is less a way out of the predicament than a denial of its existence. Realists try to avoid the predicament by turning their backs on normativity and adopting a bracing empiricism. However tough-minded this turn might seem, it too is a form of denial. Instead of seeking a way out of this predicament, the bifocal approach embraces it, adopting a thoroughly politicized hermeneutics.

Putting on bifocals helps us to reconcile the two perspectives on the politics of injustice not by choosing one or the other but by learning to shift back and forth between them. As with the glasses that I began to wear as I grew old writing this book, it takes some time to learn to make these shifts easily and to figure out that, while complementary, the two lenses are poor substitutes for one another. (If you don't wear bifocals, imagine trying to use a magnifying glass to get a good look at a bird in a tree and binoculars to read fine print.) This complementarity helps to explain—and in part to recommend—a division of labor within the field between theorists focusing mainly on the conflicts among rival ideologies and others more interested in prescription. The value added of the bifocal approach in this respect is to show how those working on either side of this division are (potential) collaborators rather than rivals.

One interesting implication of the bifocal approach is that it makes no neat distinction between "domestic" and global justice. Debates about the scope of justice, as we have seen, take this distinction as elemental, but the bifocal approach suggests that scope is merely one of the many dimensions on which competing accounts of justice will disagree. Thus it's impossible to say in any definitive way whether justice is global or statist in scope; it's a question that can only be answered with respect to particular ideological conceptions, particular claims about justice. Indeed, the bifocal approach cautions us that there is not much of value to be said about justice and injustice generally, though quite a lot might be said about how accounts of justice operate as (or through) ideologies in the world. My point is that what there is to say normatively about justice is always, inescapably, said of or from a particular partisan point of view. Thus statements such as "justice is" or "justice requires" should—for theoretical purposes—always be qualified with disclosures of the partisan position they represent. That said, an analytical perspective on the politics of injustice (on the competition among ideologies) helps us to recognize good rhetorical reasons for omitting such qualifications in political discourse. More generally, the bifocal approach renders the conflicts surrounding justice and injustice legible in terms of clashing values and ideas, as saturated with power, and as unequivocally political. What I mean is that, instead of conceiving these conflicts in terms of the error, ignorance, irrationality, unreasonableness, or immorality of those whose views differ from ours, we can treat them as manifestations of the complexity and contingency of justice and the indeterminacy and pluralism of views to which it gives rise.

In chapters 1 and 2 I criticized IMT for functioning ideologically. My argument here is consistent with that criticism, but now allows for and requires a clarification of it. The problem is not that the substantive accounts of justice that IMT generates are ideological; that's expected and unavoidable on my account. The problem is that IMT denies this ideological character and in so doing becomes distortional and engenders epistemic injustice. Similarly, I noted that many of the key arguments within global normative theory are question-begging because the normative premises to which they appeal already imply substantive positions on the questions they are invoked to resolve. I can now clarify that the problem is not the failure of these arguments to find or locate innocent or impartial first principles but rather the paralysis that the ongoing search for valid or correct principles creates. In both cases, the underlying problem is with how IMT conceptualizes justice, with its failure to understand it as ideological.

The bifocal approach that I advocate here, with its thoroughly politicized hermeneutics of justice, is a discomfiting theoretical stance. It requires theorists interested in criticizing and combating injustice to articulate and advocate substantive normative positions and simultaneously to embrace the notion that all such positions, including our own, are ideological. One critic has likened this to constantly trying to pull the rug out from under one's own feet! Clearly, I object to this characterization, but I understand that this approach will seem like a mistake and a provocation to the many scholars for whom the chief concern of political theory is to justify an ideal moral conception of justice that can animate impartial critique and provide determinate action-guidance.

ANOTHER NORMATIVITY

A primary reason why my proposed bifocal approach will seem problematic and perhaps misguided to ideal theorists (and others) is its implications for the normativity of justice claims. Most contemporary theorists treat normativity and the normative as coterminous with morality and the moral—they regard them as effectively synonymous. This is true of realists and ideal theorists alike. Both also (therefore) associate normative theorizing with the dominant, analytical approach to moral philosophy. The difference between them lies not in their *conceptualizations* of the normative but in their *attitudes* toward it: ideal theorists embrace the normative-as-moral as the key to action-guidance and transformative critique, while realists reject it as a dangerous mistake or fantasy. Their positions set up a false and unappealing dichotomy between realistic and value-driven theorizing. The bifocal approach breaks down this dichotomy, showing that while it is dangerous to imagine partisan theorizing as objective or impartial (the argument in Part I), it is also incorrect and unnecessary to reject all value-driven theorizing as delusional (the argument of the previous chapter).

The dichotomy itself is a byproduct of the overly narrow conceptualization of the normative just described. Normative claims, broadly conceived, are *should* or *ought* claims; they are propositions about how things ought to be. These claims are expressed as imperatives: people *should* keep their promises, society *ought to* take care of its most vulnerable members, and so on. The content and meaning of normative statements can vary significantly: they might be thought to express or convey purported moral truths (thou shalt not kill), social conventions (don't put your elbows on the table), personal beliefs (the death penalty should be abolished), aesthetic judgments (he shouldn't wear such drab colors), and so on. It's not always evident what kind of claim a normative claim is and not always easy to work out what the author of the claim intends in making it.

Moral claims are a supposed subset of normative claims. They are widely regarded by theorists and philosophers as possessing some special, ineluctable force—one often attributed to the supposed truth, correctness, validity, or universality of their content. That is, this special force is held to be a function or reflection of their ontological character, a quality that ought-propositions expressing content related to domains like etiquette and aesthetics are not thought to share. This difference is sometimes expressed in terms of categorical and hypothetical imperatives. Categorical imperatives express a kind of "moral absolutism," a belief that some behaviors are morally wrong or morally obligatory for all agents, regardless of their desires or motivations. They are said to provide everyone with reasons to act.[35] Hypothetical imperatives, by contrast, have an instrumental or contingent normativity; they tell agents what to do *given* particular aims and circumstances, and they bind solely through the exigencies of reason and commitment. As we've seen, IMT trades in categorical imperatives—principles of justice conceived in ideal, moral terms and held to entail binding duties. The whole point of IMT as an approach to theorizing justice is to discover and justify these categorical principles, on the assumption that (only) such principles can reliably orient critique and motivate and guide action. The methods of IMT are thought to be appropriate to ensure that we identify the right or best principles, which are assumed to possess the special attribute of morality—namely, categorical force.

The bifocal approach treats all justice claims as ideological. That means that it treats all justice claims as hypothetical imperatives, not categorical ones.† It does so because it recognizes that all justice claims are generated from within ideological systems and are thus contingent upon the concepts and interpretations that inform those systems. *Treating* justice claims this way does not mean that they *are* this way. The bifocal approach does not depend on *its being true that* all justice claims are hypothetical imperatives; nor does it depend on all ideologists regarding their justice claims as hypothetical imperatives. It conceptualizes them all as such because doing so provides powerful analytic leverage on and insight into the politics of injustice and shows deep respect for pluralism.

Very many theorists and philosophers will regard this treatment as a mistake because it denies or sacrifices (two very different things) the categorical force of morality. Principles of justice, they will worry, will lose their stringency and binding force. But there is good reason to question whether categorical imperatives really possess the mysterious qualities attributed to them. In a brilliant and iconoclastic 1972 essay, Philippa Foot skewered what she saw as vacuous arguments for the special normativity of categorical imperatives. "It is supposed," she writes, "that moral considerations necessarily give reasons for acting to any man. The difficulty is, of course, to defend this proposition, which is more often repeated than explained."[36] What further feature of moral claims, she wonders, makes them categorical, inescapable? "We must be told what it is that makes the moral 'should' relevantly different from the 'should' appearing in normative statements of other kinds."[37] Foot considers and rejects the familiar assumptions and assertions made in behalf of the special status of categorical *shoulds*, finding each to be deficient, question begging, or nonsensical. "It is obvious that the *normative* character of moral judgment does not guarantee its reason-giving force" or adequately differentiate it from hypothetical imperatives, she contends.[38]

† It actually regards *all* political oughts as hypothetical imperatives, but I stick to justice for ease of exposition.

Foot maintains that the apparent ineluctability of categorical judgments boils down to a *feeling* that we must comply with them, which feeling she attributes to our moral education.[39] "There is no difficulty about the idea that we feel we *have to* behave morally, and given the psychological conditions of the learning of moral behavior, it is natural that we should have such feelings. What we cannot do is quote them in support of the doctrine of categorical imperative."[40] Her conclusion is unequivocal: "moral judgments have no better claim to be categorical imperatives than do statements about etiquette."[41] In trying to justify moral *shoulds* through claims about what one ought to do, or must do, or has a duty to do, moralists are merely trading in illusions—"trying to give the moral 'ought' a magic force."[42]

Anticipating the objection that duty falls out of her account, Foot argues that people don't feel moral duties unless they are moral people—people who have been educated and socialized to feel a particular way about moral questions. If one is not a moral person, talk of duties and obligations and categorical imperatives is likely to leave one unmoved.[43] She rejects the Kantian notion that only actions properly motivated by duty are genuinely virtuous: "what reason could there be," she asks rhetorically, "for refusing to call a man a just man if he acted justly because he loved truth and liberty, and wanted everyone to be treated with a certain minimum respect" rather than out of a sense of moral obligation?[44] Morality is not the sole source of motivation for ethical action, Foot insists: people are prepared to fight so hard for values like liberty and justice because "these are the kinds of ends that arouse devotion."[45]

This devastating deflation of categorical normativity became, for Foot, the starting point for a conception of virtue ethics. My concerns take me in another direction (though I am convinced that virtue ethics can be comfortably accommodated within the bifocal approach). In any case, Foot understood—as I do—that many people would fear and condemn this view of hypothetical normativity as "dangerous and subversive of morality." Her eloquent, almost elegiac response is worth quoting at length:

> We are apt to panic at the thought that we ourselves, or other people, might stop caring about the things we do care about, and we feel

> that the categorical imperative gives us some control over the situation. But it is interesting that the people of Leningrad were not similarly struck by the thought that only the contingent fact that other citizens shared their loyalty and devotion to the city stood between them and the Germans during the terrible years of the siege. Perhaps we should be less troubled than we are by fear of defection from the moral cause; perhaps we should even have less reason to fear it if people thought of themselves as volunteers banded together to fight for liberty and justice and against inhumanity and oppression.[46]

I read Foot as equipping theorists with a realistic outlook on normativity. First, hypothetical normativity accurately describes the way that many people understand their political values—as contingent commitments of profound importance that motivate and guide their actions. Instead of conscripts in the service of categorical morality, my approach imagines us as volunteers inspired by our values to enlist in the service of causes we believe in. Second, this conceptualization of normativity allows theorists using the bifocal approach to make sense not just of conflicts, clashes, and struggles over power and interests but also of the competing conceptions of justice that we observe at work in politics and on which we rely when we engage in critique and prescription. Political theory needs a value orientation and substantive normative arguments to enable critique and to recommend political action; a hypothetical understanding of political normativity allows for the reconciliation of these needs with a realistic analysis of politics.

I know that many political theorists will reject this view and continue to regard principles of justice as possessed of categorical force, persevering in their efforts to justify those principles in the ways that they hope will bestow them with such force. For my part, I am simply interested in other problems—political problems to do with injustice and the role of political theory in helping to overcome it. I recognize of course that many theorists embarked on the search for categorical principles of justice also care deeply about eradicating injustice; I simply think they are mistaken in their belief about what's required to realize this aim that we share.

OBJECTIONS

To further clarify what's at stake in adopting a hypothetical conception of morality and to deepen and extend my broader argument, I want to work through several objections that have been (or might be) raised to my approach.

The first two are variations on a theme. Ideal theorists maintain, as we have seen, that only ideal moral principles of justice can reliably inform critique and guide action. Some critics have complained that my approach cannot do so because it conceives of justice claims as hypothetical imperatives, which have "only" an instrumental or contingent normativity (again: they tell agents what to do *given* particular aims, values, and circumstances). My reply is that ideology supplies those givens; the core values, concepts, and interpretations provided by an ideology can generate clear and cogent interpretations and guidance that can be shared widely among adherents of that account.[47] We can even ascribe a kind of internal validity to ideological accounts if the critiques and recommendations they generate are coherent and consistent with that core. Ideologies allow people to "posit, explain, and justify ends and means";[48] they provide perfectly adequate bases for critique and guidance. So the ideological view lets theorists account for all the things that ideal moral conceptions of justice are supposed to do (albeit differently). One of the chief advantages of treating justice claims as ideological is that doing so provides us the flexibility to theorize rival accounts of injustice as genuinely *normative* accounts without idealizing or moralizing them and without assuming anything about their truth or universality. This decoupling of internal and external validity distinguishes the bifocal approach from IMT and from realism. True, this decoupling implies that ideological accounts of justice are (immediately) authoritative solely for partisans or adherents of a particular ideology, but that simply makes my approach more realistic than its rivals.

The second variation on this theme is a familiar refrain. The most frequent and fervent objection to my approach is that it invites or embraces a dangerous moral relativism. In response, I can only say that I find claims about relativism inapposite in connection with my approach because it is not designed for or interested in adjudicating among rival value systems or ideologies. It is designed instead to help us make sense of the contentious politics of injustice. This is simply a different question from that in which IMT is primarily interested, one that does not entail or require attention to matters of truth or impartiality. Besides, nothing in my approach denies the possibility that some particular ideological perspective might be true in some moral or philosophical sense; it's just that nothing turns on that question. That my approach is *theoretically indifferent* to the truth of ideological claims does not mean, however, that it recommends or entails relativism; in this, it is reminiscent of the "anti anti-relativism" of Clifford Geertz, who emphasized that this double-negative formulation "enables one to reject something without thereby committing oneself to what it rejects."[49]

I reject the antirelativism implicit in IMT but do not embrace or endorse relativism. For we adherents to a particular ideology, nothing about the existence of competing value systems implies that they are as valid or appealing for us as ours is; nothing implies that it's impossible to make a reasoned and principled defense of our cherished beliefs. Moreover, nothing about this multiplicity need diminish our fidelity to our principled commitments. The critics might reply that my view is nonetheless deficient because it does not provide categorical reasons for everyone to act. This reply presumes what my approach rejects: that there is a special moral force of which justice claims of some special kind partake—that political oughts are or somehow can be categorical. Foot showed decisively, however, that it's nonsensical for critics to complain that hypothetical imperatives are deficient because lacking a quality of inescapability that the critics cannot identify or explain in connection with their own views. At a minimum, the burden of proof is on the other side. To me, the important question is whether hypothetical imperatives generate sufficient reasons for action for the people who subscribe to a particular ideology or value system. It is hard to doubt that they can and do: both our personal experience and our best social-scientific evidence confirm that people frequently regard their values and commitments as giving them powerful motivations for action.

One critic has, somewhat surprisingly, claimed that my approach is really the same as that taken by most ideal theorists, who also regard their arguments as contingent. What ideal theorists are doing, according to this critic, is stipulating that *if* their principles of justice are valid, agents ought to behave in the prescribed ways. Pablo Gilabert has argued that there is a difference between (1) aspiring to find principles of justice to which there are no superior alternatives, and (2) claiming to have shown that there are no superior alternatives to a particular moral principle. The difference is between ideal theory (1) and its full accomplishment (2).[50] It's true that this difference introduces a kind of contingency into IMT, but it is a different kind of contingency from that associated with hypothetical normativity. In Gilabert's schema, the contingency is related to whether the theorist has found the correct principle. In my argument, the contingency of justice claims is an intrinsic and irreducible feature of the indeterminacy and essential contestability of justice. My position might be wrong, but it's certainly different from that of IMT. Besides, one is hard-pressed to find an ideal theorist who acknowledges any contingency of the kind Gilabert describes; mostly their work is replete with claims about the binding duties and obligations that follow from (justified) moral principles. If pressed, ideal theorists probably would acknowledge that theirs might not be the correct principles, but they would not, I think, acknowledge that it's a matter of theoretical indifference whether there are correct principles. That's a big difference.

In response to all of this, critics might retrench, objecting that to abandon the search for ideal moral principles of justice possessed of categorical normativity is simply to abandon the philosophical (critical and prescriptive) work of political theory. There's nothing left to do, these critics might insist, but to enunciate some values and wade polemically into the political fray, giving "irrational free rein to the mere conviction of injustice and to eagerness for change of any sort."[51] This is simply wrong. There is plenty of important philosophical work to be done in developing coherent and persuasive accounts of injustice. I do agree, however, that this work will be different from the work that typically (pre)occupies ideal theorists. Richard Rorty made a useful distinction between philosophical *justification*, the search for moral grounds or foundations that supposedly imbue values, arguments, and critiques with binding or categorical moral force or "backup," and philosophical *articulation*, the careful formulation and expression of values, arguments, and critiques.[52] IMT engages in justification; ideologists working within my partisan perspective engage in articulation. The latter allows, as I have shown, for critique and prescription. Precisely the point of integrating the partisan lens into the bifocal theoretical apparatus is to preserve these functions while integrating them with a realistic analytical approach.

One remaining objection, mentioned earlier, concerns pulling the rug out from under one's own feet. There are really two distinct but related concerns here. One is that in conceptualizing justice as ideological, my approach undermines its critical and action-guidance functions; I've just addressed this concern. The other is that by describing justice as ideological, my approach robs it of its moral force, thereby undercutting the political claims it supports and the political actors who rely on it. If the concern is primarily rhetorical, it might be enough to reiterate my earlier observation that there are good reasons to omit qualifiers about the hypothetical normativity of justice claims in political discourse. If the concern is to do with a supposed difference in the moral *oomph* of hypothetical and categorical imperatives, it's simply a restatement of a position I have argued against at length. To recapitulate that argument: I don't worry about losing the special normative force associated with categorical imperatives because I haven't been persuaded that it exists or that it matters theoretically and because the assumption that it does has been debilitating for political theorists interested in combating injustice.

CONCLUSION

In this chapter I have proposed a bifocal theoretical framework that conceptualizes justice claims as ideological claims and enables theorists to make sense of the politics of injustice both from a realistic analytical perspective and from a partisan normative one. This approach provides a more comprehensive understanding of the politics of injustice than its competitors by integrating two crucial functions of political theory—the analysis and critique of ideologies, and substantive critique and political prescription—within a single framework. The attribution of a rehabilitated hypothetical normativity to (ideological) justice claims makes this reconciliation and integration possible and provides a solid basis for a political theory designed for the real world.

5

A Democratic Account of Injustice

In this chapter, I build on the work begun in the previous one by *articulating* a democratic account of injustice. Articulation always proceeds within a particular system of values, ideas, and commitments—within an ideology. I articulate an emancipatory democratic account of injustice, both to exemplify the kind of work theorists can do from a partisan theoretical perspective and to establish the critical and prescriptive orientation that will animate and orient my arguments in the final part of the book. Throughout the discussion I highlight the complementarity of the two theoretical perspectives of the bifocal approach and note how it enriches the partisan account developed here.

I begin with an elaboration of democracy's core values and of some of the key ideas and interpretations that stabilize the democratic conception. In presenting these concepts and the connections among them as I do, I'm making an intervention within the democratic ideology (I would once have written, "within democratic theory"), advocating my preferred conception of it. Space constraints make it impossible for me to offer anything like a complete genealogy or articulation of this conception; I can only sketch the outlines and gesture toward the rest. Since my primary purpose here is to provide a democratic account of injustice, I emphasize the critique of power relations through which democracy identifies domination, oppression, and exploitation as unjust. I then develop some epistemological and methodological implications of this account, showing why democratic political commitments also entail a commitment to a feminist account of situated knowledge that makes people's actual experiences and understandings of injustice the basis of a reflexive and provisional account of it and to a dialectical procedure that encourages critical attention to the processes through which injustice is produced and reproduced. I conclude by engaging with three prominent and sympathetic interlocutors to highlight the advantages and distinctiveness of my emancipatory account of democratic injustice and of the bifocal approach in which it operates.

That last statement requires brief clarification before we proceed. The democratic account that follows is not part of or entailed by the bifocal approach. One might agree with everything I wrote in the previous chapter and reject almost everything I write here without contradiction. The following account is an illustration of how articulation proceeds and how a particular partisan normative conception fits within the bifocal approach. That said, I also hope to make a persuasive case for my substantive position as well.

By a democratic account I simply mean one that characterizes injustice from a democratic perspective—that is, in light of democracy's core values and commitments. The work of formulating such an account involves, again, clarifying these values, developing arguments about justice and injustice informed by them, and deploying these arguments in the critique of existing social arrangements and prevailing ways of thinking. Because the bifocal approach attributes hypothetical normativity to claims about justice and injustice, I don't make any attempt to justify the values, ideas, and interpretations I present below. They reflect my own commitments, commitments I hold dear and regard as noble, worthy, and politically powerful and appealing. I use terms like *account* or *characterization* of injustice, rather than *theory* or *definition*, to emphasize that a democratic account is not an ideal moral account but an ideological one.

Democracy's core values are freedom and equality. Historically, they were invoked to justify the transfer of sovereignty to the people (in Parliament); over time, they have come to define the democratic creed itself.[1] They are "core" democratic values in the sense that all modern arguments for democracy rely on them. Freedom and equality establish the broad parameters of democracy as a political ideology; the specific meanings of the values and their relation to one another are contested, a point to which I return below.* One key idea in the emancipatory conception of democracy that I favor is the commitment to freedom and equality *for everyone*. This idea has been present from the beginning of democratic thinking, but the commitment to it has wavered. The historical-conceptual task of justifying the transfer of sovereignty shows why both freedom and equality are necessary and why both must be attributed to everyone. Individuals might be regarded as free but also unequal in their strength, talents, and so on, giving those with greater endowments an eminent title to rule; individuals equal in their endowments might be born into castes or other forms of natural or socially inescapable subjection. Only freedom and equality *together* undercut natural hierarchy and authority in the way that Locke, for instance, needed them to do. He also needed *everyone* to be regarded as free and equal; if only some people are, the possibility remains that others might be legitimately subordinated.[2] This is why Locke had to pretend he believed in the freedom and equality of women, servants, and slaves, at least initially, a pretense it took extensive work for him to nullify.[3] Positing the freedom and equality of all people is thus the definitive normative and conceptual move of democratic theory: it invalidates all

* There is some debate about whether democracy is a distinct ideology; some commentators regard it as a political method compatible with several ideologies. Ideologies always overlap to varying degrees; that said, I emphatically reject the characterization of democracy as a political method, for reasons my account makes clear.

kinds of natural authority and hierarchy and eliminates any justification for arbitrary or oppressive rule.[4]

In calling freedom and equality *core* democratic values, I don't mean to imply that they are uncontroversial, either "universally" or among democrats. They are—like all political concepts—essentially contested; their meaning is socially constructed and inherently political or politicized, which is to say that they admit of multiple and often conflicting understandings or interpretations and are fundamentally indeterminate. Put another way, the conflicts over their meaning are irresolvable—*theoretically*. Still, we can distinguish internal disagreement about the meaning of democracy and its core concepts from external challenges to democracy itself. What's distinctive of *democratic* accounts, as I have just described, is their allegiance to the idea of freedom and equality for all. Recognizing democracy as an ideology reminds us that not everyone is a democrat; many people reject one or both of these values, or think they apply only to a select group, or regard other values as paramount.

The idea that everyone should be regarded as free and equal has proven to be the most potent and disruptive political idea of the modern era. Together, freedom and equality drive the great leveling machine of democratization, which has razed traditional hierarchies and toppled authorities of all kinds. Everywhere these values are introduced or asserted, they pose an immediate and potent challenge to accepted social arrangements and power structures. For this reason, they have long been associated with emancipation, a term originally denoting the formal legal release from slavery or indenture but now implying liberation from any form of physical, psychological, or intellectual bondage.[5] I have elsewhere described emancipation as a condition of nonsubjection and emancipatory democracy as the political commitment to achieving that status for everyone. In doing so I align myself with one strain within democratic theory that stretches back (rather imperfectly) to the Diggers and Levellers in 17th-century England and includes radical theorists of the French Revolution, of abolition, feminism, and anticolonialism.[†]

[†] Goodhart, *Democracy as Human Rights*, 117ff., 136ff. Marx's critique of bourgeois rights and liberal democracy meant that many communists and socialists scorned democracy; as a result,

Freedom and equality for everyone make democracy a general and inclusive ideology. The logic that made democracy effective against the divine right of kings proved difficult to contain and wreaked havoc on social order. Following the systematic formulation of the idea that all inequalities are illegitimate and unnatural, the "profound subversive power of the democratic discourse" catalyzed its spread into increasingly wider domains, acting "as a fermenting agent upon the different forms of struggle against subordination."[6] Once this logic is unleashed, once the genie is out of the bottle, no relations of hierarchy and subordination, no traditional or "natural" authorities, are immune from critique. This tremendous subversive or leveling power of freedom and equality, which provides democracy with its emancipatory thrust, explains a great deal about the appeal and the contentiousness of democratic values. Anyone struggling against subjection might find these values appealing and quite useful precisely because they provide grounds for challenging the legitimacy of all kinds of social, economic, cultural, and political hierarchies.

These values are contentious for precisely the same reason: anyone seeking to preserve special status or privilege or to maintain oppressive hierarchies will have obvious reason to reject democracy, perhaps appealing instead to nature, order, virtue, culture, knowledge, tradition, stability, divine will, and so on. Defenders of privilege in its myriad forms frequently condemn democracy and its core values as foreign, unnatural, or heretical. It's worth noting that this was as true in the West as anywhere (and remains somewhat true today). After all, it's not as if, historically, women, working people, people of color, LGBTQ* people, and others have been regarded as free and equal in the West—culturally or philosophically. Within a bifocal framework, the contentiousness surrounding democratic values can be understood and theorized as the flip side of their appeal: what makes them attractive to some—their emancipatory or leveling logic—makes them anathema to others.

democratic theory was largely deprived of its natural connection with working-class struggles throughout the 19th and much of the 20th centuries; Samuel Bowles and Herbert Gintis, *Democracy and Capitalism: Property, Community, and the Contradictions of Modern Social Thought* (New York: Basic Books, 1986), 9n.

I stress the emancipatory character of democracy to differentiate my position from other democratic accounts, primarily the (neo)liberal account. Liberalism seeks as much equality for all as is consistent with the protection of everyone's fundamental liberties (or it seeks an equal distribution of fundamental liberties). Liberals typically portray freedom and equality as conflicting values and consistently recommend the resolution of these conflicts in favor of freedom. As a result, liberal democracy often recognizes only a narrow range of civil and political freedoms, permitting vast disparities in wealth, income, and social status. Liberal democracy might, perhaps tendentiously, be described as an attempt to limit or contain the emancipatory logic of democracy to a narrow political sphere. One way to do so, as we have seen, is through reliance on arguments about obvious or fundamental liberties—including opportunity, nondiscrimination, civil and economic liberties, and the rule of law—the preservation of which outweighs considerations of equality. (This is why liberals have historically been tempted by various forms of "enlightened despotism," whether in the salons of Frederick the Great or the stability of Singapore.)

Democracy as I understand it is much more radical, expansive, and open-ended than its liberal cousin. Emancipatory democrats see freedom and equality not as conflicting but as mutually conditioning and mutually constitutive of democracy, as working in combination to eradicate all forms of subjection in all domains of life. Indeed, in the emancipatory tradition, democracy has never been understood solely in terms of political institutions and procedures; rather, it is broadly concerned with the operation of power and its effects, with relations between superior and inferior.[7] On this view, emancipation and democratization are tied up with revolutions or transformations in social relations—with the reconfiguration of relations of power.

Historically, emancipatory democratic theorists have invoked human rights as a key concept and vocabulary of democratic empowerment.[8] The historical and conceptual links among human rights, democracy, and emancipation probably originate in the *denial* of rights in relations of subordination and in the role this denial played in fueling the democratic revolutions of the 18th century, whose declarations of rights cataloged those denials felt most acutely by aggrieved and newly ascendant political classes (hence the *bourgeois* character of the earliest manifestos). Over time, however, many people have pushed to expand the scope, the meaning, and even the catalog of rights rather than to abandon this problematic vocabulary.[9] Many activists engaged in struggles of various kinds use human rights to name and condemn the injustices they oppose.

I want to suggest that the language of human rights proves so congenial to emancipatory democrats because human rights can be used to constrain power, to criticize and challenge existing social arrangements as unjust, and to develop and protect social conditions supportive of emancipation. Put differently, human rights speak to power and its operation in all kinds of structures, processes, and social relationships. Human rights can thus be considered another key concept for democrats and a core concept of emancipatory democracy. It also happens to play a central part in the politics people make against injustice in many places around the world—including in struggles to reimagine their communities and themselves as political subjects.[10] Of course, human rights discourse can also be—has often been—used as an instrument of injustice, a tool of domination, oppression, and exploitation.[11] Sometimes this use is sheer hypocrisy, as when human rights are invoked as rhetorical cover for differently motivated actions. Sometimes, however, there are different ideological conceptions of human rights at work. Neoliberalism, for example, invokes quite a narrow understanding of liberty rights plus property in the service of its own economic and political projects.[12]

One advantage of the bifocal approach is that instead of treating these different meanings and uses of human rights as indicative of philosophical uncertainty or corruption, it invites theorists to analyze them in terms of the ideological systems from which they are deployed. Such diversity of meanings and uses is to be expected in connection with what has become a ubiquitous and indispensable political concept and discourse. That needn't—it can't be allowed to—lead to theoretical or political despair. As Edward Said put it, in grappling with the historical and contemporary abuses of the concept and vocabulary of human rights, "the thing to remember . . . is that there isn't another language at hand"; we have no choice but to try to "use that very same language to recapture the subject, reclaim it, and reconnect it to the tremendously complicated realities" that have been simplified, betrayed, diminished, or dissolved by our opponents.[13] When we understand human rights as a concept shared and contested among different ideologies, it becomes immediately clear that there is no philosophical resolution to questions about its meaning and use. As Said makes clear, the struggle over human rights is political.

DEMOCRACY, POWER, AND INJUSTICE

I want to turn from the elaboration of democracy's core values and concepts to the critique of power relations that it enables. Democracy is quintessentially concerned with the legitimate uses of power and the necessary and appropriate constraints on its operation and effects. Terms like *legitimate* and *appropriate* indicate that democracy both needs and can generate a substantive critique of power relations; the democratic account of injustice emerges from this critique. In developing this account, I hope both to sketch a compelling conception of injustice and to illustrate one of the advertised features of my approach: its capacity to integrate analytical and partisan perspectives.

To begin, we need an analysis of power. Following Barnett and Duvall, I conceptualize it as "the production, in and through social relations, of effects that shape the capacities of actors to determine their own circumstances and fate."[14] They identify four forms or expressions of power: compulsory, institutional, structural, and productive power.[15] *Compulsory* power refers to "relations of interaction that allow one actor to have direct control over another."[16] This is the power to compel with military or economic might; as the authors note, however, nonmaterial resources, such as the "naming and shaming" techniques used by international human rights and global justice campaigns, can also be forms of compulsory power.[17] *Institutional* power refers to actors exercising indirect control over others through formal or informal institutions—for instance, when powerful actors design international institutions to work to their long-term advantage and to the disadvantage of others.[18] What makes institutional power different from compulsory power is that the powerful actor rarely possesses the resources of institutional power outright. Trade regimes, for example, might be set up in ways that reflect and protect the interests and privileges of powerful states, but those states cannot fully or predictably control the decisions of the institutions that interpret and enforce the rules.[19]

IMT typically theorizes power narrowly in terms of these two of its forms. I don't mean that ideal theorists explicitly endorse or adopt this narrow view; rather, I mean that the literature as a whole *treats* power primarily in these terms. When ideal theorists discuss power, they typically focus on issues like the relative military and economic strength of states in the global system or the capacity of international organizations like the IMF or the World Bank to push through policies over the objections of governments or citizens. There are two striking limitations associated with this narrow conceptualization of power: first, it treats the effects of power as purely interactional.[20] One agent exercises "power over" another, on this view, to get the latter to do something it would not otherwise do, in Dahl's famous formulation.[21] This "power over" might be the result of a direct relation between two actors or one mediated through an institution.

The second noteworthy limitation of this narrow conception is that it treats power as flowing primarily (if not exclusively) from material resources—from bombs, bonds, and the like. This focus on interactional power and on material sources of power is hardly surprising, given the strong distributive orientation of global normative theory; it's fair to say (as many ideal theorists do explicitly say) that within IMT justice is a matter of the fair or equitable distribution of material resources—of power and wealth. Of course, ideal theorists are also concerned with basic liberties and protections (which they also typically conceive as goods distributed within society), yet most global normative theory focuses primarily, almost exclusively, on the (mal)distribution of wealth and power. On this view, *injustice* might consist in the improper distribution of such resources (as in critiques of global economic inequality), or it might result from more powerful agents using their power to establish or maintain privileged positions with respect to weaker ones through direct interactions or through institutions that "lock in" their advantages (as in critiques of global governance or global public power). In either case, within the *distributive* justice paradigm the solution to injustice is nearly always *redistribution*—of wealth, rights, income, military capacity, Security Council seats, voting shares in international financial institutions, whatever.

This narrow conception is inadequate for theorizing the full range of power relations with which a democratic account of injustice must reckon. It provides little leverage on questions about the effectiveness of norms and ideas, questions that global normative theorists might be expected to find relevant. Specifically, it ignores the *constitutive* effects of power, which have to do with "how particular *social* relations are responsible for producing particular kinds of actors."[22] While *interactional* power or "power over" is frequently understood in behavioral terms, its effects manifest in the actions of the objects or targets of power, *constitutive* power produces effects manifest in "the identities of the occupants of social positions"—their self-understandings, subjectivities, frameworks of meaning, and so on.[23]

Constitutive power is *structural* when it "concerns the constitution of social capacities and interests of actors in direct relation to one another."[24] In other words, when the relations of power are specific, as in the relation between capital and labor within capitalism, structural power is implicated. Structural power concerns the internal relations of structural positions, defining what kind of social beings actors are and producing the structural capacities of different subject positions in direct relation to one another. It allocates differential capacities to these different positions and defines the self-understandings of the subjects who occupy them. In addition, it shapes actors' ideologies in ways that often justify and reproduce these differentials and promote acceptance of their roles in existing social arrangements.[25]

Constitutive power is *productive* when it refers to "the socially diffuse production of subjectivity in systems of meaning and signification."[26] It overlaps with structural power in producing or constituting social capacities, though in a more generalized and diffuse way. Rather than focusing on structures, productive power refers to systems of signification and meaning manifest in knowledge and discourses, to how "systems of signification . . . 'microfields' or the quotidian . . . 'define the (im)possible, the (im)probable, the natural, the normal, what counts as a problem.'"[27] As an example, consider how the racialized, gendered, and Eurocentric discourse of development shapes the knowledges and subjectivities of "underdeveloped" peoples and places.[28]

IMT can't easily comprehend constitutive power because many of its justificatory strategies and many of its arguments about duty and responsibility assume idealized, autonomous moral agents. Indeed, structural power and productive power are rarely mentioned by ideal theorists, a significant and problematic blind spot. Yet to theorize constitutive power in the ideal stage would be problematic, since its operation is predicated on inequalities and differentials in power that—as with race and gender—ideal theorists exclude from consideration until the nonideal stage. Many realists also neglect constitutive power, perhaps because their zeal for description directs their attention to readily observable manifestations of power, or because their antimoralism leads them to acquiesce in power and its effects as "facts" about our world. Even those realists who do (recommend that we) engage in ideological critique seem more interested in analyzing ideologies as thought-systems and mapping their conceptual terrain than in working through their effects on social relationships and interactions.

Again, I conceptualize power as "the production, *in and through social relations*, of effects that shape the capacities of actors to determine their own circumstances and fate."[29] The emphasis on *social relations* is particularly congenial to a democratic approach, which, as I discussed earlier, is concerned with relations of superiority and subordination. This broad conceptualization of power entails a concomitantly broad conceptualization of the political as comprising social relations—past and present cultural, political, economic, and ecological relationships and processes, both formal and informal—and the workings of power in and through them. Wherever power operates, *that* is the political.

Democracy is concerned with social relations of subordination throughout the expansive domain of the political. It characterizes as unjust any social relations that create, sustain, or contribute to subordination. Injustice, on this view, is a kind of deformity in social relations. Stressing *deformity* helps to clarify that democracy is not a naive, blanket condemnation of power; rather, democracy condemns *power that produces or sustains subordination.* This preliminary account of democratic injustice vivifies the connections between democratization, injustice, and emancipation. Democratization aims at the eradication of injustice; the elimination of unjust power relations leads or contributes to emancipation. Characterizing injustice in this way explicitly (re)connects democratic theory with theorizing about injustice, a connection that's been lost in IMT.[30]

Democracy recognizes three broad categories of injustice: domination, oppression, and exploitation. Very generally, *domination* consists in arbitrary control or the *threat* of arbitrary control of people's lives; *oppression* consists in unwarranted interference in people's lives; *exploitation* consists in taking wrongful advantage of people. Each of these categories of injustice represents a modality of subordination, a particular way in which social relations produce and perpetuate subordination.

Both domination and oppression can be understood generally as types of interference. Domination emphasizes that both arbitrary interference *and the threat of arbitrary interference* violate freedom.[31] It's the realization that the threat of interference diminishes freedom and equality that makes domination distinct from oppression.[‡] By focusing our attention on the *threat* of interference, domination facilitates the theorization of how constitutive power can make people positionally or epistemically vulnerable, make them dependent upon or deferent to others, in ways that constitute

‡ On the republican view, not all interference is normatively objectionable. Paradigmatically, the law interferes in people's lives, but—in a republican constitutional state, at least—does so in a way that tracks or is responsive to people's interests and therefore does not constitute domination. So when another agent interferes *arbitrarily* in a person's life (or has the capacity to do so), when the interference takes place between agents, and when it is voluntary and intentional, it counts as domination; Buckinx, Trejo-Mathys, and Waligore, "Domination across Borders," 6.

subordination. Oppression refers to *unwarranted* interference.[§] From an emancipatory democratic perspective, oppression can be understood simply and broadly as the direct violation of people's human rights—those rights necessary for achieving and preserving emancipation.[32] This is not and cannot be a fixed list; rights understood in this way must reflect a dynamic response to people's actual experiences of oppression. Thus the definition of injustice itself must be dynamic and provisional. Exploitation means taking wrongful advantage of someone.[**] An advantage is *wrongful* on the democratic account when it is gained as a result of someone's position or vulnerability within a system of social relations. This broader definition comprises not only the important economic dimension of exploitation but also sexual exploitation, psychological manipulation, and others. Relations of exploitation show that victims of injustice are not always socially marginalized or excluded, as is too often assumed; many are deliberately *included* in social relations precisely in ways that (are designed to) take wrongful advantage of their positions or vulnerability.[33]

It's been suggested to me that one might use the term *domination* to refer to all of these injustices, but there are good reasons not to do so. For instance, the familiar interactional understanding of domination misses how structural power facilitates exploitation and how productive power can discipline subjects in ways that sharply limit their freedom; marginalization and some forms of cultural imperialism (such as epistemic domination) are examples.[34] In addition, arbitrary interference doesn't adequately rule out all forms of oppression.[35] Besides, I have

[§] For liberals, interference becomes unwarranted—it becomes oppression—when it crosses a (deontological) line, a line drawn by a person's rights, property, autonomy, etc. How the line gets drawn is a subject of intense debate. For libertarians, government is inherently oppressive, so it must be extremely limited. For liberal democrats, the oppressive nature of state power is offset by consent: government does not oppress when it is responsive, accountable—in short, when it is democratic. Yet fears of democratic masses obliterating the politically vulnerable line protecting property and privilege makes many liberals uncomfortable with their own solution to the problem of oppression.

[**] In Marxist thought, exploitation refers to the extraction of surplus value from the labor of wage workers (profit). While acknowledging the special importance of this particular form of injustice, I adopt a somewhat broader view.

never found Occam's razor to be particularly sharp: what's important is not the number of conceptual categories but the depth and rigor of the analysis they support. While domination, oppression, and exploitation do overlap, each usefully highlights particular aspects of injustice; together they emphasize democracy's concern with power differentials and positional vulnerability. Another important reason to maintain these distinctions is that they preserve a rich emancipatory vocabulary for talking about injustice. Oppression is deeply rooted in political theory and analysis and vividly evocative of a particular class of wrongs, making it a key category of political discourse for emancipatory social movements.[36] Exploitation likewise evokes a specifically class-based and particularly pervasive form of injustice central to one of the key emancipatory political traditions of modernity. Finally, highlighting the conceptual similarity among different types of injustice is politically valuable, as it facilitates the construction of broad-based forms of solidarity, as I discuss in the next chapter.

I realize that adopting the categories of domination, oppression, and exploitation risks diluting the originality of my account. After all, these concepts are familiar in global normative theory, and numerous examples can be cited (many are cited here) of studies that deploy them critically and constructively. I'm not too worried about this, partly because I think originality gets too much emphasis in political theory (more on that later). In addition, ideological analysis teaches us to expect that different ideologies will share and contest key concepts in our political discourse. As ideologists, then, we should not be surprised to find ourselves working and reworking the same concepts (nor should we be surprised when our most original inventions make little impact). In any case, the democratic characterization of injustice I offer here is distinctive in its emphasis on power, on social relations of subordination. This emphasis shifts our theoretical attention away from puzzles related to justification and toward people's actual experiences of injustice, toward the phenomenological distinctiveness of injustice discussed in chapter 1. The bifocal approach provides valuable theoretical resources for locating this phenomenon within a broader field of power relations (including ideological ones) in a way that may diminish the conceptual originality of this account but promises to enhance its social relevance and impact.

The final part of the book is devoted to showing the political and practical advantages of understanding democratic injustice within a bifocal approach, but let me give a brief example here to illustrate how that approach transforms the way political theorists think about the normative arguments that we make. Shklar and many other theorists who have argued for greater attention to injustice have struggled with the difficulty of differentiating injustice from misfortune. The answer, on the democratic account of injustice I have articulated here, is straightforward: injustices result from the operation of effects of power through social relations. So, when someone contracts a serious illness, it is misfortune; when her cancer results from the illegal disposal of toxic waste, it is injustice. When a hurricane destroys someone's home, it is misfortune; when marginalized communities are inundated, drowned because inadequate and neglected flood-control systems fail predictably in a storm surge, it is injustice. Violent storms and malfunctioning cells can do us terrible harm, but it is only when those harms are produced through social relations, when power is implicated, that they become injustices on the democratic view.

Of course, this way of drawing the distinction is politically fraught. The "facts" about whether and how social relations produce harms are themselves always contestable and frequently contested; rival ideologies will interpret them differently, in light of different values and ideas. The bifocal approach prepares us to expect disagreement of this kind, and to recognize it as *political* disagreement rather than *philosophical* uncertainty. What's contentious here is not where the distinction should be drawn on the democratic view but rather *the democratic view itself*, and no amount of philosophical justification can resolve the conflict between democracy and other ideologies. That's not to say that democrats shouldn't try to win the argument; it's rather to say something important about what kind of argument it is and how it might be won—namely, that it's a political argument (by which I mean that it's an argument arising between ideologies rather than within an ideology) and that it can only be won politically (by which I mean, through politics and persuasion in the real world and in the broadest sense). I clarify and amplify these points in Part III.

DEMOCRATIC METHODS AND KNOWLEDGE

I have been referring throughout the book to the politics of *injustice,* to a democratic account of *injustice*, and so on. I'm now able to say why. Differently situated people experience and think about existing social arrangements and prevailing ideas differently. Social relations and conditions continually change, along with people's experiences of them. As a result, the democratic commitment to emancipation for everyone—to the eradication of domination, oppression, and exploitation—requires a dynamic, provisional, and reflexive understanding of emancipation, for normative and epistemological reasons. Theorizing injustice in its own terms—in a grounded, dialectical way—captures something distinctive about our practices that our best theories of justice cannot.[37] The contingency inherent in such an account is nicely captured in John Dryzek's distinction between *democracy* as a specific set of democratic rights, procedures, and institutions, on the one hand, and *democratization* as an always unfinished process of social critique and transformation, on the other.[38] Rather than fixed moral or philosophical ideals, democracy and emancipation are moving targets.[39] I use the term *injustice* to mark this dynamism and contingency, as a reminder that justice on the democratic view can never be fully defined or achieved.

The same democratic values, ideas, and commitments that characterize injustice as domination, oppression, and exploitation—deformities in social relations that create or perpetuate subordination—generate methodological and epistemological requirements for the theorization and analysis of injustice. These requirements are entailments of democracy's generality and inclusiveness—of the notion that democrats should be concerned with *everyone's* freedom and equality. When Shklar wrote that "ever since we became 'created equal,' all our claims are supposed to matter,"[40] she brilliantly conveyed that it's the *commitment* to democracy, not some logical or rational necessity, that demands consideration of everyone. As theorists and as democrats, our commitments entail a dynamic, provisional, and reflexive understanding of injustice as well as methods that take into account the knowledge, perspective, and experience of as many people as possible.

This kind of grounded, inclusive approach considers people not as abstract or idealized moral agents but as real and potentially active participants in the co-production of knowledge and of theory. To theorize about injustice solely from our own positions—especially if those positions are structured by privileges of race, wealth, gender, education, nationality, and others—is to perpetuate, however unconsciously, a form of epistemic domination pervasive in global normative theory.[41] As we've seen, familiar methods of reasoning, such as the monological analytic methods employed in IMT, frequently reproduce domination and relations of hierarchy, reflecting what Katrin Flikschuh calls "unselfconscious philosophical parochialism." She observes that, if we accept that the "view from nowhere" is unavailable, parochialism is unavoidable; what's problematic is the presumption of general validity frequently associated with parochial views, which generates both theoretical and practical problems, including "the foisting of practical recommendations upon distant contexts on the basis of merely presumptive claims to universal validity or generalizability."[42] Margaret Kohn shares this worry, pointing to the ash heap of failed and abandoned development initiatives that relied in their design and implementation on theories shot through with metaphors and narratives reflecting colonialist assumptions and experiences rather than consulting with and learning from the people they ostensibly sought to help.[43] Flikschuh recommends what she calls "philosophical fieldwork" as a way for theorists to introduce humility into our thinking and arguments. By this, she means "taking a sideways glance" at how others think, mainly through intellectual contact with our colleagues in distant places and serious engagement with their work.[44] I certainly endorse this proposal, but I believe that much more is required.

The bifocal approach counteracts parochialism by making it an explicit premise of theoretical inquiry; part of the point of integrating two distinct theoretical perspectives is to remind us of the situated, contingent, hypothetical character—the parochialism—of any partisan point of view. A specifically democratic account further models humility in its epistemology and in its methodology. It does so in part by treating its understandings of injustice and emancipation as always provisional, as incomplete and ongoing meditations on what freedom and equality mean and require. This provisional stance is a democratically appropriate acknowledgment of the contestable and often contested meanings of our core values, and it argues for reflexivity—for the continual incorporation of changing and contested understandings into our thinking about injustice to help ensure that our theories speak directly and meaningfully to the concerns of real people, to the everyday examples of domination, oppression, and exploitation that cause so much suffering in our world. Focusing on these concerns highlights the varied and dynamic nature of injustice and its imbrication in the diverse relationships and processes through which power operates. Attentiveness to people's concrete experiences of injustice thus helps to inoculate against distortion and to make legible aspects of injustice previously invisible or opaque to theorists.

A Feminist Epistemology

The discussion so far points to the need for a democratic approach to injustice to rely on what might loosely be called feminist epistemological tools and insights.[45] In calling these *feminist* tools, I don't mean to suggest that all feminists would agree on or endorse them; rather, I mean that they have been developed by feminist theorists and from a (not *the*) feminist perspective.[46] Feminist epistemologists have long stressed that knowledge and knowing are *situated*. This means, first, that people's social positions condition what they know and perhaps what they can know. Feminists rely on grounded or standpoint epistemology to show that being in a subordinate position within a social power dynamic affords one a different and more capacious perspective on that dynamic in its totality. The goal of grounded epistemology is to generate better accounts of the world through engaged, accountable positioning;[47] this is an explicitly *democratic* goal, one dictating that theorists adopt an inclusive approach.[48]

People in subordinate subject positions—defined for example by sex, gender, race, class, ability, education, legal status, or the intersection of several of these or other factors—experience social arrangements from the dominant perspective as expressed through its rules, ideology, and impositions. Unlike those in dominant or privileged positions, however, people in subordinate positions also experience these systems as subjects or victims. For this reason, the subordinate *epistemic* position is theoretically "preferred" because it offers a different and more comprehensive vantage point on ideologies and systems of social relations. For people occupying dominant social positions, some aspects of their own behavior and of the structure of society are invisible, whereas the perspectives of those at the bottom of hierarchies can provide valuable vantage points for theory and research because significant puzzles and problems are manifest in their lives and experiences.[49] "The standpoints of the subjugated are not 'innocent' positions; on the contrary, they are preferred because in principle they are least likely to allow denial of the critical and interpretive core of all knowledge."[50]

Building on these insights and on their own experiences, black feminist theorists developed the concept of intersectionality (which is now in some sense *the* feminist epistemological position) to reveal how domination, oppression, and exploitation often overlap in ways that compound injustice even while making it invisible.[51] They recognized that multiple vectors of subordination often intersect in ways that constitute particularly vulnerable social positions. A democratic account of injustice must be attentive to these positions and their social formation. To see why, consider Alicia Garza's recent discussion of why the Movement for Black Lives must focus on racism broadly and not solely on the epidemic of police violence against black men:

> Trans women of color, including Black trans women, have an average life expectancy of 35 years old, and are the most impacted by severe unemployment (more than twice the national average). Black

> women make 64 cents to every 78 cents that a white woman makes to every dollar that a white man makes. Black women are the fastest growing prison population in this country, mostly for "crimes" of survival. Black girls are the most likely to be suspended from school. A 2012 national study determined that about one half of all people killed by the police each year are mentally ill, and that in the case of local departments, that number jumps to about 75%.[52]

As she concludes, "[i]ntersectional politics (and practice) is not just theoretical—it is the lifeline upon which we depend for our collective liberation."[53]

One reason why IMT often proves distortional is that conceiving of injustice as the lack or opposite of justice makes it difficult to recognize and account for compound injustices of the kind that intersectional analysis reveals. In addition, the nonideal mode of theorizing typically remains a monological analytic exercise; grounded, intersectional thinking attuned to the experiences of real people in real circumstances of injustice helps to reveal these precarious social positions and to facilitate better theorizing about how to address them. A democratic approach must be attentive to all subject positions within what Patricia Hill Collins called the matrix of domination—as well as to how power creates and sustains that matrix.[54]

It does so in part by shaping what we can know individually and collectively. Social relations can constrain our knowledge when prevailing discourses or ideologies (de)limit our understanding of the world; social relations can enrich our knowledge when interactions among knowers and a proliferation of perspectives and experiences contribute to the comprehensiveness and the social validity of knowledge.[55] This social dimension of epistemology reminds us that power relations shape knowledge (and ignorance) not only through experience but also through their bearing on our status as knowers. Groups or individuals whose status as knowers is challenged—because of gender, say, or because of scientific norms that denigrate indigenous knowledge—suffer epistemic injustice, compounded over time by the erosion of their social status and of their individual confidence and cognitive capacity.[56]

Heidi Grasswick observes that feminist social epistemologists struggle with the paradox that their work criticizes claims of neutrality and impartiality while simultaneously appealing to some apparent standard of objectivity in criticizing them:

> Feminist social epistemologists have felt this need to incorporate a normative dimension to their social analyses in a particularly pressing way: feminist political demands for the elimination of oppression are normative in a moral sense, but they also depend on epistemically normative claims for their justification. Their force depends on the ability to distinguish between better and worse claims to knowledge.[57]

On the bifocal approach, the main problem here is the language of "better and worse claims to knowledge," which confuses things by appealing to a seemingly objective standard of evaluation, as Grasswick indicates. The bifocal approach begins from the premise that no such standard exists—that all analysis involves interpretation and all interpretation assumes (implicitly or explicitly) a particular ideological framework. Part of the point of introducing a bifocal perspective is to show that this starting point need not mean that we give up on making evaluative claims or that we regard such claims merely as aesthetic judgments or expressions of idiosyncratic preferences. To return to the specific example, feminist critiques of neutrality and objectivity represent epistemically superior claims from within a feminist (or democratic) point of view. This stance only becomes problematic if one regards the hypothetical normativity of this particular ideological standpoint as somehow lacking or inadequate as a basis for critique. Principled critique is not compromised by its hypothetical normativity or by the specific ideological commitments that inform it; it is only possible because of and in light of them. Put another way, evaluative claims are always claims informed by a particular ideology. Better is always (only) better *from a particular point of view*. The upshot is not that we cannot make or have confidence in such claims: we can—assuming the internal validity of the account.[††] But it's a mistake to think that the question of which *framework* is best can be answered objectively, and a further mistake to think that that impossibility somehow compromises our evaluative claims.

As an illustration of how these various tools and insights can inform a democratic mode of inquiry, consider Brooke Ackerly's discussion of Third World feminist social criticism as a model of participatory social critique grounded in multipositional experience and knowledge. This modality of social inquiry is a critical reconstruction of processes of cooperative social criticism that Ackerly has observed and participated in among Third World feminists and their individual and organizational allies.[58] Ackerly defines the critic as a "facilitator of society's self-examination"—including of its critical process.[59] Critics use "guiding criteria" to help them generate knowledge through deliberative inquiry, which takes place via collaborative exchanges of views and discussion among critics and members of society. This model of collective learning seeks to incorporate those typically silenced by dominant social values, norms, and practices.[60] Ackerly shows how different interpretive and critical roles taken on by insider, outsider, and multisited or boundary-crossing critics enable different and complementary forms of criticism, including deeply informed (re)interpretation of local values and knowledge (insiders), informed theoretical skepticism (outsiders), and intersectional analysis (boundary crossers).[61]

It's immediately apparent that Third World feminist social criticism incorporates democratic and emancipatory values,[62] reflecting in this case

[††] Internal validity means roughly that the arguments and critical and evaluative standards worked out within a given ideological framework are consistent with its core values and ideas and more or less coherent with one another. Any partisan account can be scrutinized for internal validity; this is the kind of critique that realists can make because it doesn't depend on substantive normative criteria. Internal validity is not the same as internal *agreement*; key concepts and interpretations may be contested within an ideology without preventing the generation of a consistent and coherent critical account. The demands of consistency with democracy's core values and commitments mean that internal validity on a democratic or feminist account also requires that the critical and evaluative standards themselves emerge from a reflexive, iterative, and dialectical process of social engagement and reflection that cannot precede or preempt their articulation. This is the only way to avoid domination. Cf. Seyla Benhabib, *Dignity in Adversity: Human Rights in Troubled Times* (Cambridge, MA: Polity Press, 2011); "Another Cosmopolitanism," in *Another Cosmopolitanism*, ed. Robert Post (Oxford: Oxford University Press, 2006).

the values of the women and men who engage in it. There is much more to learn from their successes, challenges, failures, and self-criticism. It's also readily apparently that Third World feminist social criticism is explicitly concerned with social transformation—something Ackerly and I agree is lacking in global normative theory. While IMT contains explicit or implicit prescriptions for social change, it pays very little attention to how that change might come about or to the role of the political theorist or political theory in facilitating it.[63] I offer my own interpretation of these roles in Part III; for now, I will simply endorse Ackerly's admonition that criticism should be understood as a social project combining theoretical and practical concerns.[64]

Dialectical Thinking

I characterized injustice as a deformity in social relations where power creates or perpetuates subjection. While I grouped injustices into three broad and overlapping categories—domination, oppression, and exploitation—I also emphasized that my democratic approach requires a provisional and evolving understanding of injustice rather than a static analytic definition, in part as a way of integrating multiple understandings of injustice and holding them in productive tension.[65] The grounded, intersectional epistemology I have just been describing indicates why: people's diverse and divergent experiences of injustice, embedded in the multiplicity of social positions and relations they inhabit, mean that any fixed definition is likely to become a source of (epistemic) domination.

I am not proposing that theorists uncritically accept people's sense or experience of injustice as definitive of it; part of the point of philosophical articulation is to work out coherent conceptual accounts of the key values, ideas, and arguments of an ideology to enable critical evaluation of social arrangements and prevailing perspectives. Like Sen, I regard people's sense of injustice as a signal that demands critical evaluation. Like many signals, it can be noisy and unreliable: there might be false alarms, as when the loss of some unjustified privilege arouses anger or indignation—for instance, when men chafe against the social and cultural changes that attend women's emancipation. Alarms might also fail to sound when systemic injustices get overlooked or naturalized by dominant social norms, practices, and expectations—for instance, when structural poverty prevents people from living decent lives but the dominant ideology treats poor people themselves as responsible for their plight. The point, again, is to develop the capacity to identify and reflect critically upon people's sense and experience of injustice in ways that feed back into the ongoing (re) development of the critical framework.

One important way to do so is through dialectical thinking, by which I simply mean integrative, relational thinking about connections, disruptions, structures, and processes through time and space.[66] Thinking dialectically helps the theorist to appreciate the complexity and dynamism of a world of connection and to problematize prevailing meanings and interpretations of the world. This kind of thinking is grounded and synthetic; it supports reflexivity by interpolating people's disparate experiences and understandings of injustice into a richer—though still provisional—theoretical account of it. Perhaps most distinctively, it seeks to leverage the tensions and contradictions that arise between those experiences and the dominant understandings and interpretations of the world to gain greater theoretical insight.

It's perhaps easiest to demonstrate the advantage of dialectical thinking by contrasting it with the static, compartmentalized, and ahistorical reasoning typical of IMT. Let's begin with trade. Trade agreements—regional pacts like the North American Free Trade Agreement or the proposed Trans-Pacific Partnership (TPP) and the global trade regime of the GATT/WTO framework—have long been topics of heated discussion among global normative theorists, who frequently denounce them as unfair, benefiting the rich countries of the global North while doing considerable harm to poorer countries of the global South. One particular set of policies that often attracts critical attention concerns the refusal of rich countries with big agricultural sectors to end subsidies for domestic producers or to reduce (tariff and nontariff) barriers to agricultural imports. These policies encourage overproduction, and surpluses frequently get dumped into poor-country markets at prices below local (unsubsidized) production costs—with devastating effects on small-scale and subsistence farming.[‡‡] Global normative theorists often rightly condemn such policies and outcomes, as well as the negotiations out of which they emerge, as unfair and unjust. I have no quarrel with this conclusion. My concern has to do with the near-ubiquitous assumption that the task for global normative theory is to imagine rules and procedures that would lead to genuinely fair or just trade, which is in turn widely accepted as an unproblematic and uncontroversial good for poorer countries.

I have already discussed some of my reasons for skepticism on this point in chapter 2; here, I want to consider the danger of conceptualizing trade as a distinct and relatively autonomous system of mutual cooperation in which justice has primarily to do with the distribution of benefits and of influence within negotiation settings. This static and presentist understanding misses the relational character of trade as a historical process of dynamic interaction among peoples and polities. A dialectical approach reveals that trade has long functioned as a mechanism for the transfer of wealth from the global South to the global North and thus as an important instrument in a broader system of domination. The notorious Atlantic "triangular trade" that brought slaves from Africa to the Americas, shipped commodities to Europe, and took manufactured goods to Africa, where they were exchanged for more slaves, represents one example of this kind of transfer; another is the intraimperial trade networks that shipped raw goods from colonies to the imperial centers for manufacture and re-export, often—as with Indian cotton and British textiles—back to the countries from which the raw materials were initially purchased, usually at artificially low rates. This pattern persists today, as much global trade consists in intrafirm transfers of goods produced in one location and sold, processed, or assembled in another.

[‡‡] The protrade rebuttal points to the benefits of low-cost food for consumers in poorer countries, but usually ignores broader structural questions concerning the dislocation of agricultural workers, food security, etc.

(The destruction of local textile production in India is often described as an unfortunate byproduct of "exposure to global competition," the familiar story being that Western innovation fueled the Industrial Revolution through technological superiority that left the colonies behind—socially, economically, and developmentally. In fact, numerous policies were explicitly designed to decimate the Indian industry, which some economists now argue may have been producing at lower cost than the mills of Manchester.)

A more dialectical approach to trade also highlights the striking ways in which contemporary trade arrangements appear as a continuation of imperial patterns and techniques of domination and exploitation—suggesting that the injustices that permeate the existing trade regime might be intentional. Put differently: it is one thing to say that an unfair trade system amounts to or creates domination, quite another to realize that the point of that system might be precisely to dominate! This pattern emerges even more clearly in the light of intellectual property agreements that protect "technologies" such as terminator seeds and trigger fertilizers, which in effect criminalize traditional practices of seed saving and seed banking and ensnare farmers in spirals of unsustainable debt that enhance the power of transnational agricultural conglomerates. Similar dynamics affect small farmers in rich countries as well, though in different ways.

To mention debt also reminds us that trade is not a distinct or isolated policy domain. Contemporary trade policy is closely coordinated with the financial regime promoted by the IMF and World Bank, which make "assistance" conditional upon the adoption of neoliberal economic reforms or "austerity" policies that frequently exacerbate the debt crises they are supposedly meant to resolve. Structural indebtedness is another tool of domination and exploitation, and it has skyrocketed since the 1980s. Public and private indebtedness has served as a convenient vehicle for the redistribution of wealth to the rich, as when highly indebted governments privatize public assets at bargain prices in times of economic crisis, with the sales frequently benefiting foreign investors and well-connected public officials, or when homeowners lose their wealth to banks and investors because they can't keep up with underwater mortgages,[§§] or when governments raise taxes and cut services to finance the purchase of weapons or "development" projects whose primary beneficiaries are transnational corporations and the government officials with whom they "contract."

The point here is not to provide a detailed or comprehensive argument about pathologies of trade but to show how dialectical thinking about trade can reveal the inadequacy and the ideological character of the platitudes about "fair" exchange and "mutually beneficial effects" that dominate its discussion within IMT. Likewise, reasoning dialectically helps to disrupt simplistic and misleading binaries that structure much thinking about trade and about justice and injustice more broadly. Global normative theorists have focused intently on determining what the citizens of rich countries owe to the citizens of poor countries—on "what 'we' owe to the 'global poor.'" This way of thinking obscures the cooperation among business and elites in rich and poor countries, all of whom get enormously wealthy from global trade and finance, even as many working people in rich and poor countries are impoverished by its effects (in related but not identical ways).[***] It is often these poor-country elites who represent their countries' people in the trade negotiations that yield "unfair" agreements in the first place.

Much more could be said about the perfidies of global trade, including attempts to gut health, welfare, and environmental protections ("nontariff barriers to trade") through the creation of extrajudicial mechanisms designed to subvert local political institutions. Since my point is mainly to indicate how dialectical thinking transforms our perspective on matters central to global normative theory, let me turn instead to a second

[§§] In the United States, this process disproportionately targeted people of color, who were fraudulently sold mortgages worse than those they qualified for, which were more expensive and harder to repay when the crisis hit.

[***] Neoliberal economists are fond of citing mathematical models showing that the benefits of trade always outweigh the costs, while dismissing "political" questions about the distribution of those benefits and ignoring the long-term structural implications of trade. Never mind the transparency of such disavowals: the models themselves presume the present distribution of capital, technology, and so on as fixed and thus assume the inequalities of the present system.

example intended to draw out some additional conceptual and theoretical concerns. Dialectical thinking can help theorists to remain cognizant that present injustices have histories and to theorize those histories. Global normative theory largely ignores historical considerations, and when theorists do acknowledge the legacies of colonial rule, they typically maintain that the best way to account for them is through attention to how they affect present institutions or inequalities.[67] In fact, the neglect of history is built in to IMT: the principles of justice produced through IMT are conceived as timeless and universal, making history theoretically irrelevant. In addition, conceiving of injustice as the absence or opposite of justice establishes justice as the (a)historical baseline or steady state against which injustice appears as a kind of interruption, a departure or deviation to be corrected. This makes it extremely difficult to reckon with the past as a dynamic element of present injustice[68] or to raise questions about the historical injustices connected with the idea of justice itself, either causally or conceptually.[69]

To see this, consider developmentalism, a complex of theories and assumptions that has structured liberal and modernist thinking and shapes contemporary ideas about trade, international assistance (aid), democratization, human rights, and so on. Developmentalism is the idea that human societies develop through progressive cultural or historical stages from primitive and barbarous to advance or civilized. Thomas McCarthy points to a dilemma at the heart of the liberal notion of development: the notion that human beings who exist contemporaneously also exist at different stages of development sits quite uncomfortably with liberalism's moral universalism. The idea of progressive development is morally indefensible, McCarthy argues, but anthropologically functional and quite useful to liberals politically. In liberal thought, "war, conquest, oppression, inequality, exploitation, and the other great evils of the human condition, which are morally despicable, have served as valuable spurs to the development and spread of culture and civilization."[70] Notions of savagery and barbarity that recur throughout liberalism from Hobbes and Locke through Mill and even Marx prove difficult to expurgate, connected as they are both to liberalism's contexts of application (in which universal moral principles are applied to social realities that are described in historical or anthropological terms as "developing") and to its contexts of origin (in which developmentalism combines with universalism as a justification for empire).[71] Because liberalism is so deeply complicit in the logic of empire in this way, chimerical perversions like "developmental despotism" were always available as ideological cover for domination and exploitation.[72]

Postcolonial critics have been well aware of these problems and have largely rejected developmental thinking altogether; the difficulty is to imagine alternatives that allow us to make sense of the contemporary world without themselves reverting back to modern cultural and institutional forms permeated with developmentalist assumptions. What's needed, in McCarthy's view, is a critical reconstruction of development that can provincialize Europe;[73] this requires not the rejection of European thought but rather its rethinking and renewal from the margins.[74] Interrogating developmentalist assumptions from the perspective of those positioned outside or on the margins of mainstream theoretical concern helps both to expose the problems with those assumptions and to reveal that "the very shape and form of the international system is itself the product of imperial domination and coercion."[75]

Thinking from the margins, with and from the perspectives of subaltern and colonized peoples, helps theorists to see hidden, problematic dimensions of dominant ideas and relations and to recover histories, knowledges, and alternatives that can aid in the unthinking of familiar assumptions and frameworks. Dialectical thinking of this kind has a deep postcolonial sensibility, rooted in the impulse to expose these connections by drawing "attention to the structures, histories, and power dynamics that are not always apparent in abstract theories of justice."[76] Postcolonial theorists emphasize that key metaphors—like development—are deeply embedded in our rhetoric and our theories of contemporary justice. Powerful materialist and developmentalist assumptions, such as the notion of progression from underdevelopment to affluence and the spatial and economic coding of "we" and "the poor," are woven tightly into the fabric of concepts and narratives of global normative theory.[77] These assumptions are also deeply racially tinged, with affluence coded racially as "white," as "highly developed," and as "universal," while underdevelopment is "dark," "savage," "backward," and quite *particular*. Unless theorists expose and critically interrogate these metaphors and narratives, we miss the extent to which developmental assumptions are closely tied up with racial and racist thinking within liberalism and within global normative theory. Despite the persistent denials of the racial character of the global order—the "[whiting] out [of] the multiple ways race and racial ideology underpinned [the West's] global domination"—dialectical thinking uncovers and exposes its racial foundations.[†††]

The point of such investigations is not—or not only—to identify past injustices that must be rectified. The point is rather that past injustice lives on in our theories, our metaphors, our institutions and practices; it forms an enduring and dynamic part of the present.[78] Dialectical thinking helps theorists to appreciate why ideal moral conceptions of justice like those proffered by many global normative theorists don't seem like solutions to the problems faced by many historically oppressed groups and in fact *often seem to be the problem*.[79] To conceive present injustice as a departure from or interruption of some static and timeless notion of justice thwarts efforts to understand why injustice exists and perdures—questions the answers to which lie in the past as much as in the present. That's not only because our theories are distorted by their refusal to acknowledge that injustice has a past, but also because, as the example of developmentalism shows, metaphors, narratives, and assumptions originating in the past remain productive in the present—productive, that is, of knowledge and subjectivities. Put differently, they remain deeply implicated in contemporary hierarchies of epistemic domination, insinuating themselves into superficially impartial theories of equality, nondomination, and so on through narratives about aid, good governance, the responsibility to

[†††] Mills, "Race and Global Justice," 12–13. This "whiting out" is effected in part through the exclusion of considerations of race from ideal theory, as I argued in chapter 1. As the argument here makes clear, however, dialectical thinking challenges both the exclusion of race and gender at the moment of theoretical construction and IMT's erasure of (a highly uncomfortable) history.

protect, and many others—not to mention in the pervasive belief that a just or legitimate global order will further, and is needed to further, the interests and welfare of all. IMT can only address the legacies of past injustices, if at all, as matters of nonideal theory, but consideration at this stage of reasoning makes it impossible to consider their structural and productive impact, their effect on theorists' assumptions and ways of thinking.

Dialectical thinking is enhanced by a bifocal approach to the politics of injustice, which makes it easier to recognize the complexity and contingency of meaning, to unsettle partisan concepts and discourse that might otherwise seem like moral or historical categories with which we are stuck and which must therefore be rescued or rehabilitated. A theoretical analysis of ideological conflict over the meaning of key concepts can help us to locate the origins or bastions of injustice in particular historical moments and discursive formations, thus improving our ability to challenge injustice effectively.

CRITICAL REFLECTIONS

The foregoing discussion might raise the question of how my approach differs from that of critical theorists. Following Young, I understand critical theory broadly as "a normative reflection that is historically and socially contextualized" and that aims to provide social description and explanation that are critical, that "evaluate the given in normative terms."[80] I'm highly sympathetic with and deeply indebted to critical theory so understood, and my own approach qualifies as a critical theory on this definition. As a democratic account, it must be, as Tully describes, *critical* in the sense that enables practical arguments and facilitates the normative evaluation and critique of social arrangements while itself remaining open to constant criticism and revision in light of further experience and reasonable criticism.[81]

Oddly, while normative evaluation is central to critical theory, many critical theorists fail to be explicit about the values that inform their critiques—never mind about the normativity of those values. That may be because, as Young observed, "critical theory presumes that the normative ideals used to criticize a society are rooted in experience of and reflection on that very society."[82] For most critical theorists, "rooted in" means something like "dialectically informed by," or at least, "from the standpoint of oppressed or marginalized people," a position with which, again, I'm very sympathetic (though I do wish that they would be more explicit about this standpoint and about the value commitments that inform it). But for a subset of critical theorists actively engaged in global normative theory, those working in the Habermasian tradition of discourse ethics, "rooted in" means something more like "latent" or "inherent" or "immanent." Their approach

> contains elements of immanent, transcendent, and genealogical critique; "immanent" in that it starts from values, ideas and principles embedded in the cultures and societies it analyzes; (context-) "transcendent" in that it reconstructs these values, ideals, and principles in terms of a general, discourse-ethical account of practical reasoning; and "genealogical" in that it is self-reflectively metacritical of the historical and contemporary forms of existing reason that it seeks to reconstruct as a critical resource.[83]

I have strong reservations about this approach, reservations I shall elaborate through engagements with the work of three prominent critical theorists working in global normative theory: James Bohman, Rainer Forst, and Nancy Fraser. These thinkers share my democratic normative commitments and espouse concern with addressing existing injustices; I've benefited immensely from their work. It's precisely because of these similarities that engaging with them proves so useful in clarifying and underscoring the distinctive features of my argument. I shall contrast my approach with theirs on three points: normativity, idealization, and power.

Forst, Fraser, and Bohman all attribute categorical normativity to the evaluative standards they embrace. Forst is adamant about this, insisting that his reconstruction of the social practice of justification grounds "a categorical and overriding right and duty of justification."[84] He avers that he is happy to be a "foundationalist" when it comes to reconstructing what he calls the moral point of view of practical reason, though he insists that this point of view is neither metaphysical nor transcendental because it is anchored in "proper reflection" on the conditions of possibility of morally justified action.[85] A categorical moral foundation is necessary and appropriate, Forst holds, because critique requires "valid" norms,[86] norms objectively justified because immanent in the nature of practical reason as an activity. Without such unconditional, binding norms, he argues, "no critical thinking or theory is possible."[87]

There is an evident tension in Fraser's work between a genuine sensitivity to and appreciation of contingency, social ontology, dialectical thinking, and dialogical processes of engagement, on the one hand, and an impulse to devise "overarching" and "determinative" principles of justice and to reformulate concepts like legitimacy and impartiality, on the other. This tension is neatly encapsulated in her conception of *reflexive justice*, which she hopes incorporates "sufficient self-problematizing capacities to entertain novel claims" about the subject, scope, and scale of justice.[88] Her aim is to create a "grammar of justice" that provides for closure, which political argument requires, but which "treats every closure as *provisional.*" This *reflexive justice* should overcome the false dichotomy between agonistic models of politics, which valorize moments of opening, and discourse ethics, which valorizes moments of decision.[89] In the end, however, Fraser has difficulty reconciling a provisional understanding of justice with the justificatory work she wants her conception of justice to do, work spelled out in the "insistence that the grammar of justice be reconstituted so as to enable the subaltern to speak *in authoritative terms.*"[90] It's this idea of *authoritativeness*, which also animates Forst's view that critical thinking requires binding, unconditional norms, that leads her to formulate her normative position categorically "Henceforth, public opinion is legitimate if and only if it results from a communicative process in which all who are jointly subjected to the relevant governance structure(s) can participate as peers, *regardless of political citizenship.*"[91]

The categorical normativity of these accounts contrasts with the hypothetical normativity of my approach in two related ways.[92] First, my approach abjures the search for ideal or authoritative principles, insisting that a democratic account of injustice must not only begin as, but remain, critical and reflexive. Second, my approach forthrightly acknowledges the contingency of its normative commitments (which cautions against their ideal or categorical formulation) and in doing so also recognizes that among the chief obstacles to the eradication of injustice is the ongoing (real) political conflict among rival ideologies.

This categorical conception of normativity contributes directly to a reliance on idealization in each of these accounts, a second point of contrast. Despite their professed concerns with concrete injustices, all three thinkers rely on distortional idealizations in formulating and spinning out the principles that animate their work. Forst's argument that humans are "justificatory beings" is a highly selective and tendentious reading of one dimension of human capability, and his reconstruction of the social practice of justification as a moral principle of practical reason idealizes intersubjective relations and the social structures in which they are embedded to a remarkable degree.[‡‡‡]

Interestingly, Bohman regards his as a kind of *nonideal* theory, which he understands as theory "concerned with creating conditions that would enable people to avoid the ills of current and pervasive injustice."[93] Transnational republicanism, Bohman maintains, guides us in constructing a conception of the proper mix of institutions and individual powers needed to minimize domination and achieve the ideal of nondomination.[94] He even asserts that republicanism is inherently a critique of ideal theory because it already takes the practical and methodological priority of injustice as a fundamental methodological requirement for improving people's lives; justice consists in remedying existing injustice rather than establishing justice once and for all.[95] Bohman probably

[‡‡‡] Forst might insist that the point of reconstruction is to highlight the best, morally salient features of a practice; that may be, but it's irrelevant to whether reconstruction relies on idealization, which this response affirms that it does.

regards his theory as nonideal because he's able to characterize the republican ideal of freedom negatively—in terms of nondomination and the eradication of injustice. Still, his account relies heavily on idealizations—for instance, in conceptualizing domination as a problem of forced inclusion, he idealizes "a conception of people as members of free political communities and possessed of the relevant normative powers" necessary to secure freedom from domination.[96] "Antipower," the ability to resist domination, arises from the recognition of everyone's membership in humanity and the corresponding basic right to initiate deliberation and thus to exert equal political influence.[97] Achieving this highly idealized "democratic minimum" of effective political influence and equal status also depends upon a distributive minimum sufficient to "fulfill the necessary conditions for inhabiting statuses of individual and collective control and self-direction, and for achieving the social bases of self-respect."[98] The entire edifice, of course, rests on the foundation of a deliberative ideal taken from discourse ethics.

For Fraser, idealization is clearest in her conception of political space. She too is worried about problems of political inclusion and exclusion, arguing that the collapse of the Westphalian "frame" in which such questions were previously resolved means that there are now also difficult metapolitical questions of misframing that must be resolved. These questions arise because the territorial frame of Westphalian politics is "out of sync with the structural causes of many injustices in a globalizing world, which are not territorial in character."[99] These injustices reflect, at least in part, the exclusion that results from the division of political space into bounded polities, posing a problem of metapolitical justice that can only be resolved by a "determinative normative principle" for evaluating questions of membership and inclusion. Fraser's proposed solution is an "all-subjected" principle for inclusion in political decisions that affect those subject to governance, to be realized through new transnational political institutions and associated spaces of civil society.[100] However, as Paul Muldoon observes, "[t]o suggest, as she does on many occasions, that the Westphalian system 'gerrymanders political space' or 'partitions political space along territorial lines' is to presume that the whole world is already a political space with moveable internal boundaries."[101]

By conceptualizing the problem in terms of (re)framing, Fraser accepts and normalizes the existing neoliberal configuration of governance and spatial relations; her approach seeks to reckon with its consequences but not to question its ontology. She (mis)reads the politics of some transnational movements through this ideal lens, interpreting feminist, indigenous, environmental, and antiglobalization movements as engaged in disputes over political frames—which, again, she understands as disputes about boundaries, about political and spatial inclusion and exclusion. But many participants in such movements and in the World Social Forum process to which she often alludes reject the very institutions and cartography of governance that Fraser wants to democratize through reframing. They question the ontology of neoliberal capitalism and the epistemologies that make radical alternatives unthinkable.[102] By idealizing political space and interpreting political struggles primarily as struggles over framing, Fraser misses that contemporary movements also interrupt and challenge the history and trajectory that produced the existing configuration and the epistemic structures that normalize its characteristic injustices. They do so by breaking the continuity of systems of oppression and rupturing the normalcy that surrounds domination.[103]

Idealization is directly related to a third problem concerning power.[§§§] All three theorists conceptualize power too narrowly, in what Barnett and Duvall would call interactional terms. This is clearest in that all three prescribe transnational institutional schemes to remedy the maladies of domination they diagnose, ignoring any political opposition or ideological resistance to such schemes. While Forst characterizes the global context as "a complex system of power and domination with a variety of powerful actors," he conceives of the "multiple domination" to which people are subjected purely in interactional terms, as domination by their own illegitimate governments, local elites, and global actors.[104] As a result, his theory of "fundamental transnational justice" relies on transnational structures

§§§ Fraser is considerably better on this point than either Bohman or Forst.

of participation and justification to yield binding global norms.[105] This narrowly institutional approach cannot adequately address structural and productive power: who would justify it, in what kinds of institutions, and to whom? And how would these institutions correct for the identities and subjectivities shaped by unjust social structures and prevailing ideologies? Because Forst reconstructs practical reason as a characteristic of idealized autonomous Kantian agents formed independently of their circumstances, experiences, or social positions, he imagines that interactional forums of reciprocal justification will eradicate domination, ruling out the possibility that such processes might in fact reproduce it.

Bohman views the expansion of imperfect or incomplete principal-agent hierarchies and the forced inclusion it produces as the primary source of domination in world politics.[106] Domination results when the terms of various schemes of cooperation are set by agents not properly subject to democratic control. Bohman's solution to this challenge is a vibrant civil society and public sphere in which the capability to initiate deliberation can be institutionalized. While I am sympathetic to this aim, I worry about the conceptual and political adequacy of the conception of power underlying it. Superficially, I find talk about "schemes of cooperation" and principal-agent problems a rather anodyne vocabulary for describing relations of injustice that involve naked oppression and violent exploitation, greed, humiliation, and brutality. My deeper worry is that Bohman's idealization of humanity as a political community of free and equal citizens possessing the equal capability to initiate deliberation makes it hard to theorize the intransigence of privilege, hard to conceive of politics as a clash of values, hard to unmask structural and productive power, and thus hard to imagine how such an ideal might actually be realized.

"Antipower," which Bohman calls "the most basic normative power necessary for nondomination," is "the power over those who would dominate us, and thus control over one's life via the content of one's obligations and statuses"; it is "the positive and creative power to interpret, shape, and reformulate the contents of common obligations with others."[107] Antipower is a kind of legal or institutional power whose effective and legitimate exercise presumes the existence of transnational deliberative institutions capable of regulating all aspects of social interaction. But it's not clear whether or how such institutions might counteract constitutive power and its effects on the identities and subjectivities of Bohman's global citizens. Again, an institutional solution, which presumes the categorical normativity of its deliberative ideal, might well unintentionally reproduce such domination.[****]

The differences between my approach and those of Bohman, Forst, and Fraser can be summarized succinctly: they do not recognize themselves as ideologists. As a result, they fall back on a categorical conception of political normativity, employ idealization in justifying their claims, and in so doing neglect constitutive power in relying on institutional solutions to problems of injustice. Each adopts an essentially philosophical approach to injustice, by which I mean that each makes what ought to be the object or product of political struggle into the *basis* for political struggle.[108] They assume that their preferred normative conceptions of justice—a right to justification, or a right to membership in humanity, or a right to participatory parity grounded in communicative freedom—are theoretical *starting points* from which to work out institutional schemes designed to uphold and enforce those conceptions. Comforted by the solace of categorical norms and idealized social and political relations, theorists are unlikely to think carefully about the kinds of structural and productive power that will actively oppose and undermine such efforts. Indeed, they pay little attention to questions of how their schemes might be enacted.

In fact, the problems of global injustice do not result from uncertainty regarding the nature or details of the institutional scheme needed to realize and protect categorical norms of justice; *they result from conflict about what justice is and requires.* If we take this conflict seriously, as the bifocal approach helps us to do, injustice immediately appears as a political problem. That's not to say that there's no place for normative and

**** Bohman does discuss epistemic domination, but he understands it in oddly distributive terms and recommends an institutional solution to it as well; see Bohman, "Critical Theory," 101–10.

theoretical articulation or substantive critique; it's rather to stress that these must be understood as part of a broader political struggle that's in part about persuading others to adopt our values, to join in the fight for rights and equality, to resist domination, oppression, and exploitation.

In Part III of this book, I show how my bifocal approach, combined with the democratic account of injustice I've advocated, transforms our thinking about the politics of injustice and about the work political theory can do in combating it in the real world.

PART III

Political Theory for the Real World

6

Political Theory and the Politics of Injustice

In these final two chapters, I try to show what practical difference it makes if one adopts the approach I've developed in this book. Here I consider what work political theory and political theorists might do in support of emancipatory politics, basing much of my argument on the insight that the politics of injustice is necessarily a counterhegemonic politics. In the next chapter, I pull together the many threads of argument spun throughout this book and put them to use in an extended discussion of responsibility for injustice. Both chapters build on the bifocal theoretical framework introduced in chapter 4 and on the democratic account of injustice articulated in chapter 5.

The political theory I describe and demonstrate here takes up questions quite different from those familiar in global normative theory. It conceptualizes injustice as a political problem and shows how theory can contribute to a political response. This is political theory for the real world, informed by a realistic analysis of power, conflict, and ideology and designed to provide strategic and normative guidance for activists and citizens—theorists among them—concerned with combating injustice.

TAKING SIDES

One plain implication of my approach is that to do political theory is to take sides. Once we acknowledge that claims about justice and injustice are ideological claims, it becomes impossible to imagine that political theory or political theorists operate in some neutral, objective, or impartial domain "above the fray." Even if one were to refrain from substantive normative critique and restrict one's theoretical activities to analysis, the interpretive quality of analysis means that it, too, is shaped by ideology. Whether we like it or not, political theorists unavoidably take sides when we practice our craft.

To get a deeper sense of what this means, I want to think through the "activist political theory" proposed by Lea Ypi. She also laments that political theory often ignores the link between normative theory and the political agency required for social transformation.[1] Ypi envisions activist political theory promoting "normative views in a way that speaks to concerns arising in the real world," in part through employing a "dialectical" approach.[2] Activist political theory should be "concerned not merely with interpreting the world but also with changing it."[3] Its role "is to guide practice by putting familiar intuitions to new uses, by scrutinizing and ordering the concepts available in the tradition, by showing the inadequacy of old categories, and by bringing coherency and persuasiveness to emerging ones."[4] In Ypi's view, theorists' work should be "informed and inspired by the practical activity of real-world political agents."[5] Activist political theory therefore envisions alliances between political theorists and "avant-garde political agents," those "whose position in society renders them politically suited and morally motivated to bring about changes compatible with their ideal requirements."[6]

On these points, Ypi and I are largely in agreement. We disagree, however, on the relationship between political theory and activist politics.

Ypi seeks to develop a theory that strikes a "fundamentally appropriate" balance between ideal and nonideal theory. She calls this balanced theory *statist cosmopolitanism* because it combines cosmopolitan ideals with a nonideal or realistic conception of state-based political agency. The agents who can promote cosmopolitan justice in our nonideal world, she argues, are those who use their state-based political agency to push a cosmopolitan agenda. Ypi refers to these agents as the (cosmopolitan) avant-garde. Activist political theory is "informed by relevant (avant-garde) instances of political practice," which contribute to the "emergence, articulation, revision, and development of a particular family of normative political theories," prescriptive theories about "how political societies *should* be arranged, how agents *ought* to behave, and what politically effective and motivationally sustainable steps *could* be taken to transform existing social and political relations."[7]

Ypi distinguishes progressive from regressive claims for political change using a dialectical method, which for her means "learning from the trials, failures, and successes of the past." Progressive or avant-garde practice "outperforms" its rivals insofar as it can "articulate existing concerns and commitments at a fundamentally appropriate causal and normative level," can "reflect on the function and purpose of political institutions in a way that preserves and adds content to the positive normative commitments of previous theories whilst avoiding their morally problematic aspects," and can "raise new, unforeseen questions related to the development of political institutions reformed in accordance with their requirements."[8]

There's a clear tension in Ypi's approach between her claim that the avant-garde is progressive because it is "conceptually additive" in this way and her insistence that the "substantive set of commitments promoted by avant-garde political agents" can be justified "by analyzing; what a fundamentally appropriate account of global justice should look like and by comparing cosmopolitanism to its rival theoretical alternatives [*sic*]."[9] The claims arising from avant-garde agency, she states, "are not sufficient by themselves to illustrate why a particular theory is more fundamentally appropriate than another: a significant amount of work is done through pure normative argument" based on "specific first order values."[10] The tension is that activist political theory requires not just that theorists take sides, but also that they take the *right* side. Ypi wants theory to be informed and inspired by activists' work—but only those activists advancing the right substantive theory of justice in the right way.

The problem stems from her desire to identify the avant-garde now, using her "dialectical" method (whose criteria, one of her critics notes, are question begging).[11] David Miller attributes this desire to the influence of Ypi's "Germanic muses" and her progressive view of history (which he claims has long since lost whatever plausibility it might once have had).[12] Whatever the case, Miller rightly insists that we can't rely on the cunning of reason to make clear for us which are the progressive and regressive movements.[13] One solution for Ypi, he suggests, would simply be to define the avant-garde as those who promote particular principles or values—social equality, statist cosmopolitanism, whatever. This would be a coherent approach in itself, he writes, but it doesn't provide Ypi with the relationship she wants between theory and practice, because on this view the values have to come first.[14]

This suggestion brings me full circle to taking sides. Ypi's political commitments counsel her to let practice guide theory, but her ontological commitments say otherwise. The real problem for her, I think, is not that she wants practice to inform values but that she wants it to deliver the right values—she wants the values (and thus the practice) to be correct. In other words, Ypi wants political theorists to engage in politics and ally with activists without thereby becoming ideologists. Putting the point this way makes clear the difference between her activist political theory and the kind of political engagement recommended by my approach, which doesn't recognize any impartial conceptual or other criteria for identifying progressive or avant-garde movements or correct principles of justice. Evaluations of progress necessarily rely on criteria supplied by the evaluator's ideology. If theorists want to engage in normative critique oriented toward social transformation, or if we want to engage actively in political struggles alongside activists, we have to take sides—and we have only our political commitments to guide us in choosing which side to take.

THE POLITICS OF INJUSTICE

The idea that all justice claims are ideological claims has significant implications not just for theorists choosing sides but also for how we think about the politics of injustice and about the work of political theory and political theorists in connection with it. Of course, not every injustice will be ideologically contested: many very different worldviews will converge in condemning wrongs like murder and theft, so that there will be little or no ideological conflict over them. (There may, however, be some—for instance, about how much weight should be attributed to social conditions and to individual responsibility in explaining and addressing these wrongs.) Many injustices, however, will be subjects of ideological conflict; their very characterization as injustices will be a matter of contention. What's really at stake in these cases is the meaning of (in)justice itself and the rival interpretations of the world implicated in answering that question. I referred to such conflicts in chapter 4 as the politics of injustice. Again, the bifocal approach helps us discern the two complementary aspects or dimensions of this politics. Through the analytic lens, we focus on ideological conflicts—on contested claims about (in)justice, the different meanings and configurations of concepts and rival interpretations that support those claims, and the political clashes that play out over them. Through the partisan lens, we focus on defining specific claims, parsing their meaning, interpreting and critiquing the world—on what Rorty called articulation. Combining the two perspectives provides guidance on strategy and tactics for engaging in political struggles around injustice in light of those particular articulations, including questions of agency and implementation.

As political theorists who advocate for particular substantive accounts of justice—as ideologists—most of us engage in this work of articulation, though perhaps without recognizing it in these terms. But we mostly neglect questions about strategy and tactics and agency and implementation.[15] IMT gives theorists implicit permission to ignore or neglect these questions because its categorical conception of normativity makes justice seem self-enacting.* It simply doesn't recognize or accept the irreducibility of conflict over the meaning of (in)justice itself. Partly as a result, global normative theorists treat questions about the actual adoption and implementation of their proposals as an unwelcome afterthought because these questions force them to confront politics. Often, after laying out detailed plans for policy and institutional reform guided by carefully reasoned principles of justice, theorists conclude by observing that the realization of these programs will require political will—and stop there, or perhaps after some encomiums to civil society and past struggles for reform. In effect, they point to political will as the *solution* to the problem of agency rather than as a central part of the problem to be resolved.†

The bifocal approach helps and encourages us to view these questions differently, in ways that upend our familiar thinking and practices. It does so by integrating the partisan and analytic perspectives. In chapter 4, I pointed out that IMT has a monocular view of the politics of injustice, seeing it exclusively through the partisan lens. Likewise, realists see only half the picture, viewing politics solely through the analytical lens. The bifocal approach offers us stereoscopic clarity on the politics of injustice, showing that struggles over meaning are not only or even mainly philosophical disputes but rather partisan political struggles in the real world. My approach thus shows that to challenge injustice requires engaging in counterhegemonic politics.

Recall that ideologies impose meaning and influence people's behavior by "decontesting" key concepts and interpretations, limiting or closing off contestation over them. The more successfully an ideology decontests its key concepts and interpretations within a particular social setting, the more dominant it becomes. This success is a function of power. An ideology can be constructed, promulgated, and promoted through institutional

* One reviewer of this book was adamant that no one thinks this; another offered a defense of morality as self-enacting!

† My own first book, *Democracy as Human Rights*, engages in some of this cloud-castle building and invokes precisely these "mechanisms" of change, along with some more concrete possibilities. I now think that much of the argument of the final two chapters of that book requires significant reconsideration and reformulation—i.e., that it is wrong.

power (laws, the judicial and political systems), structural power (class relations, the organization of production and consumption), and productive power (control of the media, popular culture, public discourse). Already-powerful groups will therefore have huge advantages in ideological struggles. The success of an ideology is also, however, a function of the appeal of its ideas—of how well the worldview it constructs speaks to people's experiences and emotions, helps them to make sense of their situations, and so on. Sheer force might allow a bizarre or unappealing ideology to become dominant for a time, but, as Gramsci stressed, successful ideologies are dialectical; they consider the need to appeal to (Gramsci would write, to win the consent of) people in subordinate positions.[16]

Sometimes an ideology becomes so dominant that it successfully shuts down contestation over many of its key concepts and interpretations and becomes hegemonic. Hegemony doesn't imply or require complete dominance; there will always be pockets of resistance and contestation, always resources for thinking otherwise (elsewhere, in the past, even in neglected or contradictory aspects of the prevailing view). When an ideology becomes hegemonic, many of its key concepts and interpretations become widely accepted, taken-for-granted ways of making sense of the world. When this occurs, these concepts and interpretations become what Gramsci called "common sense."[‡] A hegemonic ideology gets reinforced through institutions, structures, identities, and subjectivities that increasingly come to incorporate and reflect it, so long as it can successfully manage the tensions and contradictions it inevitably generates—inevitably, because of the indeterminacy of politics and of the pluralism and the essential contestedness of political concepts to which it gives rise.

I don't want to delve too deeply into Gramsci's or subsequent socialist thinking about hegemony (partly because it reflects a Marxist understanding of ideology as distortion that I eschew). For my purposes, it's enough to see that many injustices will originate and persist because a

‡ This usage conflicts with standard English language usage, in which common sense means practical knowledge or good judgment. Gramsci's term "good sense" comes closer to this meaning. See Jones, *Antonio Gramsci*, 54–55.

dominant or hegemonic ideology does not recognize them as injustices; it normalizes or naturalizes them such that many people take them for granted as acceptable or at least unavoidable features of our world. (Another way to think about this is that people find it difficult to articulate their disagreement with or opposition to systems of meaning and interpretation that have been successfully decontested.) The notion of hegemony suggests one way that we might read Shklar's comments about the compatibility of "normal justice" and injustice. On this reading, normal justice reflects the prevailing common sense; it will be "compatible with" injustice in that some aspects or elements of common sense will be rejected or contested by people whose values, ideas, or experiences lead them to assign meaning and interpret the world differently.

When I call the politics of injustice a counterhegemonic politics, I mean that struggles over injustice frequently require recontesting key elements of a hegemonic ideology, challenging the dominant meanings and interpretations that naturalize or normalize those injustices. This recontestation can transpire in two related ways: through the promulgation of alternative ideologies that construct the world differently by relying on different meanings and interpretations of it, and through tapping into what Gramsci called people's "good sense," knowledge and understanding based in their lived experience. Good sense helps people to navigate the world, in part by allowing them to negotiate aspects of it that common sense fails to illuminate or to characterize it in a way that's compatible with their needs.[17] There's a consciousness opened up by tensions and contradictions between the "common sense" way of understanding the world and people's "good sense" in which alternative imaginaries can emerge. (Dialectical thinking helps both in identifying and accentuating those tensions and in formulating alternatives that speak to them.) To give a very brief, concrete example: a caste system and its common-sense understanding of justice will license some beliefs, ideas, and practices that some people will find unjust because of their experience and knowledge of the world or because they subscribe to conflicting belief-systems. A politics that challenged caste would have to recontest fundamental elements of the dominant ideology itself.

When I say that the politics of injustice is necessarily counterhegemonic politics, all I mean is that it must be a politics that recognizes and acts on the realization that struggles over injustice are in large part struggles over values, ideas, and interpretations. It must, for this reason, be a transformative politics as well, a politics that aims to change prevailing thinking about (in)justice by challenging existing social arrangements and the ideology that informs them. Global normative theorists have not typically thought of (in)justice in these terms. While many theorists offer powerful substantive critiques of the dominant ideology and the social arrangements it supports, few pay much attention, if any, to how these critiques fit into what I've described as the broader politics of injustice. Again, they've neglected questions of uptake and implementation and thought little about what it might mean to formulate their arguments in ways that would orient and animate collective political action, build effective political alliances, and so on. The bifocal approach shows the urgency of paying greater theoretical attention to the counterhegemonic, transformative politics of injustice. In the following sections I consider how this perspective might shape the work we do as political theorists.

COUNTERVAILING POWER AND COLLECTIVE POLITICAL ACTION

Since ideologies are created and maintained through power, counterhegemonic politics must develop countervailing power to challenge the prevailing common sense. Countervailing power is not a modality of power. It refers to the vector—the political direction—in which power is exercised: against hegemonic power, that is, against power deployed consistently with or in support of the dominant ideology. Countervailing power is a vital consideration because any realistic analysis of politics makes clear that those whose status and privilege are threatened by an emancipatory democratic political project will vigorously oppose and forcefully resist it.

Again, it's hard to find any sense in the global normative theory literature that realizing justice might depend upon a transformative political struggle against the dominant ideology and its supporting configuration of power relations. The bifocal approach helps us to see that the transformation of power relations and of the social structures in which they are embedded and reflected depends on the successful (re)assertion or reinterpretation of democratic values as part of a broader counterhegemonic strategy.[18] This will involve struggles against specific or local injustices, struggles that are important and desirable in their own right and which also contribute to a broader transformative politics. But they are not identical with or exhaustive of such a politics, just as struggles against particular disease outbreaks contribute to public health but are not identical with it. In both cases, the difference concerns the alteration of the background conditions that engender the more immediate problems. Successful counterhegemonic politics requires the marshaling and deployment of countervailing power against the dominant ideological formations that normalize and perpetuate injustice.

Discursive Politics

In thinking about what this kind of politics might look like, I've found John Dryzek's work on discursive politics invaluable. Dryzek defines a discourse as "a shared set of concepts, categories, and ideas that provides its adherents with a framework for making sense of situations," a framework that comprises "judgments, assumptions, capabilities, dispositions, and intentions."[19] If "ideas" are interpreted expansively to encompass values and beliefs, Dryzek's conception of discourse becomes nearly identical to the definition of ideology that I have been relying on throughout this book. (I shall read him in this way.) Counterhegemonic politics must push back against injustice at this discursive or ideological level. It must, that is, specifically seek to recontest the meanings and interpretations that constitute the dominant view. It must do so both through arguments and through collective political action. Dryzek's insight is to show how closely these are related in practice.

As he argues, "[d]iscourses are a matter of action as well as words, for actions in the social realm are always accompanied by language that establishes the meaning of action."[20] Discourses and deliberation are much richer, more complex ideas than the anodyne version of deliberation favored by many liberal democrats. Discursive action comprises words and arguments along with a panoply of social activities intended to influence behavior and (re)shape frameworks of meaning.[21] So, for example, it also includes strikes, protests, demonstrations, occupations, educational efforts, electoral campaigns, civil disobedience, social media activism, and a host of other practices.[§] Discursive political engagement is most likely to succeed when undertaken reflexively, that is, with "sensitivity to the degree to which actions themselves help create the contexts for action."[22] Discourses are "amenable to influence from the reflective choices of human agents" and can be made the targets of "popular reflection and conscious action."[23] Thus discursive action in the broadest sense has counterhegemonic potential precisely because "practices help constitute, reconstitute, and sometimes challenge discourses."[24]

Among the daunting tasks of theorizing counterhegemonic politics is thinking though the complex and multifaceted relations among local struggles against concrete injustice, the normative and conceptual vocabulary in which those struggles are articulated, the specific ideas and concepts they target, and the strategies and tactics—the discursive engagements—likely to be most effective in advancing alternative values and ideas while also ameliorating those local injustices. Political theory has not done a good job of this, or even made much of an attempt. This is one way in which alliances with activists already involved in counterhegemonic struggles can be enormously beneficial. Theorists can learn from the experts who

[§] Emancipatory democratic politics will be predominantly nonviolent, though it may well make use of tactics including the destruction of property, the disruption of social order, and the deliberate provocation of violent responses from agents of unjust power structures. I cannot take up the difficult question of whether and in what circumstances such tactics are a legitimate response to egregious injustice; for a good treatment of this topic, with which I am largely sympathetic, see Shane O'Neill, "Struggles against Injustice: Contemporary Critical Theory and Political Violence," *Journal of Global Ethics* 6, no. 2 (2010).

engage daily in the work of grounded theorizing about these questions. (I take this to be a key insight of Ackerly's model of Third World feminist social criticism.) Such alliances are held together, always somewhat fragilely, by the glue of shared or overlapping ideological commitments.

An example will help to illustrate these points. The "Fight for $15" is a campaign for a $15 per hour minimum wage and union representation in the United States (see fightfor15.org). Presently, the US federal minimum wage is $7.25 per hour; for an employee who works 40 hours per week every week of the year, this yields an income of $15,080—above the (absurd) official federal poverty line of $11,880 for individuals but below the line of $16,020 for a household of two. Minimum wage workers toil full time (if they can get the hours) in often physically demanding jobs that typically offer few or no benefits and no paid days off for illness or vacation. Such workers frequently cannot afford to live near their places of employment, meaning that they endure long and costly commutes (worsened by the chronic underfunding of public transit) to live in neighborhoods that often feature violence, poor housing, and execrable public schools (thanks to a grotesque schools-funding scheme based on local property values). Many of these people cannot support themselves and their families, and many more live one crisis—a broken arm or refrigerator, an absent babysitter—from homelessness and destitution.

In a very immediate way, then, the Fight for $15 is a struggle against a concrete injustice, and the remedy it seeks, a living wage and union representation, is quite specific to that particular injustice. At the same time, however, this campaign to end poverty wages also challenges the wider neoliberal discourse. It does so in a variety of ways using diverse tactics, one of which is relying on the leadership and the direct public testimony of workers themselves. It's moving and sobering to hear story after story of hard work, personal and family struggles, callous treatment, and employer retaliation in response to their activism. Many speak eloquently of the degradation they experience in their jobs and as a result of their poverty, as well as of their desire to be treated with respect and dignity. Many also understand their situation in structural terms, identifying greed, exploitation, lack of educational and employment opportunities, and a political system that caters to the rich as the root causes of their problems.

The prominent role of workers in this movement itself challenges dominant assumptions about who counts as an authority to speak on economic matters and about how we learn and what we know about the economy. Their experience also directly contradicts neoliberal platitudes that "hard work pays off." It belies the notion that "flexible" labor markets and limited social protections benefit workers, many of whose schedules are designed to make them ineligible for overtime and benefits, for instance by breaking their shifts into two blocks separated by several hours "off" from work. (Think about what a split shift means for a worker with young children who might reside an hour or more from home by public transit.) By raising questions about work, wages, and profits, about corporate political influence, and about vast and growing socioeconomic inequality, among others, and by doing so from their situations as low-wage employees, these activists disrupt the prevailing common sense. Thus the broader discourse around the Fight for $15—including strikes, marches, legislative efforts, social media and public awareness campaigns, and so on—is clearly oriented toward changing norms, expectations, and practices around low-skilled employment and toward challenging the pillars of neoliberal ideology itself. This discursive strategy proves highly effective in building alliances because it allows workers to communicate their struggles and demands with others who share their broader ideological commitments and critiques, even though their life experiences may be quite different. It also shows how the immediate and broader struggles are linked: strikes, rallies, protests, informational campaigns, and other tactics bring immediate pressure on employers and help to raise awareness and to educate people more broadly about the exploitation of these vulnerable workers.

The campaign, initially spearheaded by fast-food workers, has spread quickly to other sectors and has met with astounding success nationally, having achieved legislative, executive, or popular action to enact state and local minimum wages of $15 per hour in many jurisdictions within the next few years and winning significant increases in many more.[25] Equally significantly, this campaign has helped to reorient public discourse around economic issues toward fairness and justice—a tectonic shift. This campaign exemplifies the kind of counterhegemonic politics from which political theorists have much to learn—and to which, I shall argue below, we have much potentially to contribute as well.

While Dryzek helps us to see that discursive political engagement of this sort can be tremendously effective, I differ with his broader understanding of its role in effecting social transformation in two important and related ways. First, he sometimes writes as if merely the agglomeration of many reflexive discursive actions will add up to systemic transformation, a view in harmony with his general preference for decentralization in discursive politics.[26] In my view, counterhegemonic politics requires greater coordination if it is likely to be successful, a point to which I return below. Dryzek is optimistic on this point because—and this is our second disagreement—he believes that processes of "reflexive modernization" are working to undermine hegemonic discourses and to create spaces for discursive engagement.[27] My worry is that this quasi-teleological view often leads him to set aside his own insights into the close connections between discourses and power and thus to misapprehend what's required to achieve broader social transformation (as opposed to localized victories).

It's important in this connection not to equate counterhegemonic politics with emancipatory politics. Boaventura de Sousa Santos, with whom I agree on almost everything, sometimes seems to assume that all counterhegemonic struggles and practices can be interpolated into a coherent, principled emancipatory movement (a view similar in its way to Dryzek's faith in reflexive modernization). He sees an emancipatory impulse in all counterhegemonic movements, but this confuses two meanings of emancipation. Any disruptive, counterhegemonic struggle is emancipatory with respect to the reigning hegemony and in the bare sense in which release from or resistance to hegemonic constraints is a kind of emancipation. But this is very different from the much more substantive emancipatory democratic commitment I have been advocating and that Santos shares. The problem, as Laclau and Mouffe emphasize in their seminal analysis of the possibilities for radical democratic politics, is that emergent social antagonisms have no set ideological complexion or direction. In fact, the "democratic revolution," with its subversive logic of freedom and equality, establishes a terrain of contestation on which diverse ideologies can flourish. Neither reason nor history, progress nor morality determines which of those ideologies will prevail; an emancipatory counterhegemonic discourse must be constructed—it is a political project.[28]

So while I agree wholeheartedly with Santos that the theoretical challenge for proponents of emancipatory politics is to "construct an ethical and political position without grounding it in any absolute principle,"[29] I think he's mistaken in thinking (if he thinks) that such a politics can do without clear democratic commitments—which need not be absolute in the way I infer he's worried about. Put differently, an emancipatory democratic politics must be constructed, and it must be *democratic*; it must insist on its core values, even while it reflexively understands them as contingent, provisional, and protean.** It may be possible to identify some genuinely emancipatory elements in the thinking and practice of counterhegemonic movements that are not completely or consistently democratic; it's also a separate question.

Articulation and Translation

Amassing countervailing power does not require creating a unified or overarching political movement; there are numerous dangers in such an attempt from a democratic point of view. The challenge is rather to build the kind of reflexive, intersectional solidarity among movements (a "movement of movements") than can coordinate and advance this kind of politics.[30] Again, many critical theorists—along with sociologists, anthropologists, historians, and others—are engaged in scholarship that advances this crucial work. In this section I briefly highlight two important

** The conception of political normativity introduced in chapter 4 and the methods and epistemology developed in chapter 5 show how this is possible.

aspects of it to which political theorists in particular might usefully contribute: articulation and translation.

Articulation, as we have seen, can refer to the careful formulation and expression of values, arguments, and critiques; this is the philosophical work that Rorty contrasted with justification, the search for foundations or moral grounding. I don't want to suggest that there's an unbridgeable gulf between these two labors, but there is an unmistakable difference in emphasis and style. Justification involves trying to establish that certain values and ideas are the right ones, that they are true, valid, immanent, unrejectable, or whatever. Articulation involves fashioning values and ideas into clear concepts, arguments, and critiques with the aim of clarifying their meaning and practical significance. Many global normative theorists (and analytically inclined political theorists more generally) expend a lot of effort on justification, hoping that it will imbue their arguments with categorical force. Of course, they also engage in conceptual clarification and develop arguments and critiques—though frequently in a rather didactic way. Good articulation, again, emphasizes the meaning and practical significance of certain values, stressing their political appeal and usefulness. So, for instance, my account of emancipatory democracy stresses its leveling power and its emancipatory thrust and highlights the work they have done historically.

Consider the practical difference it makes—in our writing, in our teaching, in our activism—when instead of trying to show that one ought to hold certain values, one instead explores what certain values imply politically and how they can be used. As a concrete example, let me discuss my own experience teaching human rights—experience informed by years of research and writing on the subject, and by my (modest) activist experience. For a long while, I hewed to the conventional wisdom in teaching my political theory seminar on human rights by organizing it around questions to do with the universality of human rights, the various justifications for them, the critiques of universalism and of those justifications, and examples that encouraged students to work through these debates by thinking about them in connection with particular problems or controversies. The course left students skeptical about the validity of human rights and unsure whether they should champion them or adopt a sort of resigned relativism.

Now I teach the course very differently, making the case that human rights are political tools designed to do very specific political work: constrain the powerful, criticize and challenge existing social arrangements and hierarchies, and institutionalize protections against domination, oppression, and exploitation. I explain what it is about the conceptual structure of human rights arguments that makes them effective in doing this work and what makes them prone to (mis)use by the powerful. I also invite students to think about who might find arguments like these useful, who might be opposed to them, and why. Instead of looking at the work of philosophers seeking to justify human rights, we look at the work of activists (and not just "progressive" ones) who use them in their struggles; we also read some blistering critiques of human rights theory and practice, past and present. Students come away from the course understanding that there's something important at stake in debates over human rights beyond philosophical arguments and thinking about the controversies surrounding rights in much more politically sophisticated ways. I'm not trying to tell anyone how to teach human rights—or how to do political theory, for that matter. I'm merely trying to illustrate the differences between justification and articulation by pointing out that scholarship and pedagogy in support of emancipatory social transformation look very different from scholarship and pedagogy in pursuit of the truth.

Another important distinction between articulation and justification is that the former is an ongoing, recursive process. At least on the democratic view that I've been advocating, the commitment to reflexivity requires the continual *rearticulation* of the meanings of injustice and emancipation in light of changing circumstances and perspectives. New forms and permutations of injustice emerge as power relations and the ideologies in which they operate evolve; new knowledge about injustice and emancipation is continually produced through engagements with differently situated people in different contexts. Good articulation must critically evaluate all of this input and synthesize it into a dynamic and evolving understanding of democracy.

One crucial aspect of articulation that I want to emphasize is framing. By framing I mean devising persuasive vocabulary and narratives for promoting and popularizing the meanings and interpretations central to an ideology. Successful discursive frames must resonate with people's daily lives and struggles. Political theory hasn't paid much attention to framing, apart from discursive theorists like Dryzek, perhaps because it seems too much like marketing or because it seems unnecessary when concepts are supposed to enjoy categorical force and to be self-enacting. But for theorists concerned with combating injustice—with emancipatory social transformation—it would be a mistake to dismiss or neglect the construction of alternative discursive frames; the very notion of counterhegemonic struggle implies changing how people understand and interpret the world. One effective technique for framing is to identify and accentuate those gaps between people's common-sense and good-sense understandings of the world to frame alternatives—as the Fight for $15 movement does so effectively in countering the neoliberal story about the labor market with a narrative about (un)dignified work.

Framing is also important because bad political frames or narratives can be self-defeating. In a fascinating discussion of this danger, Martin Kirk explains that international antipoverty NGOs have developed an impressive capacity to affect the public agenda using consumer-marketing strategies that "sell" the urgency of particular emergencies to the public and raise impressive sums of money. Yet these strategies rely on a frame emphasizing the direct provision of services to the poor, a framework that reinforces perceptions of poverty as an intractable problem to be ameliorated through charitable giving. As the NGOs themselves understand, this frame cannot address the structural causes of poverty or effect changes in public attitudes about poverty. It

> is not suitable to the task of delivering profound and long-term shifts in public attitudes. It can stimulate immediate pressure by getting large numbers of the public to support "a good cause," but it is inherently limited in the scale of what it can achieve. It depends on what the public understands to be necessary, possible, and acceptable—which,

> because of the ubiquitous and oppressive charity frame described above, is limited to fund-raising for services that deliver help directly to "the poor" and to only marginal policy change, both of which fall short of what NGOs themselves believe is actually required.[31]

As Kirk's example makes clear, framing matters. Some efforts to address problems and to "do good" might inadvertently reinforce the common sense that engenders and perpetuates those problems in the first place. One of my primary objections to IMT, as I have noted repeatedly, is that it frequently (and probably inadvertently) reinforces neoliberal assumptions and ideology. It does so because its idealizations (predictably) replicate the prevailing common sense. The bifocal approach equips political theorists to help develop effective, appealing, inclusive, and perspicacious frames without losing sight of the strategic considerations and broader emancipatory aims in play.

Thinking of the politics of injustice in terms of discursive politics and effective framing highlights the importance of making connections among the disparate groups and movements engaged in various forms of opposition to injustice. As Laclau and Mouffe emphasized, there is no guarantee that such groups will align themselves with progressive or emancipatory political forces. Even among those groups that can be bound together by the glue of shared values and commitments, the potential points of contact and cohesion are not always readily apparent. It's thus imperative to identify and explore the equivalences among groups and to theorize, carefully and critically, the differences among them with the aim of developing a movement that is resolutely democratic and emancipatory and that construes multiplicity as a resource for, rather than an obstacle to, intersectional solidarity.[††]

Realizing this aim requires that we find ways to render people's varied knowledges, experiences, and practices mutually intelligible and to promote reciprocal understanding among those engaged in emancipatory

[††] In each of these aspects of articulation, the grounded epistemology and dialectical reasoning to which the democratic approach is committed prove helpful. The concerns, knowledge and

struggles against injustice in different contexts; it requires translation (which is the second significant contribution theory can make to building countervailing power).[32] There are two related aspects of this work, what I'll refer to as horizontal and vertical translation. Horizontal translation is necessary because there is no single notion or experience of injustice; its character varies in different contexts and produces diverse forms of resistance and opposition. This multiplicity can enrich our understanding of injustice, but it creates a challenge that's at once epistemological and political: how to make common cause among movements and people who might not immediately recognize one another as engaged in similar struggles, as potential allies or comrades. To

> promote counter-hegemonic practices that combine ecological, pacifist, indigenous, feminist, workers' and other movements, and to do so in a horizontal way and with respect for the identity of every movement, an enormous effort of mutual recognition, dialogue and debate will be required.[33]

The political aim of such an effort is to facilitate learning and collaboration among the various forces working against injustice in ways that enable a coherent and cohesive emancipatory politics. To make the possibility of such collaboration legible requires the translation of practices, including "forms of organization, objectives, styles of action and types of struggle."[34]

Vertical translation refers both to the redescription and rearticulation of situated struggles and knowledges in a broader vocabulary of emancipatory democratic politics and to the adaptation and use of these broader discourses in local struggles against injustice. "Downward vertical translation occurs when local activists interpret and adapt global discourses to their specific circumstances and purposes, as occurs frequently (for example) in human rights activism."[35] Through such translations, however,

experience of people enduring and opposing injustice provide important normative guidance for democratic inquiry and invaluable insight into the kinds of narratives and arguments that might resonate with them.

it's not just that a global discourse gets fitted to a particular context; ideally, the larger discourse itself is enriched and transformed. This "upward" vertical translation is not only about interpolating particular knowledges and experiences into a shared vocabulary but also crucially about the continual dialectical reformulation of the larger discourse itself.

We can see such processes of translation at work in the extraordinary politics of opposition to the Dakota Access Pipeline that emerged in 2016 at the Standing Rock Sioux Reservation of the Lakota and Dakota peoples. As Jeanne Morefield and I wrote,

> The fight to stop the pipeline from transgressing on territory sacred to the Sioux (territory that once belonged to them by treaty right) is at one and the same time a fight to protect the water, to resist further theft, and to rectify historical wrongs. It is thus simultaneously a movement in which struggles over the past, present, and future are inextricably linked. By reflecting upon, rather than deflecting, the history of American continental imperialism, the Standing Rock movement is able to connect that past directly to the contemporary struggles for First Nation rights, for a livable planet, and for alternatives to the rapacious logic of capitalism that again threatens life as we know it. In addition, this modality of reflective politics offers a compelling alternative to liberal universalism, one in which the situatedness of the resistance in the particularity of a distinctive local context vivifies and amplifies the global resonance of that resistance by clarifying points of convergence and divergence with similar struggles elsewhere.[36]

As this example makes clear, the point of translation is emphatically not to assert the priority or superiority of a more general emancipatory discourse, to suggest any deficiency in local experiences or vernacular vocabularies, or to promote a singular or unified discourse of emancipation. The point is that for a diverse and pluralistic movement of movements based on intersectional solidarity to function as a counterhegemonic force requires that we devise techniques for promoting mutual intelligibility and reciprocal understanding as well as the reflexive interpolation of myriad struggles against injustice into an always-provisional and emerging discourse of emancipatory politics.

My distinction between vertical and horizontal translation differs from and cuts across Santos's distinction between *translation of practices*, which as I noted above includes work to make different objectives, organizational forms, styles of action, and types of struggle mutually intelligible, and *translation of knowledge*, which involves interpretive work among cultures and aims at deep mutual understanding and reciprocal recognition.[37] I think that Santos sometimes overstates the difficulty of translation in general because he worries about the real epistemological difficulties that arise in the translation of knowledge. It's not clear, however, that deep cross-cultural understanding is a *precondition* for collaboration, as these worries sometimes lead him to suggest: such understanding is most likely to emerge *through* collaboration and the dialogues it initiates and through which it proceeds. It's through such engagements that we come to recognize the inadequacies in any understanding of emancipation that presents itself as a complete or ideal conception.[38] It's about the process.

Articulation and translation are practices through which political theorists can enact the grounded, reflexive epistemology of emancipatory democracy in a practical and politically constructive way.[‡‡] Again, to be very clear, the point of this work is not to discover some least common denominator to which various struggles might be reduced, to construct an idealized account of injustice or of emancipation, or to dictate a political vocabulary or program to anyone. The aim is "to create intelligibility, coherence and association in a world that sees itself enriched by multiplicity and diversity."[39]

To do so requires that we imagine and construct a counterhegemonic politics that is not itself hegemonic in its presumptions or its projects. In

‡‡ Santos emphasizes that only representatives of social groups (movements and NGOs) can carry out the work of translation because "knowledges and practices exist only as mobilized by social groups"; Santos, *Rise of the Global Left*, 143. This might be true for some types of deeper intercultural knowledge, but I see no reason to doubt that scholars, working in collaboration with activists, can ably undertake much of this work.

framing things this way I'm parting ways with Laclau and Mouffe, who insist that democracy—which they define as the logic of the elimination of relations of inequality and subordination—is an incomplete and inadequate political project.[40] They believe that an alternative hegemonic project is necessary to replace the existing hegemonic formation and that it must include the articulation of proposals for the positive organization of the social. They frame the contrast as one between a strategy of opposition and a strategy for the construction of a new order. Radical democracy must avoid the extremes of the ideal city and of "reformism without a project," they argue, and it must do so in a way that embraces utopian thinking.[41]

A WORLD ENRICHED BY MULTIPLICITY AND DIVERSITY

I'm skeptical of this call for a utopian democratic hegemony—at least if it means the construction of a single utopian project. Laclau and Mouffe's worries about reformism without a project reflect a false dichotomy between (purely) oppositional politics and (hegemonic) utopian politics. The dichotomy is false because oppositional politics can be generative– and needn't be merely "reformist." Consider three very brief examples. Two decades ago, a number of groups with roots in the environmental justice movement developed a principled framework for democratic collaboration among diverse social actors. This framework, the Jemez Principles for democratic organizing, enjoins activists to be inclusive, to engage in bottom-up organizing, to allow and enable people to speak for themselves, to work together in solidarity and mutuality, to build just relationships among themselves, and to commit themselves to self-transformation through their politics and process.[42] These principles vividly illustrate how shared *opposition* to injustice grounded in multiple disparate experiences of domination, oppression, and exploitation can engender *positive* political prescriptions for relations of recognition, respect, and mutual understanding without requiring consensus.

My second example is, again, Standing Rock. In December 2016, Lakota elders and pipeline protesters, including a group of military veterans, held a "forgiveness ceremony." As Morefield and I explained, relying on an account by Toyacoyah Brown,

> During the ceremony, veterans apologized for the US Army's role in dispossession, violence, and genocide and acknowledged their ongoing connection to an institution that continues to enable those same injustices (often in the name of the same resource extractive capitalism) around the world today. The response of Lakota Elder Chief Leonard Crow Dog to this public expression of regret was to offer forgiveness and then to move immediately and seamlessly to the broader issues at stake, first calling for "world peace," then acknowledging Lakota sovereignty, and finally ending with the observation that "we do not own the land, the land owns us." Crow Dog's double pivot—from the particular to the global and then back to the local—shows how it is possible to reshape the possibilities of the present by reconfiguring the past. This move transforms the encounter from one between supplicants and confessors to one characterized by parity and reciprocity and made possible by the courage and humility of all parties.[43]

This remarkable encounter, we concluded, shows how "the bonds and knowledge created through shared acknowledgment and forgiveness transform the past and the present in ways that foster 'alternative knowledges' while reminding us that another world is possible."[44]

That hope in the possibility of another world makes a neat segue to my final example, the World Social Forum process.[§§] The Forum is an ongoing effort to theorize and construct a diverse politics anchored in shared opposition to neoliberalism.[45] The conscious reference by participants to the Forum as a process highlights the generative dimensions of its

§§ The phrase "another world is possible" has become closely associated with the Forum as well as with the politics of the global Left more generally.

work, which include building discursive power, deepening the critique of neoliberal hegemony and its injustices, and imagining alternative futures. Many critics who dismiss the Forum as an ineffective talk shop, a sort of jamboree of the global Left with no leaders and no clear demands, miss that the point is the process itself, which is to discover and build precisely the kind of emancipatory politics that might effectively challenge neoliberal hegemony without substituting another hegemony in its place.

Each of these examples helps us to glimpse a political future for that world which understands itself as enriched by multiplicity and diversity and regards them as a resource, and each prefigures that future, imperfectly. Rather than conceptualizing this future as a utopian project, with its connotations of perfection and singularity, I prefer to think of it in terms of the cultivation of a utopian imaginary, one concerned with the conditions of possibility for the proliferation of many contemporaneous utopias. This utopian imaginary is summarized in the ethos of "one no, many yesses" underlying the nascent solidarity being constructed by the alter-globalization movement.[46] Surprisingly, it was Robert Nozick who first (to my knowledge) proposed a "framework for utopias" in the often-neglected third part of *Anarchy, State, and Utopia*.[47] My objections to Nozick's libertarian approach in that book are too numerous to document, but in that third section he was grappling with a problem not unlike the one I have been discussing here: how to reconcile democratic commitments to freedom and equality for all with a multiplicity of ways of being in the world. His proposed solution, a framework for the coexistence of many utopian communities, remains provocative.

I take something like these same concerns to be Gerald Gaus's motivation in condemning what he calls the tyranny of the ideal. I want to give his argument serious attention, as it's the best recent attempt I know to work out the practical implications of a utopian imaginary in a pluralistic way. As we've seen, Gaus is critical of Sen's "climbing" approach to comparative justice, worrying that it will lead to suboptimal maxima (to getting stuck on lower peaks). But he also worries about the pursuit of a single ideal of justice in a diverse society. In his view, Rawls's notion of a well-ordered society "is ultimately a mirage, yet one that tyrannizes over our thinking and encourages us to turn our back on pressing problems of justice in our own neighborhood"; it "is a dangerous illusion."[48] Gaus urges us, as theorists and as citizens, to eschew what he calls the "optimizing stance," the insistence on pursuing a particular social optimum,[49] and instead to embrace what he calls an "Open Society."

According to Gaus, "to know justice and just social states as well as possible, requires an open, diverse society, in which innumerable perspectives simultaneously cooperate and compete, share and conflict."[50] Instead of a single-minded ascent to the summit (the optimizing perspective), we should launch a multitude of expeditions in which various "teams" explore the "landscape" of justice, ultimately leading to the emergence of "competing theories of the ideal." This kind of exploration can only take place in an Open Society, which "provides a framework in which these different perspectives can search, share, debate, and, yes, dismiss each other's insights, while engaging in other cooperative social relations."[51] They do so by "[constructing] an artificial, public social world that all can share, given our various perspectives on justice."[52]

Gaus describes the Open Society as a "liberal framework in which different republican communities of inquiry" agree to coexist by agreeing on a "moral constitution" for the regulation of public life.[53] Like many liberals before him, he does not regard this "moral constitution" as a constraint on the various substantive views people might hold in a diverse society. As a result, he, like many liberals before him, doesn't take deep conflicts about fundamental matters of justice seriously enough, treating the liberal ideal as if it were not actually a substantive ideal of justice but merely a necessary, reasonable, and unobtrusive framework in which other ideals can be pursued. Though he acknowledges "fringe communities" that might find nothing appealing in such an arrangement and withdraw into the certainties of their own perspectives, Gaus nonetheless regards the Open Society both as a good in itself and as a necessary mechanism in the pursuit of justice.

By treating the Open Society as a reasonable compromise or accommodation rather than a substantive ideal, Gaus's liberalism denies—as liberalism always has done—its own ideological character and substantive commitments and shields the injustices that those commitments have historically protected from critical scrutiny and political thematization. Gaus's proposal also assumes—again, in typical liberal fashion—that conflicts among rival conceptions of justice can be managed through the mechanisms of liberal democratic accountability. This assumption entails the view that victims of liberal justice will and should be content to lose repeatedly within a rigged system whose procedural conception of fairness upholds the status quo. In Gaus's case, the rigging takes place through the device of what he calls the "socially eligible set of rules" for governing society, rules that "everyone" agrees are better than no rules and are thus eligible for adoption.[54] This seemingly benign device gives an effective veto to the powerful, who prefer no (change in the) rules to rules that might undermine their privileged positions.*** Thus Gaus's Open Society, like most liberal frameworks of justice, only recognizes as injustice what those in dominant social positions regard as unjust.

Gaus worries about fringe communities that take their marbles and go home, but I worry more about how framing liberalism as a reasonable compromise or a minimal framework for managing disagreement excludes radical claims about injustice altogether. Imagine a group that questions private property and challenges the social violence on which our society depends. Its views might be inadmissible, and policies based on them "ineligible," in the Open Society because the rich and powerful would (correctly) view them as threats to their privilege and thus as far worse than no (change in the) rules. Consensus and reasonableness function in the Open Society as they inevitably function within liberal theories, as constraints on radical critique and radical politics. In place of the tyranny of the ideal, Gaus offers us yet another iteration of liberal despotism, whose hallmark is its refusal to recognize itself as an ideology.

Gaus's proposal highlights the difficulty of attempting to institutionalize multiplicity and diversity. Still, I believe that the idea of a framework of utopias remains a politically fertile and potentially productive

*** Think of the rules the rich and poor agree to in Rousseau's account of the transition out of the state of nature.

one. A democratic reconceptualization of that idea might interpret the emancipatory democratic project as a *process* in which the condition of possibility for contemporaneous utopias is the reflexive continuation and deepening of democratization itself. This process must involve the repair and emancipatory transformation of relationships and ways of thinking damaged by ongoing histories of injustice. It can be, as my brief examples suggested, generative, intersectional, solidaristic, and counterhegemonic. It is also inherently open-ended. This indeterminacy may be the best guarantee that multiplicity and diversity really might enrich the world, because they can do so only through the continual renewal and reformulation of the democratic aspiration for emancipation that the complexity and contingency of politics invites and requires.

It is impossible to know in advance whether a successful counterhegemonic politics can be fashioned from these resources and on these terms. It's a practical, not a theoretical, question—one to which our democratic political commitments enjoin us to seek an answer.

PROFESSIONAL POLITICAL THEORY AND COUNTERHEGEMONIC POLITICS

Before concluding, I want to reflect briefly on some of the professional and institutional challenges for scholars considering undertaking the kind of work I've been describing here. Our discipline prizes originality; for philosophers and political theorists (and many others), publication and career prospects turn on producing a distinctive body of scholarship judged not for its practical impact but rather on its "visibility" in top outlets with high "impact factors." Those outlets prize novelty, even idiosyncrasy, not relevance. This is not to denigrate scholarship of any kind; it's just to note that professional incentives make it difficult to build on the work of others or to admit agreement. Compounding this, most of us have been well socialized into a tradition that lionizes the lone, brilliant thinker whose genius begets ideas that transform the world. Without dismissing the virtues of independent thinking or denying that a few thinkers *have* made monumental contributions, I want to suggest that this model is unrealistic for most of us and anyway profoundly undemocratic. It is unrealistic because very few of us can make the sort of heroic contributions we have been taught to strive for—and because the work of combating injustice is not, as the foregoing discussion makes plain, work that any of us can adequately perform alone. That work requires ongoing collaboration within and beyond the academy that is difficult to achieve institutionally, harder to support financially, and unlikely to be rewarded in any case. The lone-genius model is undemocratic because it is predicated upon an epistemology that imagines knowledge to be out there awaiting discovery through objective or impartial inquiry, rather than something to be produced cooperatively and from a particular point of view. It is also undemocratic in its idealization of positions, resources, and working conditions of scholars privileged with appointments at prestigious colleges and universities or analogous posts.

There are institutional obstacles to this work as well. As scholars, many of us labor in institutions that in practice discourage collaborative and interdisciplinary work, however piously they are celebrated in word. We are rewarded for originality and yet, at the same time, discouraged by tenure and promotion processes from taking big intellectual risks. We are admonished to maintain our "neutrality," to avoid "partisanship" in teaching and in research in the name of "objectivity." These worries about objectivity are related to what Onora O'Neill recently called a "positivist hangover"—a lingering sense that there is no intellectually credible or responsible way to advance or defend normative claims.[55] They are strongly amplified by universities themselves, especially public universities, which are anxious to avoid any controversy that might inflame social media or anger state legislators who could (it remains mathematically possible) cut funding for higher education.

It's vital to remember that this hangover was brought on in part by concerted efforts over the past seven decades or so, beginning in earnest in the McCarthy era (at least in the United States), to divide intellectuals from activists. So universities make it hard for faculty and students to work with social justice advocates, even as they celebrate the corporate partnerships with faculty and schools that are proliferating at an alarming rate and generating unsettling "sponsored research" in growing quantities. Meanwhile, it's impossible to ignore the links among declining funding for higher education, the phenomenal growth of a student loan racket that transfers public and individual wealth to private corporations and investors in the name of "increasing access to higher education," the expanding reliance on precariously employed faculty (who administrators hope are less likely to make trouble and know are easier to dismiss if they do), the growing dependence of universities upon corporate sponsorship (which facilitates the suppression or preemption of inconvenient research), the open advocacy of neoliberal orthodoxy within the business and economics curricula, the explosion of corporate-backed MBA degree programs, the infiltration and transformation of university administrations by holders of such degrees (who often lack experience as faculty), and the fervent embrace of STEM training by those administrators as a pretext for eviscerating the university of the critical disciplines.

If these observations seem like a departure from the line of argument I have been developing, recall that my focus in this chapter is on the work of political theory and political theorists. This work takes place in a particular social context shaped by neoliberal hegemony, a context that profoundly conditions our ability to conduct our scholarship. That context and the power relations shaping it must also therefore be theorized and resisted as part of any counterhegemonic politics, and such efforts constitute another part of the work we can do as scholars in support of the politics of injustice.

CONCLUSION

Conflict about injustice in the real world is often ideological conflict—that is, conflict arising from the divergent values, ideas, and interpretations people hold. To get to grips with injustice requires that we treat it as a political, not (merely) a philosophical, problem. Doing so means that political theorists have to take sides, to embrace the ideological character of claims about justice and injustice and engage in counterhegemonic politics. Theorists can, in particular, help to build countervailing political power by articulating arguments and critiques that challenge the prevailing common sense and by translating concepts and practices among movements and across cultural and political contexts. The aim of such countervailing power is to challenge hegemonic social formations and achieve social transformation through discursive political action. From a democratic perspective, that transformation should be in the direction of a diverse, intersectional, solidaristic movement of movements dedicated not to a single utopian project but rather to creating the conditions of possibility for the realization of many utopias. This aim can only be realized through a reflexive, open-ended, and continual process of repair, renewal, and (re)generation.

This chapter has outlined what political theory and political theorists might do to combat concrete injustices. The final chapter illustrates what political theorizing in this modality might look like by applying the bifocal approach and democratic values to the question of responsibility for injustice.

7

Taking Responsibility for Injustice

Responsibility has become a hot topic within global normative theory in large part because recent critiques of IMT's relevance and practical benefits have led scholars working within that approach to recognize the importance of better connecting their ideal theories of justice to the everyday injustices the theories are meant to address.[1] In this chapter, I take up this question of responsibility for injustice.[*] It's an important question in itself, and also one that lets me illustrate the radical difference the bifocal approach makes in how we think about problems like this one. I shall argue that responsibility for injustice must be reconceptualized as a political rather than a philosophical question. The bifocal approach reveals responsibility to be a social practice influenced by power and ideology,

* Much of the material here originally appeared in Michael Goodhart, "Interpreting Responsibiilty Politically," *Journal of Political Philosophy* 25, no. 2 (2017). I am grateful to the editor and publishers for giving me permission to reuse it here (in heavily revised form).

highlighting that what's ultimately at stake in our judgments about responsibility is the meaning of injustice itself. The chapter is constructed around an extended engagement with the work of Iris Marion Young, whose thinking on this subject (and many others) has been formative for me.

RESPONSIBILITY: A PHILOSOPHICAL PROBLEM?

Despite important differences in their approaches,[2] political theorists and philosophers typically think of agents as morally responsible for injustice when two conditions obtain: the agents' behavior—their acts, attempts, and omissions—leads to or results in some wrongful event or condition (*causation*); and, that behavior is proscribed or violates moral requirements (*culpability*).[3] Few people doubt that when injustice follows straightforwardly from the culpable behavior of some agent, that agent "is responsible" or should be "held responsible" for it. This conception of responsibility captures a widely held understanding (at least in the West) of common-sense morality,[4] one that seems to connect agency to redress in the right way by linking causation and blameworthy behavior with an obligation to make amends, to put things right.

This familiar *philosophical* approach to responsibility treats it as a determination based on the moral and empirical facts of a particular case; it regards culpability and causation as questions we can get to the bottom of through careful analysis and argumentation. That is, it conceives of both the normative and empirical dimensions of responsibility as factual determinations—and frequently conflates or collapses them together.[5] Treating responsibility this way allows theorists to put agents on the hook for injustice by linking their culpable behavior causally to a particular injustice, providing a powerful justification for compelling agents to change their ways or to compensate those who have been wronged. Many theories of global justice, while not necessarily framed this way, are attempts to establish causation and to clarify what counts as wrongful behavior in a transnational context for the purpose of establishing who is responsible for injustice. Arguments about the proper principles of justice, their scope, and the effects of the global order on the poor can all be construed as arguments partly about who is responsible for injustice.

Moral or philosophical responsibility is only one species of responsibility: legal liability often (but not always) tracks moral responsibility (they diverge, for instance, in cases of strict liability). In addition, relationships can give rise to responsibility: I might have a special obligation to clear my neighbor's sidewalk of snow simply because she needs the help and is close to me.[6] Some theorists maintain that we have responsibilities to help others by virtue of our capacity to do so without giving up anything of moral significance.[7] Further, certain social roles create responsibility: societies designate people to be lifeguards or firefighters so that otherwise diffuse responsibilities can be efficiently discharged.[8]

I'm not interested in undertaking a comprehensive survey or analysis of responsibility; I'd rather like to ask why argument about moral responsibility has proven so disturbingly ineffective in the face of systemic injustices like hunger, poverty, and sweatshops—injustices originating in complex social systems, structures, and processes. One plausible answer is that moral reasoning is only persuasive when it speaks to events or conditions that can be clearly and straightforwardly attributed to specific agents on the basis of having been caused by their blameworthy behavior; on this view, morality refers to the "domain of those things which can readily, or perhaps unmistakably, be put down to some particular agents' account."[9] If morality is only persuasive when the moral and empirical facts of the matter are clear, this would explain why global normative theorists have found questions of responsibility to be so frustrating: systemic injustices are characterized by empirical complexity, ethical ambiguity, and epistemological uncertainty that make factual determinations of responsibility difficult.[†] Causal connections between specific agents and particular injustices are often highly attenuated or indeterminate;

[†] This conception also makes the problem of historical responsibility difficult because the initial causes or historical wrongs—though not necessarily the perpetuating causes or the enduring harms—lie in the past and so cannot be easily assigned to contemporary agents.

theories about how the world works, which might help in establishing such connections, are incomplete and often contradictory. In addition, we lack clear intuitions about culpable behavior in such cases. Moreover, scholars disagree about how to think about these problems—about which assumptions hold, what factors matter and how much, and so on. Such complications "leave our thinking about responsibility in some disarray."[10]

Most theorists have responded to these challenges by tracing subtler chains of causality or developing innovative or more nuanced philosophical arguments about culpable behavior in the global context—by doubling down on the philosophical approach, trying harder to determine the moral and empirical facts surrounding systemic injustice. Two prominent theorists, David Miller and Iris Marion Young, have despaired of better casuistry and developed models of responsibility based in social connection that are explicitly designed to get to grips with responsibility for systemic injustice. Miller's connections approach to responsibility differentiates between two concepts of responsibility: outcome and remedial responsibility.[11] Outcome responsibility begins with agents and asks how they can reasonably be credited or debited with the results of their conduct.[12] Outcome responsibility is backward looking; it seek the facts of moral responsibility in past behavior. Remedial responsibility, by contrast, is forward looking. It begins with "patients," those who are suffering, and asks who should bear the burden of helping them. Remedial responsibility is a duty to put a bad situation right.[13] Sometimes this duty follows from some agent's being identified as outcome-responsible for the situation. We *identify* responsibility, in Miller's view, when we inquire who fits the relevant conditions for being responsible (who has culpably caused an injustice). We *assign* responsibility when we attach costs and benefits to agents regardless of whether they fulfill conditions for being responsible.[14]

When an agent is identified as outcome responsible, the agent is also—therefore—typically held remedially responsible.[15] This connection between outcome responsibility and remedial responsibility links agency and redress in the right way, Miller argues; it attaches costs and benefits to those agents who can be debited or credited with the results. Sometimes, as with systemic injustice, outcome responsibility is unclear.[16] The challenge in these cases is to find principles for assigning remedial responsibility that are morally weighty enough to justify sanctioning agents for failing to discharge it.[17] In assigning remedial responsibility, Miller proposes consideration of factors such as (nonculpable) causation, agents' capacity to help in remedying a situation, community ties linking agents to those affected by an injustice, and any benefits that might accrue to agents as a result of it.[18] There is no algorithm for assigning remedial responsibility on the basis of such connections, he argues; careful weighing of the relevant factors and good judgment are essential.[19]

In assessing what he calls the "intolerable" poverty in our world today, Miller laments that there is a large gap between this moral assessment and the identification of outcome responsibility. He believes that the poor bear most of the outcome responsibility for their poverty, but he admits that at least some lies elsewhere and that in any case they require assistance.[20] Miller recommends formal global mechanisms for assigning remedial responsibility in cases like this, yet at the same time doubts that these assignments can overcome the opposition that they will inevitably arouse. This contingency or indeterminacy surrounding such assignments makes it difficult and contentious, ethically and politically, to impose substantial costs for remedial responsibilities upon anyone. The result is a "justice gap" between what the poor can legitimately demand and what the rich can legitimately be obligated to pay.[21] Unfortunately, this "justice gap" swallows up all of the distinctiveness of Miller's approach, reinforcing the philosophical model of responsibility he set out to overhaul.[22] He fails, on his own terms (i.e., resolving the problem of remedial responsibility in cases of systemic injustice), because he continues to regard outcome responsibility as a factual determination that can be gotten right. Social connection proves an insufficiently weighty basis for assigning costly remedial responsibilities, leaving us back where were started.[23]

Iris Marion Young attempted a more definitive break with the philosophical approach, which she referred to as the liability model to emphasize its concern with blame or culpability. Her social connection model is specifically designed to address what she calls *structural* injustices, which exist when social processes place large categories of people under systematic threat of domination or deprivation of the means to develop and exercise their capacities.[24] This model rests on three premises: that the backward-looking liability model is unworkable and inappropriate in cases of structural injustice; that responsibility for structural injustice is shared and forward looking; and that shared responsibility must be discharged politically. Young rejects the liability model because she finds it inappropriate to blame "connected but removed actors" for their role in producing structural injustice (which is frequently unintended) and equally inappropriate to absolve people who contribute by their actions to processes that result in injustice.[25] She insists that the actions of individuals cannot be causally disentangled from structural processes in a way that would allow the tracing of specific aspects of the outcome for which those individuals might be blamed.[26]

Young focuses instead on the social processes out of which "obligations of justice" arise among people connected through them. "The 'social connection model' of responsibility says that all agents who contribute by their actions to the structural processes that produce injustice (including victims of injustice) have responsibilities to work to remedy these injustices."[27] Structures, according to Young, "denote the confluence of institutional rules and interactive routines"; they encompass resources and physical structures that create the relatively stable contexts in which individuals act, "presenting actors with options" and providing "channels" that both enable and constrain action.[28] Structures define social positions and the relations among those positions. Some people are positioned within structures in ways that leave them vulnerable to the systematic threat of domination and deprivation—that is, they experience structural injustice.[29]

Actions and interactions that transpire within structures "often have future effects beyond the immediate purposes and intentions of" actors, such that they "often have collective results that no one intends."[30] "Many large-scale social processes in which masses of individuals believe that they are following the rules, minding their own business, and trying to accomplish their legitimate goals" can nonetheless produce structural injustice.[31] The ground of an individual's shared responsibility for this injustice lies in the fact of her participation in structural processes that have unjust outcomes; she "shares with others the responsibility to transform these processes to reduce and eliminate the injustice they cause."[32] This responsibility is shared because "the harms are produced by many of us acting together within accepted institutions and practices, and because it is not possible for any of us to identify just what in our own actions results in which aspects of the injustice that particular individuals suffer."[33] In short, Young's model assigns responsibility for recent and ongoing structural injustice to those whose actions contribute to its production.[34]

On this view, shared responsibility can only be effectively discharged by joining with others in collective action. None of us can change social processes or institutions on our own; precisely because some injustices are structural, they require the intervention of many people acting in concert.[35] Shared responsibility is political, then, in that it requires "public communicative engagement with others for the sake of organizing our relationships and coordinating our actions most justly."[36] "We call on one another to take responsibility *together* for sweatshop conditions, without blaming anyone in particular" for those conditions or the structures that encourage them.[37] Using the example of homelessness, Young suggests that one way of discharging shared responsibility might be "trying to persuade others that this threat to well-being is a matter of injustice rather than misfortune and that we participate together in the processes that cause it. We would then enjoin one another to work on our collective relationships and try to transform the necessary practices."[38]

I find Young's insights into the political discharge of responsibility compelling, and they have influenced my own thinking about discursive political engagement. Yet I find the social connection model on the whole disappointing. Like Miller, Young remains constrained by the very philosophical conception of responsibility with which she intended to break. She rejected that model as backward looking and inappropriately focused on blame and set out to develop a forward-looking alternative. That alternative model makes responsibility a function of social connection, and she's especially interested in cases where the connection consists in routine, accepted behavior (such as shopping for low-priced clothing). While Young strips these connections of liability or culpability, her model remains backward looking nonetheless: the social connections that concern her (necessarily) originate in the past. While she does not regard these connections as blameworthy, she nonetheless *moralizes* them—that is, treats them as giving rise to moral responsibilities. The shared responsibility for structural injustice arising from connection is, in her view, an "[obligation] of justice."[39] Seemingly, the *empirical* fact of connection suffices to establish *moral* responsibility in Young's view: "we bear responsibility because we are part of the process" that produces injustice.[40]

Moralizing connection in this way tethers responsibility to the past.[41] More importantly, it reproduces the relationship between responsibility and determinations of moral and empirical fact that defines the philosophical approach. The key difference is that Young takes blame out of the equation—a mistake about which I'll have more to say below.

A POLITICAL APPROACH TO RESPONSIBILITY

The philosophical approach struggles to identify responsibility for systemic injustice because it treats responsibility as a determination based on normative and empirical facts and because the facts are unclear in such cases. From the bifocal perspective, the difficulty in ascribing responsibility for systemic injustice is not that the facts are mired in complexity, ambiguity, and uncertainty. Rather, it's that our familiar way of thinking about responsibility simply doesn't identify agents as responsible for the roles they play in creating and sustaining systemic injustice. That's less a matter of factual complexity, ambiguity, and uncertainty than a particular social judgment informed by prevailing values and interpretations of the world. What Young proposes is really that we reach a different conclusion about the moral and political facts; she makes a different determination about responsibility based on her reading of social connection. The problem is that she treats this determination as if it were a philosophical conclusion, a matter we might get right.

I take a radically different approach, following the lead of Marion Smiley, who conceives of responsibility as a practical judgment based on the facts of the particular situation and on broader social norms, expectations, and practices that obtain in the wider sociocultural context.[42] According to Smiley, when we say that someone is or should be held responsible for some injustice, we are making a practical judgment that applies these social conventions to the facts of a specific case. Crucially, for Smiley and for me, there are no objective or categorical bases for these judgments about responsibility; both the "facts" and our social conventions must always be *interpreted*.[43‡]

Different interpretations of the "facts" arise when people bring different values, beliefs, and experiences to their consideration of particular cases. For example, many conceptions of justice might condemn the use of excessive force by police, yet people whose beliefs or life experiences make them alive to structural racism might nonetheless see a police shooting of an unarmed black man very differently than people whose outlook or social position lets them imagine that society is colorblind. Even our assessments of the "facts" about the dangers that officers face and about the difficulty of making accurate split-second decisions regarding threats and options will be interpreted though these lenses. People may also agree on the "facts" but appeal to very different conceptions of justice when making judgments about responsibility. For example, people might agree that there is too much poverty and inequality in society but rely on different values and ideas in thinking about who should be held responsible for these ills. Socialists might appeal to equality or cite exploitation in blaming capitalists, while neoliberals might excoriate a "culture of dependency" and blame the poor themselves as lazy or irresponsible. Decisions about which "facts" to consider, how to weigh them, and what values best apply in a given situation are always decisions that express and reflect our

‡ In the previously published version of this argument, my debts to Smiley are clearer because I use her vocabulary throughout the article. Here, equipped with the full bifocal apparatus, I frame the argument differently. Those debts, however, remain. Indeed, it was partly in thinking through these questions with Smiley that the need for a bifocal approach became clear to me.

normative or ideological commitments. This means that judgments about responsibility for injustice—like those about the meaning of injustice itself—will always be contentious.

That said, the collective application of social conventions to the "facts" of particular cases reflects an iterated and irreducibly interpretive social practice of *ascribing* responsibility—a term I prefer to *identifying* (too categorical) and to *assigning* (insufficiently socially embedded). As a social practice, responsibility will be shaped by power relations and by the dominant ideology. This influence will encourage convergence in our judgments, many of which may settle into something like "truths" about responsibility, especially when our normative intuitions about culpability align and when causation is straightforward. At the opposite extreme, even the understanding that responsibility is mainly about culpable causation might be contested and revised. As a rule, convergence will be more likely—though we shouldn't expect anything like complete agreement or uniformity. The indeterminacy of the political and the pluralism and essential contestedness it engenders militate against full consensus.[§]

Because responsibility is a social practice, our judgments about it are necessarily contingent and therefore malleable, subject to contestation and revision. These judgments might evolve slowly, reflecting gradual shifts in shared attitudes, beliefs, and understandings, or they might change rapidly, as a result of conscious efforts to target and transform them. Viewed through the analytical lens of the bifocal approach, responsibility comes into focus as a likely terrain of disagreement and contestation. This contestation might be over various interpretations of the "facts" about causation, or it might be over which conception of justice one should appeal to in assessing culpability. The bifocal perspective also implies that we should *expect* our thinking to be in disarray in cases of systemic injustice like those that concern global normative theorists, not so much because the

[§] Unlike a Kantian reconstruction, my account of this practice does not seek to distill immanent or transcendent principles of responsibility; it is rather an interpretation or characterization of practice, one that highlights the irreducible contingency of judgments about responsibility. See Ronald Dworkin, *Freedom's Law: The Moral Reading of the American Constitution* (Cambridge, MA: Harvard University Press, 1996), 63.

"facts" are particularly messy but because people's values, interpretations, and life experiences are so disparate in such cases. So, for example, we can read the line of protests stretching from the Zapatista uprising in 1994 through the battles of Seattle, Genoa, and Pittsburgh to Standing Rock, the Fight for $15, and the populist backlash of 2016 as challenges to neoliberal claims of nonresponsibility for poverty, inequality, social insecurity, and environmental degradation.

The contingency and malleability of judgments about responsibility make them ripe for transformation through discursive political engagement. To shift collective thinking about responsibility requires collective action designed to change people's minds; only coordinated efforts to make people view the facts differently or modify or reconsider their values and ideas are likely to reshape judgments about responsibility. The Occupy movement and the Movement for Black Lives explicitly attempt to challenge prevailing judgments about responsibility by disrupting common sense and offering alternative narratives about injustice and responsibility through discursive political engagement of many types.

The bifocal approach suggests that such movements are more likely to succeed the more clearly and persuasively they articulate their values, ideas, and understandings and the more effectively they can be translated into discourses that resonate widely and facilitate alliances with sympathetic groups and individuals. One particularly effective tactic is to awaken that consciousness dormant in the gap between common sense and people's lived experiences of injustice. The Movement for Black Lives has made brilliant and astute use of social media—especially video—in transforming perceptions about police brutality in ways that speak to the fascinating potential of those media to translate lived experience itself in ways that others can experience directly and viscerally.

This is where Young went wrong. She clearly saw the value of this kind of persuasion through collective political action: "Political contestation about structural injustice," she wrote, "entails making arguments that some of the suffering of people is in fact injustice."[44] But because she conceptualized responsibility philosophically, as a matter of fact about social connection, she could only understand political action as a means of *discharging* shared responsibility, a way of fulfilling the responsibility we already have by virtue of our connection to injustice. The bifocal approach shows us that political action can be *constitutive* of responsibility, in that discursive political action can redefine responsibility by reshaping prevailing interpretations of the world or even the meaning of injustice itself.

THE POLITICS OF RESPONSIBILITY

Put differently, the bifocal approach shows that responsibility is determined politically, not philosophically. It is not a puzzle to be solved through careful analysis but rather a battle to be won through persuasion. Skeptics might object that there is nothing particularly new in this interpretation: persuading people to change their views about responsibility is what political theorists who write about this topic are trying to do. At one level there is no denying this. But there is nothing in the recent literature on responsibility in global normative theory to suggest that scholars recognize it as socially constructed or appreciate the political significance of that fact, no indication—save in Young's work—that the key tasks in persuading people are political and discursive rather than primarily philosophical. To put the point differently, the extant literature on responsibility is replete with analytic arguments that purport to determine, based on the moral and empirical facts, who has responsibility for injustice. I have no desire to question the value or utility of such arguments, but—especially when couched in turgid disciplinary prose published in peer-reviewed journals and read (if at all) primarily in graduate seminars—they represent only a fraction of what's necessary. Persuasion that seeks to (re)shape social conventions must also happen in bars, on social media, in the streets; it must rely on strikes, protests, petitions, education, organizing, electoral politics—on a broad range of discursive strategies and tactics for changing people's minds. This does not mean that there is no role for rigorous normative arguments about responsibility; it means placing those arguments into a much richer and more complex theoretical and political context.

At a minimum, then, my approach highlights some extremely important aspects of responsibility that have been sorely neglected in recent debates. The full implications are, however, much more radical. I've argued that the politics of injustice is about contesting the very meaning of injustice itself and that practices of responsibility and blame are a field on which these battles play out in the real world. That's why I think Young makes a mistake in forsaking blame; it's a potent and valuable tool, one there is good normative and political reason to hold on to.[45] For instance, if the continual search for bargains foreseeably leads to the structural injustice of sweatshops, why shouldn't we consider it blameworthy—at least once the connection is understood—and hold people responsible for it? Their behavior might be acceptable *now*, but that's precisely one of the judgments that many antisweatshop activists are seeking to transform through their efforts to raise awareness of the consequences of that behavior and to make people think about their responsibility in another way (to make them feel guilty about their consumption habits).

Giving up on blame led Young to a second serious mistake: when combined with her moralization of all social connection, abjuring blame leads her to conclude that victims have as much responsibility for injustice as do others who are connected to it.[46] So, on her view, sweatshop workers are responsible for the injustice of their own conditions. Workers are of course part of the system that exploits them, but to conflate their obvious interest in changing this exploitative system with a moral responsibility to do so—a responsibility shared with those who exploit them—is to get things badly wrong (and in a way that bolsters the neoliberal discourse of personal responsibility Young criticizes).[47] It doesn't help much to insist that calling the workers responsible does not amount to blaming them, since the same holds for the owners and managers who do the exploiting!

Young recognizes the tension here, acknowledging that some of the injustice experienced by sweatshop workers "is properly the responsibility of specific culprits under a liability model"—she cites violations of labor laws by factory owners and managers and states' failure to punish them.[48] Yet she also insists that many of the actors who we might blame for the workers' exploitation—the culprits—can claim with some justification that they too operate under constraints beyond their control that make them vulnerable to economic and institutional pressures.[49] They too are caught up in the uncoordinated and largely unintentional social processes that ultimately give rise to structural injustice.[50] Young is deeply conflicted on this point: she does not want to ignore the objectionable behavior of factory owners, managers, and state regulators, but she is reluctant to blame them when larger structural factors are at work.

From a bifocal perspective, we can see that part of the difficulty she's confronting arises because she has a monocular vision of responsibility for injustice. What I mean is that Young still treats responsibility as a philosophical determination, so she overlooks the larger power dynamics in play, missing that what's at stake here is not the "facts" about responsibility but the struggle over the meaning of injustice itself. Indeed, Young's account is remarkable for its treatment—or rather, neglect—of power. Her model erases important distinctions among different kinds of connection, obscuring the normative distinctiveness of power relations and making it hard to generate a critique of how power creates and sustains structural injustice or shapes our judgments about responsibility. This is clear in Young's discussion of power and privilege as "parameters of reasoning" about responsibility that let us determine "what is required morally of agents in respect to rectifying structural injustice."[51] These parameters help us to "respond to the intuition that different agents properly have different kinds and degrees of forward-looking responsibility for injustice" deriving largely from their social positions.[52] According to Young, those with greater actual or potential power and influence over processes that produce injustice, those who enjoy relative privilege in relation to structures of injustice, those who have a particular interest in realizing justice (including the victims of the injustice), and those who are in a position to draw on existing resources to promote change should all take responsibility proportionate to their positions within structures that produce injustice.[53]

To see why this matters, consider again Young's discussion of the global garment industry. That discussion elides that some people get quite rich as a direct result of the low wages and unsafe, oppressive working conditions that typify sweatshop production—it ignores that *some workers are exploited by capitalists*. This is hardly a shocking revelation, I realize; my point is that there is a telling difference between regarding sweatshop laborers as *exploited* by *capitalists* and conceiving of workers as "put under systematic threat of domination or deprivation of the means to develop and exercise their capacities" by "social processes."[54] When all connections are morally equivalent, the responsibility of workers becomes identical to that of their exploiters, and the operation and effects of power get ignored or erased.

Moreover, treating power merely as a factor in calibrating degrees of shared responsibility assumes that unjust outcomes are unintentional and thus ignores how power *engenders* injustice by shaping structures and conditioning social norms and expectations in the first place.[55] I'm referring not so much to individual owners and managers, who might be excused for bowing to competitive pressures, as to corporations and institutions that advocate policies facilitating the mobility of international (financial) capital, promoting hypercompetitive markets, encouraging so-called austerity policies that cut corporate tax rates and slash social protections, and attacking worker organizations and solidarity—all of which function systematically to suppress wages, compound workers' vulnerability, and augment profits. Many of these same agents actively promote standards of acceptable social behavior based on neoliberal conceptions of liberty, responsibility, and free markets that effectively normalize or excuse structural injustice. Young's account gives her no critical leverage on any of these problems because it moralizes all social connection and abandons blame.

The bifocal perspective provides a much clearer understanding of how power shapes our judgments and practices of responsibility, making it both possible and strategically essential to take its operation into account. Recall that Barnett and Duvall define power as "the production, in and through social relations, of effects that shape the capacities of actors to determine their own circumstances and fate."[56] Most theorists of responsibility consider power, if at all, in its *interactional* modalities; that is, they pay attention to the outcomes of compulsory or institutional power in the form of concrete injustices for which power-wielders might be responsible.

Constitutive power, on the other hand, produces effects manifest in "the identities of the occupants of social positions"—their self-understandings, subjectivities, frameworks of meaning, and so on.[57] Constitutive power is pretty much ignored in most accounts of responsibility because, I suspect, it doesn't register in the familiar philosophical formula—that is, it doesn't cause concrete injustices in any straightforward way.

On the bifocal approach, constitutive power is central to a comprehensive view of responsibility because it is deeply implicated in the construction and promulgation of the ideologies that shape the practice of responsibility—that shape our interpretations of the world and our judgments about responsibility. To see the practical implications of taking constitutive power seriously, consider once more Young's discussion of sweatshops. She views sweatshops and other examples of systemic injustice as the result of unintended consequences arising from agents' pursuit of their aims and interests "for the most part within the limits of accepted rules and norms" and regards this as behavior for which they should not be blamed.[58] I have already observed that by treating all connections as morally equivalent, Young seems to overlook some fairly obvious forms of interactional power, such as the direct oppression and exploitation of workers. She likewise ignores constitutive power: many of the social processes she characterizes as unintentional or as complex, compound consequences of seemingly insignificant or harmless individual behavior are actually products of constitutive power—specifically, of a carefully orchestrated, decades-long program of neoliberal economic policy designed to serve the interests of capital and to restore class power.[59] The race to the bottom in labor protections, the general lack of regulation and enforcement of human rights and workplace safety, states' and workers' vulnerability to the rapid withdrawal of investment capital, the precariousness created by austerity programs designed to dismantle social safety nets (where they existed at all)—these "social processes" were carefully designed and implemented as part of an explicit neoliberal agenda dating back at least to the infamous Powell Memorandum of 1971 and traceable to the formation of the Mont Pelerin Society decades before.[60]

Moreover, the bifocal approach helps us to see that "accepted rules and norms" are themselves produced through the operation of power. Smiley observed that we generally hold people to blame for negligence but don't blame states or the rich for failing to head off poverty.[61] *That's because neoliberalism encourages us to see poverty as natural and unavoidable and to blame it on the poor themselves.* The bifocal perspective not only clarifies this crucial point but also helps us to imagine a *political* response. Young might be correct that most people pursue their aims and interests innocently, as it were, but it is precisely these rules and norms, this notion of innocence, that must be problematized, theorized, and changed if anyone is to be held responsible for the injustices engendered by sweatshops—as many activists recognize. Rather than accept neoliberal conventions as constraints on our thinking about responsibility, as Young's approach effectively does, my approach invites a counterhegemonic critique of them.

So Young highlights the role of fashion tastes and trends in creating a demand for cheap apparel that contributes to the injustices of sweatshop labor; she is right to do so, but she never adequately theorizes how neoliberalism profoundly shapes popular thinking through the generation of specific knowledges and subjectivities that must themselves be interrogated and challenged.[62] Tastes and trends are consciously constructed through pervasive (and very costly) advertising campaigns orchestrated by the corporations that benefit from the manufacture and sale of clothing—and thus from the exploitative conditions in which it is produced.[63] Such campaigns unfold in a cultural context where freedom and self-expression have largely become modalities of consumption—or in which consumption is the primary modality of expressing freedom. Further, our (modern, Western) expectations about everything from work conditions and standards of living in core and peripheral economies (ours and theirs) to the nature of trade and development are structured by and saturated with neoliberal ideology and associated constructs of race and development, as we saw in chapter 5. Even what counts as "knowledge" about how the global economy works—about "rational" economic behavior, about the "laws" of the market and so on—reflects neoliberal common sense.

Mounting an effective critique of the exploitation of sweatshop labor is impossible unless we adopt a theoretical framework that allows us to conceptualize these effects of constitutive power and to challenge the dominant norms and expectations regulating the behavior of the relevant actors—in this case, including investors, executives, managers, state officials, individual consumers, and so on—as ideological formations. Only then can we formulate a political response. Put differently, any attempt to change people's thinking about responsibility requires a critique of power and ideology and simultaneously represents a challenge to them.

One reader has complained that my emphasis on hegemony is unnecessary and overstated since there are plenty of critics of neoliberalism working within global normative theory. This criticism illustrates precisely why an approach like mine is essential. There *are* certainly many theorists who are critical of some of neoliberalism's effects, primarily of the unfairness and inequality it generates. But criticizing these effects is hardly the same as a critique of neoliberal ideology and hegemony as such. As I have shown repeatedly, criticisms of neoliberalism's effects can and do reproduce neoliberal hegemony, however unintentionally, by accepting its basic assumptions (about the benefits of trade, the efficiency of markets, the meaning of freedom and opportunity, and so on) and idealizing them, turning them into constraints on our political imagination. Without an explicit focus on constitutive power and its effects, global normative theory can become an unwitting accomplice to neoliberal injustice.

My critique of Young's argument and of neoliberal hegemony does reflect a particular partisan or ideological point of view (which might be part of what the unhappy reader dislikes). This perspective is not entailed by the bifocal approach; I use it to illustrate how that approach integrates and utilizes partisan and analytical critique in a way that clarifies the political nature of responsibility. Whether people should contest particular judgments about responsibility or the broader ideologies in which they are enmeshed are questions that the bifocal approach cannot answer definitively; they hinge on people's particular values, beliefs, and motivations. The substantive critique offered here reflects my own emancipatory democratic commitments, commitments shared by many global activists—from the antisweatshop movement to the World Social Forum—who work to hold corporations, financial capitalists, and neoliberal politicians responsible for systemic injustice. My arguments and their activism can be interpreted as part of a broader political struggle to reshape prevailing interpretations and conventions that obfuscate responsibility for the social, economic, and cultural injustices of neoliberal globalization.[64] There are many prominent intellectuals and politicians, however, who endorse neoliberalism; to them, there is nothing admirable or heroic about opposing low-cost production in developing countries, protesting free trade agreements, denouncing austerity budgets, or demanding living wages. They see antisweatshop activists not as heroes but as ignoramuses—or subversives. It's because people do disagree over interpretations, including the substantive account I am using to illustrate my argument, that a bifocal political approach to responsibility is essential.

TAKING RESPONSIBILITY FOR INJUSTICE

To take responsibility can mean "to own up to one's responsibility" (as when someone acknowledges her decisions and their consequences or accepts the costs and burdens imposed as a result of her behavior) or "to assume responsibility when one has no obligation to do so" (as when someone volunteers or accepts responsibility for clearing up a mess she encounters). I'm particularly interested in this second meaning because it provides us with a useful way to make sense of an important aspect of many people's engagement in struggles against systemic injustice.

In a discussion I find quite troubling, Young characterized Danes who rescued or protected Danish Jews from the Nazis during the occupation as acting out of shared responsibility.[65] Recall that on her account, shared responsibility always arises out of a social connection to the processes that create injustice. In arguing that the Danes had shared responsibility for the plight of their Jewish neighbors, Young in effect suggested that they somehow contributed to this injustice and were discharging their moral responsibility—even though their only connection to the arrests and deportations appears to be their joint subjection to the Nazi terror state.[66] It seems frankly perverse to allocate shared responsibility to the Danes, just as it is to attribute shared responsibility to sweatshop workers for their own exploitation and mistreatment.[**]

Doing so misses the heroism of the Danes, who risked their lives in resisting an injustice they could not ignore. I see Young's antisweatshop activists as heroes in an analogous way: while their circumstances are quite different from those of the Danes, prevailing judgments about responsibility and common sense tell these activists that they bear no responsibility for sweatshops—indeed, that there is no injustice associated with sweatshops! Neoliberal ideology absolves them (and us) of responsibility by extolling markets as fair and efficient mechanisms for allocating benefits and burdens, by normalizing poverty-wage work in abhorrent conditions as consensual contractual labor that must (by definition) make workers better off, by promoting an ethos of consumer sovereignty in which my individual consumption choices are constitutive of my own freedom and autonomy and unconnected to the conditions of their production and distribution—in short, by depicting production, distribution, and consumption as apolitical and socially costless.

To me, the point of Young's examples is (or should have been) to highlight the heroism of people taking responsibility for injustice even when—as in this case of activists—they are not responsible for it (on the prevailing ideological view). The very point of antisweatshop activism is to educate people about the implications of their choices and habits, to try to change popular thinking so that consumers begin to regard themselves and others as responsible for the effects of their behavior. Activists are seeking to change how people think about injustice itself, not as a way of discharging responsibility but in hopes of pinning the blame where they believe it belongs. Some of these people might explain their motivation for

** I think Young goes astray here because the two different notions of responsibility that Gould identified in her model track the two different meanings of taking responsibility. She conflates these, just as she conflates the (moral) responsibility she links with causing or contributing to injustice with the forward-looking sense of responsibility people often feel to or for others. See Gould, "Varieties of Global Responsibility."

acting in terms of responsibility, but we should not let this distract us: the language of responsibility is commonly used to express the feeling that one "must do something" for any number of reasons—including anger, compassion, class solidarity, self-interest (in the case of sweatshop workers themselves), or a desire to alleviate suffering. My point is that people's political commitments frequently motivate them to act even when they have no clear "moral obligation" to do so. The bifocal approach helps us to appreciate the meaning and significance of their action in an appropriately political way.

POLITICAL THEORY FOR THE REAL WORLD

I've argued here that questions about responsibility for injustice are irreducibly political. Our judgments about them are contingent, and therefore malleable; they can be transformed through collective political action that (re)contests prevailing meanings and interpretations of the world and challenges dominant configurations of power. The social practice of responsibility is thus a terrain of ideological contestation. As a way of concluding the chapter and the book, I want to consider some objections to this argument. Doing so affords me the opportunity to recapitulate my main claims and the key features of my approach.

The first objection I want to consider is that, even assuming we know which conventions ought to change, and in what direction, the political interpretation of responsibility creates a dilemma: either there is no moral imperative to alter conventions, in which case there is no basis for cajoling others to change their views; or there is a moral imperative to change them, in which case we need to know to whom this imperative applies and thus need a substantive account of responsibility of the type that I have declined to provide. My approach begins from the realistic assumption that people adhere to different systems of values and beliefs—to different ideologies—and that people determine which conventions need to change, and how, with reference to them. Sincerely held values and beliefs certainly provide powerful guidance and motivation for how to behave and what to do. That there might be multiple and conflicting normative imperatives *among* ideologies doesn't constitute an interpretive or motivational problem within any given ideology, as I argued in chapter 4. An ideology is perfectly able to—its function is to—generate what philosophers like to call "action-guidance." Furthermore, nothing about my view implies that there is no normative or empirical basis for the various accounts of responsibility to which people subscribe; on the contrary, their judgments about responsibility are informed by their values and ideas and by their interpretations of the world. Politically, their task is not to justify these beliefs but to get others to see things their way.

A skeptic might (did) retort that while there may be psychological bases for cajoling people to change their views, my account provides them with no moral bases for doing so, no moral imperative to change their minds. This retort correctly characterizes my position: as I argued in chapter 4, I understand all political oughts as hypothetical rather than categorical (moral) imperatives. I do so because I am not persuaded that moral oughts possess the elusive magical powers that philosophers have been wont to attribute to them. Again, however, it's simply wrong to imagine that there are no bases for persuading people. I argued at length in chapter 6 that a realistic analysis of the politics of injustice shows that discursive political engagement can be effective in challenging prevailing norms and assumptions and instigating people to question their ideological commitments and to think differently about injustice. I also showed that to be successful, such politics must be conceived as a form of counterhegemonic politics and take power relations explicitly into account.

My argument in this chapter has been precisely that the politics of responsibility for injustice is counterhegemonic politics—politics oriented to problematizing entrenched social judgments about responsibility for systemic injustices like sweatshops. I've shown how and why responsibility is a political problem that demands a political response and illustrated the kinds of critiques and forms of activism that a democratic account of injustice recommends. Not everyone will agree with my treatment of claims about injustice and responsibility for it as ideological claims, but that disagreement does not make the argument wrong or deficient; it only makes it controversial.

Another objection—which has been raised in numerous permutations by various readers—is that my approach fails to take such and such appropriately into account. For example, a friend has insisted (and I simplify) that my approach fails to take *history* properly into account, that it ignores the obvious historical responsibility of colonial powers for many enduring injustices in our world, such as poverty in the global South (a position with which I substantively agree). The objection isn't quite accurate: my approach can accommodate blaming former colonial powers for poverty—*or any other substantive position.* What my friend really objects to, I think, is that my approach does not treat (her preferred account of) responsibility as a matter of moral and empirical fact and that it refuses to rule out some substantive positions (she regards) as normatively deficient. That, however, is not a failure of the approach; *it is the key feature of the approach.* Treating all normative claims as ideological is what makes the approach realistic, what allows it to avoid moralization and idealization and to provide insight into the conflictual politics of injustice. I've shown that this approach can be integrated with substantive normative critique and prescription and argued that the partisan theorizing we do as ideologists is actually enriched—made more politically relevant—by this bracing form of realism. My bifocal approach likewise makes our political analysis itself more realistic by giving proper attention to the critical and transformative ambitions of political actors and movements.

Suppose, however, that my friend were right. Suppose there were some correct moral basis for determining responsibility. Unless we also believe that morality is somehow self-enacting, it would still require concerted political effort to see the correct view accepted and enacted. That is, it would still require persuading enough people of this view to shift our dominant social conventions and change prevailing practices of judgment and blaming so that we could hold the "right" agents responsible. Thus even if I am wrong about the hypothetical normativity of political oughts, much of my account of the politics of injustice remains relevant.

This discussion of responsibility for injustice highlights the advantages of the bifocal approach to injustice that I've developed throughout this book, one that breaks clearly with IMT and with political realism. It integrates analytic and normative perspectives within a single theoretical framework designed to enable effective political action through counterhegemonic discursive politics. My approach is consciously designed for the real world, in which the overriding imperative for social justice activists and people of goodwill is to challenge concrete injustices and effect social transformation. On this view, responsibility for injustice is a political, not a philosophical, problem, and the meaning of injustice itself is a matter to be contested, an object of political struggle.

NOTES

INTRODUCTION

1. I borrow the term *global normative theory* from Katrin Flikschuh, "The Idea of Philosophical Fieldwork: Global Justice, Moral Ignorance, and Intellectual Attitudes," *Journal of Social Philosophy* 22, no. 1 (2014), using it to refer to the political theory literature on global justice, responsibility, and related topics. I exclude *transitional* justice, which addresses challenges of restoring peace and balancing retribution and reconciliation in postconflict or postauthoritarian societies; for a good overview, see Joanna R. Quinn, "Transitional Justice," in *Human Rights: Politics and Practice*, 3rd ed., ed. Michael Goodhart (Oxford: Oxford University Press, 2016). This important literature has evolved mostly separately from the approach I challenge here.
2. Charles W. Mills, "'Ideal Theory' as Ideology," *Hypatia* 20, no. 3 (2005): 169.
3. See Michael Goodhart, "Constructing Global Justice: A Critique," *Ethics and Global Politics* 5, no. 1 (2012).
4. Peter Singer, "Famine, Affluence, and Morality," *Philosophy and Public Affairs* 1, no. 3 (1972).
5. *Theory* is often credited with launching a renaissance of political theory, one that Brian Barry and many others associated with the decline of utilitarian argument; Vittorio Bufacchi, *Social Injustice: Essays in Political Philosophy* (Basingstoke, UK: Palgrave Macmillan, 2012), 18. I would locate the start of political theory's renewal in the mid-1960s, in the reaction against the so-called empirical theories of democracy (see Henry Kariel, ed., *Frontiers of Democratic Theory* [New York: Random House, 1970], for an introduction). Whatever the case, the waning influence of utilitarianism is not in much dispute.
6. These early "global Rawlsians" included Brian Barry, *The Liberal Theory of Justice* (Oxford: Clarendon Press, 1973); "Humanity and Justice in Global Perspective," in *Ethics, Economics, and the Law: Nomos 24*, ed. J. Roland Pennock and John W. Chapman (New York: New York University Press, 1982); Robert Amdur, "Rawls' Theory of Justice: Domestic and International Perspectives," *World Politics* 29, no. 3 (1977); Charles R. Beitz, *Political Theory and International Relations* (Princeton, NJ: Princeton University Press, 1979); "Economic Rights and Distributive Justice

in Developing Societies," *World Politics* 33, no. 3 (1981); and later, Thomas W. Pogge, *Realizing Rawls* (Ithaca, NY: Cornell University Press, 1989).

7. John Rawls, *A Theory of Justice* (Cambridge, MA: Harvard University Press, 1971), 3.
8. See David Harvey, *A Brief History of Neoliberalism* (Oxford: Oxford University Press, 2005), 19; Loïc Wacquant, *Punishing the Poor: The Neoliberal Government of Social Insecurity* (Durham, NC: Duke University Press, 2009), 307.
9. Wacquant, *Punishing the Poor*, 307.
10. Ibid., 311ff. This regulation also takes place at the individual level through a distinctive regime of self-discipline undertaken by subjects formed in the wider ideological environment of neoliberalism; see Wendy Brown, *Undoing the Demos: Neoliberalism's Stealth Revolution* (Boston: Zone Books, 2015); Michel Foucault, *The Birth of Biopolitics: Lectures at the Collège de France, 1978–1979* (New York: Picador, 2010).
11. David Harvey, "Neoliberalism as Creative Destruction," *Geografiska Annaler: Series B, Human Geography* 88, no. 2 (2006). It does so for a "new global ruling class in the making" (Wacquant, *Punishing the Poor*, 306); cf. Leslie Sklair, *The Transnational Capitalist Class* (Oxford: Wiley-Blackwell, 2000). This class comprises, among others, the chief officers of transnational corporations, high-ranking national politicians and bureaucrats, and top officials of various international organizations, including international financial institutions like the International Monetary Fund, the World Trade Organization, and the World Bank, as well as the professionals who work for them. In short: the Davos set.
12. See Thomas Piketty, *Capital in the Twenty-First Century*, trans. Arthur Goldhammer (Cambridge, MA: Belknap Press of Harvard University Press, 2014); Branko Milanovich, *The Haves and the Have Nots: A Brief and Idiosyncratic History of Global Inequality* (New York: Basic Books, 2011); Wacquant, *Punishing the Poor*; Harvey, "Neoliberalism as Creative Destruction."
13. George Monbiot, "Neoliberalism—the Ideology at the Root of All Our Problems," *The Guardian*, April 15, 2016, https://www.theguardian.com/books/2016/apr/15/neoliberalism-ideology-problem-george-monbiot.
14. John Williamson, ed., *The Political Economy of Policy Reform* (Washington, DC: Institute for International Economics, 1994); "What Washington Means by Policy Reform," in *Latin American Adjustment: How Much Has Happened?*, ed. John Williamson (Washington, DC: Institute for International Economics, 1990).
15. Naomi Klein, *The Shock Doctrine: The Rise of Disaster Capitalism* (New York: Metropolitan Books, 2007).
16. Martin Seliger, *Ideology and Politics* (London: Allen and Unwin, 1976), 14.
17. Harvey, *Brief History of Neoliberalism*, 3; cf. John S. Dryzek, *Deliberative Global Politics: Discourse and Democracy in a Divided World* (Cambridge: Polity Press, 2006), 7.
18. Antonio Gramsci, *Selections from the Prison Notebooks of Antonio Gramsci*, trans. Quintin Hoare and Geoffrey Nowell Smith (New York: International Publishers, 1971).
19. Thomas S. Kuhn, *The Structure of Scientific Revolutions*, 3rd ed. (Chicago: University of Chicato Press, 1996).

CHAPTER 1

1. Michael Goodhart et al., "Introduction: Unthinking the World-System," in *Social Movements and World-System Transformation*, ed. Jackie Smith et al. (New York: Routledge, 2016), 1.
2. Gerald Gaus, *The Tyranny of the Ideal: Justice in a Diverse Society* (Princeton, NJ: Princeton University Press, 2016), 34.
3. Ingrid Robeyns, "Ideal Theory in Theory and Practice," *Social Theory and Practice* 34, no. 3 (2008): 341.
4. Matt Sleat, "What Is a Political Value? Political Philosophy and Fidelity to Reality," *Social Philosophy and Policy* 33, nos. 1–2 (2016): 263. The internal quotations are from David Estlund, "Utopophobia," *Philosophy and Public Affairs* 42, no. 2 (2014): 113–15.
5. Adam Swift, "The Value of Philosophy in Nonideal Circumstances," *Social Theory and Practice* 34, no. 3 (2008): 381; cf. G. A. Cohen, "Facts and Principles," *Philosophy and Public Affairs* 31, no. 3 (2003).
6. Rawls, *A Theory of Justice*, 8; cf. *The Law of Peoples; with, "The Idea of Public Reason Revisited"* (Cambridge, MA: Harvard University Press, 1999), 90.
7. See Lea Ypi, "On the Confusion between Ideal and Non-ideal in Recent Debates on Global Justice," *Political Studies* 58, no. 3 (2010): 538.
8. Simon Caney, "Addressing Poverty and Climate Change: The Varieties of Social Engagement," *Ethics and International Affairs* 26, no. 2 (2012): 209.
9. Robeyns, "Ideal Theory," 352.
10. Ibid., 350; A. John Simmons, "Ideal and Nonideal Theory," *Philosophy and Public Affairs* 38, no. 1 (2010). The terms *ideal* and *nonideal* theory are deployed inconsistently in the literature, making both the distinction and the division of labor between them controversial; see Zofia Stemplowska, "What's Ideal about Ideal Theory?," *Social Theory and Practice* 34, no. 3 (2008): 322; Robert Jubb, "Tragedies of Non-ideal Theory," *European Journal of Political Theory* 11, no. 3 (2012): 230; cf. David Wiens, "Prescribing Institutions without Ideal Theory," *Journal of Political Philosophy* 20, no. 1 (2011): 46.
11. Simmons, "Ideal and Nonideal Theory."
12. Ibid., 34.
13. Judith N. Shklar, *The Faces of Injustice* (New Haven, CT: Yale University Press, 1990), 16.
14. Ibid., 86.
15. Ibid., 23; cf. Jeff Spinner-Halev, *Enduring Injustice* (Cambridge: Cambridge University Press, 2012), 63ff.
16. Shklar, *The Faces of Injustice*, 19.
17. Ibid., 87. Spinner-Halev similarly argues that enduring injustice—roughly, present injustices that flow from historical wrongs—sometimes stands on its own as something that justice cannot overcome (*Enduring Injustice*, 120).
18. Holly Lawford-Smith, "Ideal Theory—a Reply to Valentini," *Journal of Political Philosophy* 18, no. 3 (2010). There might well be other reasons to engage in IMT; Stemplowska, "What's Ideal about Ideal Theory," 320–24, argues that IMT helps us to understand what a commitment to a given set of values entails; cf. Jubb, "Tragedies of Non-ideal Theory," 231.

19. Eva Erman and Niklas Möller, "Three Failed Charges against Ideal Theory," *Social Theory and Practice* 39, no. 1 (2013): 9.
20. Keith Horton, "How Academics Can Help People Make Better Decisions Concerning Global Poverty," *Ethics and International Affairs* 26, no. 2 (2012): 272.
21. Cf. Glen Newey, "Two Dogmas of Liberalism," *European Journal of Political Theory* 9, no. 4 (2010): 450.
22. Ibid.
23. Raymond Geuss, *Philosophy and Real Politics* (Princeton, NJ: Princeton University Press, 2008); Bernard Williams, *In the Beginning Was the Deed: Realism and Moralism in Political Argument*, ed. Geoffrey Hawthorn (Princeton, NJ: Princeton University Press, 2005), 2.
24. Matt Sleat, "Bernard Williams and the Possibility of a Realist Political Theory," *European Journal of Political Theory* 9, no. 4 (2010): 486.
25. William A. Galston, "Realism in Political Theory," *European Journal of Political Theory* 9, no. 4 (2010): 386; cf. Bonnie Honig, *Political Theory and the Displacement of Politics* (Ithaca, NY: Cornell University Press, 1993).
26. Richard North, "Political Realism: Introduction," *European Journal of Political Theory* 9, no. 4 (2010): 384.
27. Eva Erman and Niklas Möller, "Political Legitimacy in the Real Normative World: The Priority of Morality and the Autonomy of the Political," *British Journal of Political Science* 45, no. 1 (2015): 228. Strangely, they also contend "that all coherent and plausible conceptions of political legitimacy must hold onto the ethics first premise" (216). It's puzzling to insist that ethics must come first and at the same time to argue that no one actually endorses the view that morality should take precedence over politics.
28. Newey, "Two Dogmas of Liberalism," 450.
29. Rawls maintained that in a pluralistic society the burdens of judgment will lead reasonable people to disagree about comprehensive doctrines of the good. John Rawls, *Political Liberalism* (New York: Columbia University Press, 1993), 56–57. He is nonetheless confident that they will be able to agree on a political conception of justice via overlapping consensus. This happy result reflects that "reasonableness" does a lot of behind-the-scenes work in Rawlsian liberalism.
30. Bernard Yack, "Putting Injustice First: An Alternative Approach to Liberal Pluralism," *Social Research* 66, no. 4 (1999): 1103.
31. Cf. Williams, *In the Beginning*, 77.
32. Erman and Möller, "Three Failed Charges"; Robeyns, "Ideal Theory," 352; Zofia Stemplowska, "What's Ideal about Ideal Theory," 321; Lisa H. Schwartzman, "Abstraction, Idealization, and Oppression," *Metaphilosophy* 37, no. 5 (2006): 579–80; Laura Valentini, "On the Apparent Paradox of Ideal Theory," *Journal of Political Philosophy* 17, no. 3 (2009): 337–39.
33. Mills, "Ideal Theory as Ideology," 178. Mills identifies as a nonideal theorist, a position somewhat at odds with his biting critique of ideal theory. He seems to understand the term differently from others who adopt it.
34. Onora O'Neill, "Bounded and Cosmopolitan Justice," *Review of International Studies* 26 (2000): 67ff.; cf. Mills, "Ideal Theory as Ideology."

35. Charles R. Beitz, "Rawls's Law of Peoples," *Ethics* 110, no. 4 (2000): 680.
36. Mills, "Ideal Theory as Ideology," 172.
37. Onora O'Neill, *Bounds of Justice* (Cambridge: Cambridge University Press, 2000), 180.
38. Ibid., 165ff.
39. Ibid., 120.
40. Anne Phillips, "Egalitarians and the Market: Dangerous Ideals," *Social Theory and Practice* 34, no. 3 (2008): 446.
41. Ibid., 447.
42. Rawls, *The Law of Peoples.*
43. Allen Buchanan, "Rawls's Law of Peoples: Rules for a Vanished Westphalian World," *Ethics* 110, no. 4 (2000): 717–18.
44. See Mills, "Ideal Theory as Ideology," 173ff.
45. Robeyns, "Ideal Theory," 360.
46. Ibid., 355ff.
47. Ibid., 357–58; cf. Schwartzman, "Abstraction, Idealization, and Oppression"; Valentini, "On the Apparent Paradox."
48. Thomas McCarthy, "Political Philosophy and Racial Injustice: From Normative to Critical Theory," in *Pragmatism, Critique, Judgement: Essays for Richard J. Bernstein*, ed. Seyla Benhabib and Nancy Fraser (Cambridge, MA: MIT Press, 2004), 158–59; cf. Phillips, "Egalitarians and the Market."
49. Rawls, *A Theory of Justice*, 8. For the debate on strict compliance, see Erman and Möller, "Three Failed Charges"; Jubb, "Tragedies of Non-ideal Theory," 231; Liam B. Murphy, *Moral Demands in Nonideal Theory* (Oxford: Oxford University Press, 2000); Michael Phillips, "Reflections on the Transition from Ideal to Non-ideal Theory," *Noûs* 19, no. 4 (1985): 553; Schwartzman, "Abstraction, Idealization, and Oppression," 586; Stemplowska, "What's Ideal about Ideal Theory," 320–34; Valentini, "On the Apparent Paradox," 353.
50. On how such deflective claims shield ideologies from critique and self-reflection, see Jeanne Morefield, *Empires without Imperialism: Anglo-American Decline and the Politics of Deflection* (New York: Oxford University Press, 2014).
51. Wacquant, *Punishing the Poor.*
52. Tommie Shelby, "Justice, Deviance, and the Dark Ghetto," *Philosophy and Public Affairs* 35, no. 2 (2007).
53. Ibid., 128.
54. Ibid., 150.
55. Ibid., 157.
56. Ibid.
57. Ibid., 154.
58. Ibid. I accept his conclusion (158–60) that, in such cases, combating *injustice* is mainly a political task.
59. Ibid., 158.
60. McCarthy, "Political Philosophy and Racial Injustice"; Mills, "Ideal Theory as Ideology"; O'Neill, *Bounds of Justice*, 152.
61. McCarthy, "Political Philosophy and Racial Injustice," 10.

CHAPTER 2

1. Rawls, *A Theory of Justice*, 11, 16.
2. Rawls, *A Theory of Justice*, rev. ed. (Cambridge, MA: Harvard University Press, 1999), 16.
3. Ibid., 512. Ironically, Rawls ignored his own admonitions in his two-stage contractual process in *The Law of Peoples*; see Goodhart, "Constructing Global Justice," 13ff.
4. Rawls, *A Theory of Justice* (1999), 516. To do so requires strong assumptions that provide the initial choice situation with sufficient determinacy; none of these assumptions holds in the global context; see Goodhart, "Constructing Global Justice."
5. Goodhart, "Constructing Global Justice," 17.
6. Charles Jones, *Global Justice: Defending Cosmopolitanism* (Oxford: Oxford University Press, 1999), 14n.9.
7. Gillian Brock, *Global Justice: A Cosmopolitan Account* (Oxford: Oxford University Press, 2009), 47; cf. Darrel Moellendorf, *Cosmopolitan Justice* (Boulder, CO: Westview Press, 2002).
8. Brock, *Global Justice*, 48–49.
9. Ibid., 48.
10. Ibid., 49–50.
11. Ibid., 50.
12. Ibid., 51.
13. Ibid., 52.
14. Ibid., 181.
15. Ibid., 304–5.
16. As Rawls always understood; see Goodhart, "Constructing Global Justice," 17–18.
17. Brock, *Global Justice*, 119.
18. Ibid., 51, 62–63.
19. Ibid., 120.
20. Ibid., 119.
21. Ibid., 222.
22. Ibid., 227.
23. Ibid., 223–27.
24. Ibid., 227.
25. See Phillips, "Egalitarians and the Market," 446.
26. Wacquant, *Punishing the Poor*.
27. Devaki Jain, "To Be or Not to Be: Problems of Locating Women in Public Policy," *Economic and Political Weekly* 42, no. 8 (2007).
28. Ha-Joon Chang, *Bad Samaritans: The Myth of Free Trade and the Secret History of Capitalism* (New York: Bloomsbury Press, 2008).
29. Goodhart, "Constructing Global Justice."
30. Brock, *Global Justice*, 232.
31. David Singh Grewal, "Network Power and Global Standardization: The Controversy over the Multilateral Agreement on Investment," in *Global Institutions and Responsibilities: Achieving Global Justice*, ed. Christian Barry and Thomas W.

Pogge (Oxford: Blackwell, 2005). Developing countries did gain concessions on access for manufactured goods to rich-country markets, but they "accepted" rules on intellectual property and on "nontariff barriers to trade"—public goods like health and environmental protections—that massively favored the rich; grossly unfair rules on agricultural trade were left virtually unchanged. See, e.g., Bhagirath Lal Das, *The WTO Agreements: Deficiencies, Imbalances, and Required Changes* (New York: Zed Books, 1998).

32. Arash Abizadeh, "Cooperation, Pervasive Impact and Coercion: On the Site (Not Scope) of Distributive Justice," *Philosophy and Public Affairs* 35, no. 4 (2007): 323.
33. See O'Neill, *Bounds of Justice*, 189.
34. Luis Cabrera, *Political Theory of Global Justice: A Cosmopolitan Case for the World State* (New York: Routledge, 2004), 17.
35. David Miller, *National Responsibility and Global Justice* (Oxford: Oxford University Press, 2007), 16.
36. Ibid., 18. Miller slides problematically between state and nation, as his critics have long complained. For a critique of this position, see Andrew Hurrell, "Global Inequality and International Institutions," *Metaphilosophy* 32, nos. 1–2 (2001): 37. Hurrell points out that Miller provides no criteria for identifying relevant thresholds of relational intensity and notes that institutional arrangements don't merely reflect static, preexisting communities but actually help to shape communities.
37. Mathias Risse, *On Global Justice* (Princeton, NJ: Princeton University Press, 2012), 10, 52–53.
38. Laura Valentini, *Justice in a Globalized World: A Normative Framework* (Oxford: Oxford University Press, 2011), 78.
39. Cabrera, *Political Theory of Global Justice*, 81.
40. Ibid., 20.
41. Ryan Pevnick, "Political Coercion and the Scope of Distributive Justice," *Political Studies* 56, no. 2 (2008).
42. Michael Blake, "Distributive Justice, State Coercion, and Autonomy," *Philosophy and Public Affairs* 30, no. 3 (2001); cf. Thomas Nagel, "The Problem of Global Justice," *Philosophy and Public Affairs* 33, no. 2 (2005).
43. Valentini, *Justice in a Globalized World*
44. Rawls, *The Law of Peoples*, is the best-known statist example.
45. Jones, *Global Justice*, 14 n. 29.
46. Rawls, *A Theory of Justice* (1999), 7.
47. Early proponents of (versions of) this view included Barry, *Liberal Theory of Justice*; Beitz, *Political Theory and International Relations*; Pogge, *Realizing Rawls*.
48. Charles R. Beitz, "Cosmopolitan Ideals and National Sentiment," *Journal of Philosophy* 80, no. 10 (1983), argued that the proper moral conception of the person in fact justified global principles of justice, including distributive justice, a view shared by Moellendorf, *Cosmopolitan Justice*.
49. Abizadeh, "Cooperation, Pervasive Impact," 357.
50. Andreas Føllesdal, "The Distributive Justice of a Global Basic Structure: A Category Mistake?," *Politics, Philosophy and Economics* 10, no. 1 (2011): 62.

51. Abizadeh, "Cooperation, Pervasive Impact," 344.
52. Ibid.
53. Nancy Fraser, *Scales of Justice: Reimagining Political Space in a Globalizing World* (New York: Columbia University Press, 2008), 38.
54. David Miller, "Justice and Global Inequality," in *Inequality, Globalization, and World Politics*, ed. Andrew Hurrell and Ngaire Woods (Oxford: Oxford University Press, 1999), 188.
55. Simon Caney, *Justice beyond Borders: A Global Political Theory* (Oxford: Oxford University Press, 2005), 35–38.
56. Ibid., 107.
57. Risse, *On Global Justice*, 83.
58. The original example appears at Caney, *Justice beyond Borders*, 110; I am indebted to Risse's enlightening discussion of Caney, including of this example; Risse, *On Global Justice*, 81–84.
59. Joshua Cohen and Charles Sabel, "Extra Rempublicam Nulla Justitia?," *Philosophy and Public Affairs* 34, no. 2 (2006): 149.
60. Risse, *On Global Justice*, ix.
61. Lea Ypi, *Global Justice and Avant Garde Political Agency* (Oxford: Oxford University Press, 2011), 86–87, 104ff.
62. Ypi, "On the Confusion."
63. Valentini, *Justice in a Globalized World.*
64. Mary Kaldor, "Transnational Civil Society," in *Human Rights in Global Politics*, ed. Tim Dunne and Nicholas J. Wheeler (Cambridge: Cambridge University Press, 1999); Jan Aart Scholte, *Democratising the Global Economy: The Role of Civil Society*, (Centre for the Study of Globalisation and Regionalisation, University of Warwick, 2003); Jackie Smith, "Global Civil Society? Transnational Social Movement Organizations and Social Capital," *American Behavioral Scientist* 42, no. 1 (1998).
65. Helena De Bres, "The Many, Not the Few: Pluralism about Global Distributive Justice," *Journal of Political Philosophy* 20, no. 3 (2012).
66. Cohen and Sabel, "Extra Rempublicam Nulla Justitia," 149.
67. Ibid., 159, citing Nagel, "Problem of Global Justice," 122.
68. Cohen and Sabel, "Extra Rempublicam Nulla Justitia," 174.
69. See De Bres, "Many, Not the Few," 338.
70. For a summary see Risse, *On Global Justice*, 327ff.
71. Following Andrea Sangiovanni, "Justice and the Priority of Politics to Morality," *Journal of Political Philosophy* 16, no. 2 (2008).
72. Ibid., 148.
73. Valentini, *Justice in a Globalized World*, 92. cf. Ypi, *Global Justice*, 50ff.
74. Sangiovanni, "Justice and the Priority," 150.
75. Paul Pierson and Theda Skocpol, "Historical Institutionalism in Contemporary Politial Science," in *Political Science: State of the Discipline*, ed. Ira Katznelson and Helen V. Milner (New York: Norton, 2002); Paul Pierson, *Politics in Time: History, Institutions and Social Analysis* (Princeton, NJ: Princeton University Press, 2004).
76. Galston, "Realism in Political Theory," 394.

77. Mathias Risse, "How Does the Global Order Harm the Poor?," *Philosophy and Public Affairs* 33, no. 4 (2005): 351.
78. Mathias Risse, "What We Owe to the Global Poor," *Journal of Ethics* 9, nos. 1–2 (2005): 90.
79. Mathias Risse, "Do We Owe the Global Poor Assistance or Rectification?," *Ethics and International Affairs* 19, no. 1 (2005): 16.
80. Risse, "How Does the Global Order Harm," 357–58.
81. Risse, "What We Owe," 85–86.
82. Risse, "How Does the Global Order Harm," 356.
83. Risse, "What We Owe," 92.
84. Cf. Leif Wenar, "What We Owe to Distant Others," *Politics, Philosophy, and Economics* 2, no. 3 (2003), who claims that complexity and uncertainty undermine our confidence that remedial actions can be effective in reducing poverty. He concludes (roughly) that the obligations of rich westerners are limited to inexpensive programs we are sure will be effective.
85. Risse, "What We Owe," 90, 110–12. In later work, Risse proposes additional "membership rights" for all people, rights derived from common ownership of the earth and "common citizenship"; see *On Global Justice*, esp. 130–51.
86. Thomas W. Pogge, "Severe Poverty as a Human Rights Violation," in *Freedom from Poverty as a Human Right: Who Owes What to the Very Poor?*, ed. Thomas W. Pogge (New York: Oxford University Press / UNESCO, 2007).
87. Thomas Pogge, "'Assisting' the Global Poor," in *Global Ethics: Seminal Essays*, ed. Thomas Pogge and Keith Horton (St. Paul, MN: Paragon House, 2008), 535.
88. Thomas W. Pogge, "The Influence of the Global Order on the Prospects for Genuine Democracy in Developing Countries," *Ratio Juris* 14, no. 3 (2001): 331.
89. Pogge, "Assisting the Global Poor," 541; cf. Pogge, "Influence of the Global Order"; Thomas W. Pogge, "Achieving Democracy," *Ethics and International Affairs* 15, no. 1 (2001).
90. Pogge, "Assisting the Global Poor," 541–45.
91. Pogge, "Influence of the Global Order," 338. He rejects arguments from history and culture, arguing that things change too fast for such arguments to explain much and because they assume away any global role.
92. Pogge, "Severe Poverty," 30.
93. Ibid.; Thomas Pogge, *World Poverty and Human Rights*, 2nd ed. (Cambridge: Polity Press, 2008). I can't explore here the deeply weird implication that it's OK for the rich to go on harming the poor as long as they pay compensation. Notice once again that there is no obligation to make redress or reparation for past wrongs in Pogge's view, because the harm of imposing occurs wholly in the present.
94. Pogge, "Assisting the Global Poor," 534; cf. Margaret Kohn, "Postcolonialism and Global Justice," *Journal of Global Ethics* 9, no. 2 (2013): 190.
95. Pogge, "Assisting the Global Poor," 534ff.
96. Pogge, *World Poverty and Human Rights*, 26.
97. E.g., Christian Barry and Gerhard Øverland, "The Feasible Alternatives Thesis: Kicking Away the Livelihoods of the Global Poor," *Politics, Philosophy, and Economics* 11, no. 1 (2012); Pablo Gilabert and Holly Lawford-Smith,

"Political Feasibility: A Conceptual Exploration," *Political Studies* 60, no. 4 (2012); Holly Lawford-Smith, "Understanding Political Feasibility," *Journal of Political Philosophy* 21, no. 3 (2013); Erman and Möller, "Three Failed Charges."

98. Thomas Pogge, "The Health Impact Fund: Enhancing Justice and Efficiency in Global Health," *Journal of Human Development and Capabilities* 13, no. 4 (2012). See http://healthimpactfund.org/. For a critique, see Sakiko Fukuda-Parr and Proochista Ariana, "Health Impact Fund—Raising Issues of Distribution, IP Rights and Alliances," *Intellectual Property Watch*, September 26, 2011, https://www.ip-watch.org/2011/09/26/health-impact-fund-%e2%80%93-raising-issues-of-distribution-ip-rights-and-alliances/.
99. The pathbreaking study is Ronald Rogowski, *Commerce and Coalitions: How Trade Affects Domestic Political Alignments* (Princeton, NJ: Princeton University Press, 1989).
100. See Milanovich, *Haves and Have Nots*; Piketty, *Capital in the Twenty-First Century*.
101. Sklair, *The Transnational Capitalist Class*.
102. For a comprehensive catalogue of the "worse," see Klein, *The Shock Doctrine*.
103. Harvey, "Neoliberalism as Creative Destruction."
104. Cf. Beitz, "Rawls's Law of Peoples," 680.
105. Rainer Forst, "Toward a Critical Theory of Transnational Justice," in *Global Justice*, ed. Thomas W. Pogge (Oxford: Blackwell, 2001), 174.

CHAPTER 3

1. Michael Freeden, "Interpretative Realism and Prescriptive Realism," *Journal of Political Ideologies* 17, no. 1 (2012): 1.
2. North, "Political Realism," 381.
3. Galston, "Realism in Political Theory," 386.
4. Ibid., 403.
5. John Horton, "Realism, Liberal Moralism and a Political Theory of Modus Vivendi," *European Journal of Political Theory* 9, no. 4 (2010): 433–44.
6. William E. Scheuerman, "The Realist Revival in Political Philosophy, Or: Why New Is Not Always Improved," *International Politics* 50, no. 6 (2013): 799, 801.
7. Horton, "Realism, Liberal Moralism," 433; Raymond Geuss, "Realism and the Relativity of Judgement," *International Relations* 29, no. 1 (2015): 13.
8. Williams, *In the Beginning*; Sleat, "What Is a Political Value"; Terry Nardin, "The New Realism and the Old," *Critical Review of International Social and Political Philosophy* 20, no. 3 (2017); cf. Scheuerman, "Realist Revival."
9. Richard Bellamy, "Dirty Hands and Clean Gloves: Liberal Ideals and Real Politics," *European Journal of Political Theory* 9, no. 4 (2010): 415; Williams, *In the Beginning*, 3.
10. Galston, "Realism in Political Theory," 393–94.
11. I shall largely leave aside those realists who focus primarily on the conduct of politicians and with the problem of "dirty hands" (e.g., Bellamy, "Dirty Hands";

Mark Philp, "What Is to Be Done? Political Theory and Political Realism," *European Journal of Political Theory* 9, no. 4 [2010]).

12. Geuss notes that even if some principles were somehow shown to be true or validated by reason, it would not follow that they would be universally recognized or obeyed (*Philosophy and Real Politics*, 10).
13. Duncan Bell, "Political Realism and International Relations," *Philosophy Compass* 12, no. 2 (2017), e12403; "Realist Challenges," in *Handbook of International Political Theory*, ed. Chris Brown and Robin Eckersly (Oxford: Oxford University Press, forthcoming).
14. Cf. Enzo Rossi, "Review: Reality and Imagination in Political Theory and Practice: On Raymond Geuss's Realism," *European Journal of Political Theory* 9, no. 4 (2010): 504.
15. Janosch Prinz and Enzo Rossi, "Political Realism as Ideology Critique," *Critical Review of International Social and Political Philosophy* 20, no. 3 (2017): 350.
16. Amartya Sen, "What Do We Want from a Theory of Justice?," *Journal of Philosophy* 103, no. 5 (2006): 216; cf. Prinz and Rossi, "Political Realism as Ideology Critique," 350.
17. Sen, "What Do We Want," 216–17.
18. Amartya Sen, *The Idea of Justice* (Cambridge, MA: Belknap Press of Harvard University Press, 2009), ix.
19. Sen, "What Do We Want," 218.
20. Ibid., 226.
21. Sen, *The Idea of Justice*, 99.
22. Sen, "What Do We Want," 222; cf. *The Idea of Justice*, 102.
23. Sen, *The Idea of Justice*, 228–71; cf. *Development as Freedom* (New York: Alfred A. Knopf, 1999). For an introduction to the capabilities approach, see *Inequality Re-examined* (Cambridge, MA: Harvard University Press, 1992).
24. Amartya Sen, "Open and Closed Impartiality," in *Global Responsibilities: Who Must Deliver on Human Rights?*, ed. Andrew Kuper (New York: Routledge, 2005); *The Idea of Justice*, 124ff.
25. Sen, "What Do We Want," 229ff.; cf. *The Idea of Justice*, ch. 6.
26. Gaus, *Tyranny of the Ideal*, 7.
27. Ibid., 67.
28. Ibid., 7; cf. Simmons, "Ideal and Nonideal Theory."
29. Gaus, *Tyranny of the Ideal*, 75–82.
30. Sen, *The Idea of Justice*, 12–14.
31. Some commentators confuse the plurality of reasons with incommensurability of values (e.g., Ian Shapiro, "Review: The Idea of Justice," *Journal of Economic Literature* 49, no. 4 [2011]: 1256), but the two problems are different. The latter refers to the difficulty of reducing all considerations of justice to a single value metric; Sen, *The Idea of Justice*, 239–41. Part of the attraction of the capabilities framework is precisely its multidimensionality, but, as Shapiro points out, Sen never shows us how that model can actually be used to make the kind of pairwise comparisons of complex social realizations that his comparative approach calls for; Shapiro, "Review: The Idea of Justice," 1257.

32. Sen, "Open and Closed Impartiality," 71–72.
33. Sen, *The Idea of Justice*, 2–4. Sen sometimes worries that the plurality of reasons reduces the likelihood of plural grounding or overlapping consensus, making it harder for people to converge on particular judgments. At other times, he's concerned with a kind of intratheoretical indeterminacy, the possibility that one could mount, say, a utilitarian defense of each distribution; Shapiro, "Review: The Idea of Justice," 1256.
34. Sen, *The Idea of Justice*, 16,101.
35. Chris Brown, "On Amartya Sen and *The Idea of Justice*," *Ethics and International Affairs* 24, no. 3 (2010): 314.
36. Pablo Gilabert, "Comparative Assessments of Justice, Political Feasibility and Ideal Theory," *Ethical Theory and Moral Practice* 15, no. 1 (2011); Emil Wannheden, "Justice and the Capability Approach," in *Human Development and International Cooperation* (University of Florence, 2013).
37. Martha C. Nussbaum, "Capabilities as Fundamental Entitlements: Sen and Social Justice," *Feminist Economics* 9, nos. 2–3 (2003): 43–50. Unlike Sen, Nussbaum thinks that an Aristotelian, essentialist account of capabilities and human functioning can be "universal"; e.g., "Human Functioning and Social Justice: In Defense of Aristotelian Essentialism," *Political Theory* 20, no. 2 (1992); "Capabilities and Human Rights," *Fordham Law Review* 66, no. 2 (1997); "Capabilities as Fundamental Entitlements"; "Beyond the Social Contract: Capabilities and Global Justice," *Oxford Development Studies* 32, no. 1 (2004).
38. Brooke Ackerly, *Just Responsibility: A Human Rights Theory of Global Justice* (New York: Oxford University Press, 2018).
39. Michael Mann, *The Sources of Social Power*, vol. 1: *A History of Power from the Beginning to A.D. 1760* (Cambridge: Cambridge University Press, 1986); P. J. Taylor, "Embedded Statism and the Social Sciences: Opening Up to New Spaces," *Environment and Planning A* 28 (1996).
40. Sen, *The Idea of Justice*, xix.
41. Brown, "On Amartya Sen," 315.
42. Shapiro, "Review: The Idea of Justice," 1258.
43. Sen offers a list of obvious injustices but without any accompanying conceptual analysis to explain or support it; Bufacchi, *Social Injustice*, 6–7.
44. Sen, *The Idea of Justice*, viii.
45. Shklar, *The Faces of Injustice*, 83.
46. Stuart Hampshire, *Justice Is Conflict* (Princeton, NJ: Princeton University Press, 2000), xii.
47. Barrington Moore Jr., *Reflections on the Causes of Human Misery and upon Certain Proposals to Eliminate Them* (Boston: Beacon Press, 1970), 1–2.
48. Ibid., 11, 52.
49. Williams, *In the Beginning*, 23, 26.
50. As Bell argues, these charges don't stick to IR realists in quite the same way ("Realist Challenges"). Lorna Finlayson has recently argued that realism needn't entail conservatism; see "With Radicals Like These, Who Needs Conservatives? Doom, Gloom, and Realism in Political Theory," European Journal of Political Theory 16, no. 3 (2017).

51. Judith N. Shklar, "The Liberalism of Fear," in *Political Thought and Political Thinkers*, ed. Stanley Hoffmann (Chicago: University of Chicago Press, 1998), 11–12.
52. See Ackerly, *Just Responsibility*, chs. 2–3.
53. Williams, *In the Beginning*, 3.
54. Ibid.
55. Ibid., 4.
56. Ibid., 5.
57. Ibid., 6–7.
58. Ibid., 12.
59. Ibid., 7.
60. Ibid., 5.
61. Ibid., 36–37.
62. Ibid., 11.
63. Ibid., 37.
64. Ibid., 56.
65. Ibid., 26.
66. Ibid., 72.
67. Ibid.
68. Ibid., 19.
69. Ibid., 64.
70. Ibid., 19.
71. Ibid., 52–61.
72. Cf. Scheuerman, "Realist Revival," 808.
73. Morefield, *Empires without Imperialism*.
74. Williams, *In the Beginning*, 6.
75. Many contemporary realist political theorists in fact only analyze reality in the most abstract and generalized way; Scheuerman, "Realist Revival," 799.
76. Geuss, *Philosophy and Real Politics*, 9.
77. Ibid., 11.
78. Ibid., 13.
79. Ibid., 14.
80. Ibid., 37–55.
81. Janosch Prinz, "Raymond Geuss' Radicalization of Realism in Political Theory," *Philosophy and Social Criticism* 42, no. 8 (2016): 782.
82. Ibid., 781.
83. Ibid., 780–81.
84. Geuss, "Realism," 7.
85. Ibid., 13.
86. Geuss, *Philosophy and Real Politics*, 59.
87. Raymond Geuss, *History and Illusion in Politics* (Cambridge: Cambridge University Press, 2001), 144.
88. Geuss, *Philosophy and Real Politics*, 62–63.
89. Geuss, *History and Illusion in Politics*, 145.
90. Michael Goodhart, "Human Rights and the Politics of Contestation," in *Human Rights at the Crossroads*, ed. Mark Goodale (Oxford: Oxford University Press,

2013); cf. Katherine Eddy, "Against Ideal Rights," *Social Theory and Practice* 34, no. 3 (2008).

91. Cf. Neil Stammers, "Social Movements and the Social Construction of Human Rights," *Human Rights Quarterly* 21, no. 4 (1999).
92. Karen Zivi, *Making Rights Claims: A Practice of Democratic Citizenship* (New York: Oxford University Press, 2012); Brooke Ackerly, *Universal Human Rights in a World of Difference* (Cambridge: Cambridge University Press, 2008).
93. Ackerly, *Universal Human Rights*; Michael Goodhart, *Democracy as Human Rights: Freedom and Equality in the Age of Globalization* (New York: Routledge, 2005).
94. Cf. Galston, "Realism in Political Theory," 398.
95. Geuss, "Realism," 15.
96. Ibid., 16.
97. Sleat, "What Is a Political Value,"255ff.
98. Ibid., 260–61.
99. Ibid., 262.
100. Ibid., 270. This position is nearly indistinguishable from practice-dependence.
101. Ibid., 272.
102. Prinz, "Raymond Geuss' Radicalization," 783.
103. Ibid., 781.
104. Prinz and Rossi, "Political Realism as Ideology Critique," 357.
105. Ibid., 359.
106. Edward Hall and Matt Sleat, "Ethics, Morality and the Case for Realist Political Theory," *Critical Review of International Social and Political Philosophy* 20, no. 3 (2017): 282.
107. Ibid., 284.
108. Prinz and Enzo Rossi, "Political Realism as Ideology Critique," 360ff.
109. Horton, "Realism, Liberal Moralism," 444–46; Freeden, "Interpretative Realism and Prescriptive Realism," 2, 10.

CHAPTER 4

1. Shklar, *The Faces of Injustice*, 23; Shelby, "Justice, Deviance," 157.
2. E.g., James Bohman, "Republican Cosmopolitanism," *Journal of Political Philosophy* 12, no. 3 (2004); Cécile Laborde, "Republicanism and Global Justice: A Sketch," *European Journal of Political Theory* 9, no. 1 (2010); Terry Macdonald and Miriam Ronzoni, "Introduction: The Idea of Global Political Justice," *Critical Review of International Social and Political Philosophy* 15, no. 5 (2012): 523.
3. Macdonald and Miriam Ronzoni, "Introduction: The Idea of Global Political Justice," 523.
4. Ibid.
5. Ibid., 524.
6. Not all theorists of GPJ recognize a sharp distinction with distributive approaches. Laura Valentini, for instance, sees no tension between liberal justice and legitimacy; "Assessing the Global Order: Justice, Legitimacy, or Political Justice?," Critical Review of International Social and Political Philosophy 15, no. 5 (2012).

7. Barbara Buckinx, Jonathan Trejo-Mathys, and Timothy Waligore, "Domination across Borders: An Introduction," in *Domination and Global Political Justice: Conceptual, Historical, and Institutional Perspectives*, ed. Barbara Buckinx, Jonathan Trejo-Mathys, and Timothy Waligore (New York: Routledge, 2015).
8. Barbara Buckinx, "Global Actors and Public Power," *Critical Review of International Social and Political Philosophy* 15, no. 5 (2012): 537.
9. Buckinx, Trejo-Mathys, and Waligore, "Domination across Borders," 540–41.
10. Macdonald and Ronzoni, "Introduction: The Idea of Global Political Justice."
11. Andrew Hurrell and Terry Macdonald, "Global Public Power: The Subject of Principles of Global Political Legitimacy," *Critical Review of International Social and Political Philosophy* 15, no. 5 (2012): 557.
12. Ibid.
13. Ibid.
14. Ibid., 557–58.
15. E.g., Miriam Ronzoni, "Two Conceptions of State Sovereignty and Their Implications for Global Institutional Design," *Critical Review of International Social and Political Philosophy* 15, no. 5 (2012).
16. Valentini, "Assessing the Global Order," 601.
17. Manfred Steger, *Globalization: A Very Short Introduction*, 3rd ed. (Oxford: Oxford University Press, 2013), 103.
18. Cf. Michael Freeden, *Ideologies and Political Theory: A Conceptual Approach* (Oxford: Oxford University Press, 1996), 3.
19. These negative connotations originate in the reaction against the French Revolution and in the Marxist critique of bourgeois ideology; see ibid., 15–25.
20. Seliger, *Ideology and Politics*, 14, my emphasis.
21. Freeden, *Ideologies and Political Theory*, 76ff.
22. Ibid., 123.
23. Michael Freeden, "What Should the 'Political' in Political Theory Explore?," *Journal of Political Philosophy* 13, no. 2 (2005): 124.
24. Freeden, *Ideologies and Political Theory*, 44, 75.
25. Ibid., 30ff.
26. Freeden, "What Should the Political," 115.
27. Ibid., 116.
28. Ibid., 118; cf. W. B. Gallie, "Essentially Contested Concepts," *Proceedings of the Aristotelian Society* 56 (1955–56).
29. Freeden, *Ideologies and Political Theory*, 6.
30. Freeden, "What Should the Political," 134; cf. "Interpretative Realism and Prescriptive Realism," 3.
31. Freeden, "What Should the Political," 131.
32. Ibid., 132; cf. "Interpretative Realism and Prescriptive Realism."
33. Karl Mannheim, *Ideology and Utopia: An Introduction to the Sociology of Knowledge*, trans. Louis Wirth and Edward Shils (San Diego: Harvest/Harcourt, 1955), 2–3.
34. Ibid., 6.
35. Stephen Finlay and Mark Schroeder, "Reasons for Action: Internal vs. External," in *Stanford Encyclopedia of Philosophy*, ed. Edward N. Zalta (Fall 2017 ed.), 1.2.2.

36. Philippa Foot, "Morality as a System of Hypothetical Imperatives," *Philosophical Review* 81, no. 3 (1972): 309.
37. Ibid.
38. Ibid., 310, my emphasis.
39. Ibid.
40. Ibid., 312.
41. Ibid.
42. Ibid., 315. Foot shares with Elizabeth Anscombe this view that the seeming "inescapability" of moral *shoulds* traces to our early training and socialization—a view not terribly distant from Hume's and one I find persuasive. I'm grateful to Katharina Nieswandt, whose fascinating doctoral dissertation has taught me a great deal about these matters.
43. Ibid., 314–15.
44. Ibid., 314.
45. Ibid.
46. Ibid., 315.
47. Cf. Richard Yetter Chappell, "Truth and Relativism," *Philosophy, et cetera*, July 10, 2004, http://www.philosophyetc.net/2004/07/truth-and-relativism.html.
48. Seliger, *Ideology and Politics*, 14.
49. Clifford Geertz, "Distinguished Lecture: Anti Anti-relativism," *American Anthropologist* 86, no. 2 (1984): 264. Geertz may have been playing on the stance of "anti anticommunism" adopted by some Marxists who wanted to disavow Stalinism.
50. Gilabert, "Comparative Assessments of Justice," 43. To be clear, I don't know whether Gilabert is the critic who raised this objection.
51. Simmons, "Ideal and Nonideal Theory," 34.
52. Richard Rorty, "The Priority of Democracy to Philosophy," in *The Virginia Statute for Religious Freedom*, ed. Merrill D. Peterson and Robert C. Vaughn (Cambridge: Cambridge University Press, 1988), 260.

CHAPTER 5

1. Goodhart, *Democracy as Human Rights*, ch. 6; cf. Anthony Arblaster, *Democracy*, 2nd ed. (Minneapolis: University of Minnesota Press, 1994); David Held, *Models of Democracy*, 2nd ed. (Stanford, CA: Stanford University Press, 1996).
2. See Goodhart, *Democracy as Human Rights*, 53.
3. Ibid., ch. 3; Carole Pateman, *The Sexual Contract* (Stanford, CA: Stanford University Press, 1988).
4. See *The Sexual Contract*, 39.
5. Goodhart, *Democracy as Human Rights*, 137.
6. Ernesto Laclau and Chantal Mouffe, *Hegemony and Socialist Strategy*, 2nd ed. (London: Verson, 2001), 155.
7. Ian Shapiro, *Democratic Justice* (New Haven, CT: Yale University Press, 1999), 30; Elizabeth Anderson, "What Is the Point of Equality?," *Ethics* 109, no. 2 (1999): 312; cf. Michael Walzer, *Spheres of Justice: A Defense of Pluralism and Equality* (New York: Basic Books, 1983), xii–xiii.
8. Goodhart, *Democracy as Human Rights*, ch. 6.

9. Cf. Laclau and Mouffe, *Hegemony and Socialist Strategy*, 154ff.
10. See Zivi, *Making Rights Claims*. In the vocabulary I introduce below, these are struggles for constitutive power.
11. I have considered various aspects of this problem elsewhere; see Michael Goodhart, "Origins and Universality in the Human Rights Debates: Cultural Essentialism and the Challenge of Globalization," *Human Rights Quarterly* 25, no. 4 (2003); *Democracy as Human Rights*; "'None So Poor That He Is Compelled to Sell Himself': Democracy, Subsistence, and Basic Income," in *Economic Rights: Conceptual, Measurement and Policy Issues*, ed. Shareen Hertel, Alanson Minkler, and Richard A. Wilson (Cambridge: Cambridge University Press, 2007); "Europe's Democratic Deficits through the Looking Glass: The European Union as a Challenge for Democracy," *Perspectives on Politics* 5, no. 3 (2007); "Human Rights and Global Democracy," *Ethics and International Affairs* 22, no. 4 (2008); "Global Democracy through Transnational Human Rights"; "Democratic Accountability in Global Politics: Norms, Not Agents," *Journal of Politics* 73, no. 1 (2011).
12. See Goodhart, "Origins and Universality."
13. Edward W. Said, *Humanism and Democratic Criticism* (New York: Columbia University Press, 2004), 132. It must await another book to work through these complexities in any adequate way.
14. Michael Barnett and Raymond Duvall, "Power in Global Governance," in *Power in Global Governance*, ed. Michael Barnett and Raymond Duvall (Cambridge: Cambridge University Press, 2005), 3.
15. Ibid., 3–4.
16. Ibid., 3.
17. Ibid., 15.
18. Ibid., 3.
19. Ibid., 15–17.
20. Ibid., 11.
21. Robert Dahl, "The Concept of Power," *Behavioral Science* 2, no. 3 (1957): 202–3.
22. Barnett and Duvall, "Power in Global Governance," 9.
23. Ibid., 10.
24. Ibid., 3.
25. Ibid., 18.
26. Ibid., 3.
27. Ibid., 21. The internal quotation comes from Clarissa Rile Hayward, *De-facing Power* (Cambridge: Cambridge University Press, 2000), 35.
28. Thomas McCarthy, "Liberal Imperialism and the Dilemma of Development," in Buckinx, Trejo-Mathys, and Waligore, *Domination and Global Political Justice*; Kohn, "Postcolonialism and Global Justice." I return to this discussion later on.
29. Barnett and Duvall, "Power in Global Governance," 3, my emphasis.
30. Cf. James Bohman, "Critical Theory, Republicanism, and the Priority of Injustice: Transnational Republicanism as a Nonideal Theory," *Journal of Social Philosophy* 43, no. 2 (2012).
31. See Philip Pettit, *Republicanism: A Theory of Freedom and Government* (Oxford: Oxford University Press, 1997). For a good, brief summary of Pettit's

evolving views, see Buckinx, Trejo-Mathys, and Waligore, "Domination across Borders," 4ff. For a concise bibliography of the literature, see their footnote 10 on page 4. Some theorists prefer Pettit's earlier conceptualization of nondomination in terms of *antipower* to his more recent formulations; see James Bohman, "Domination, Global Harms, and the Priority of Injustice: Expanding Transnational Republicanism," in Buckinx, Trejo-Mathys, and Waligore, *Domination and Global Political Justice*; Terry Macdonald, "Antipower, Agency, and the Republican Case for Global Institutional Pluralism," in Buckinx, Trejo-Mathys, and Waligore, *Domination and Global Political Justice*.

32. Goodhart, *Democracy as Human Rights*, ch. 7.
33. I am grateful to Roger Rouse for a very valuable discussion of these issues.
34. E.g., Michel Foucault, "The Subject and Power," *Critical Inquiry* 8, no. 4 (1982); also Iris Marion Young, *Justice and the Politics of Difference* (Princeton, NJ: Princeton University Press, 1990), ch. 2.
35. Steven Wall, "Freedom, Interference and Domination," *Political Studies* 49, no. 2 (2001).
36. Young, *Justice and the Politics of Difference*, 39.
37. Duncan Ivison, "Indigenous Peoples, Injustice, and Global Politics," in Buckinx, Trejo-Mathys, and Waligore, *Domination and Global Political Justice*, 213.
38. Dryzek, *Deliberative Global Politics*, 93–94; 160–61. Neither Dryzek nor I wish to deny the significance of elections and parliamentary government to democracy; the point is to appreciate their importance as parts of and in relation to a broader framework of policies and institutions that constrain the exercise of power and enable meaningful political agency; Goodhart, "Human Rights and Global Democracy."
39. John Markoff, "A Moving Target: Democracy," *European Journal of Sociology* 52, no. 2 (2011).
40. Shklar, *The Faces of Injustice*, 86.
41. See Kohn, "Postcolonialism and Global Justice"; Charles W. Mills, "Race and Global Justice," in Buckinx, Trejo-Mathys, and Waligore, *Domination and Global Political Justice*.
42. Flikschuh, "Idea of Philosophical Fieldwork," 19–21.
43. Kohn, "Postcolonialism and Global Justice," 194ff.
44. Flikschuh, "Idea of Philosophical Fieldwork," 19ff.
45. For an excellent introduction to and overview of feminist social epistemology see Heidi Grasswick, "Feminist Social Epistemology," in *The Stanford Encyclopedia of Philosophy*, ed. Edward N. Zalta (Winter 2016 ed.), on which I have relied heavily in the discussion that follows.
46. See Boaventura de Sousa Santos, João Arriscado Nunes, and Maria Paula Meneses, "Introduction: Opening Up the Canon of Knowledge and Recognition of Difference," in *Another Epistemology Is Possible: Beyond Northern Epistemologies*, ed. Boaventura de Sousa Santos (London: Verso, 2007), xxix–xxxiii.
47. Donna Haraway, "Situated Knowledges: The Science Question in Feminism and the Privilege of Partial Perspective," *Feminist Studies* 14, no. 3 (1988): 590.
48. S. Laurel Weldon, "Inclusion and Understanding: A Collective Methodology for Feminist International Relations," in *Feminist Methodologies for International*

Relations, ed. Brooke A. Ackerly, Maria Stern, and Jacqui True (Cambridge: Cambridge University Press, 2006), 64–65.

49. Sandra Harding, "Rethinking Standpoint Epistemology: What Is 'Strong Objectivity'?," in *Feminist Epistemologies*, ed. Linda Alcoff and Elizabeth Potter (London: Routledge, 1993), 54.
50. Haraway, "Situated Knowledges," 584. In other words, the subjugated have a better chance of being in on "the god trick."
51. See Patricia Hill Collins, *Black Feminist Thought: Knowledge, Consciousness, and the Politics of Empowerment* (Boston: Unwin Hyman, 1990); Kimberlé Crenshaw, "Mapping the Margins: Intersectionality, Identity Politics, and Violence against Women of Color," *Stanford Law Review* 43, no. 6 (1991).
52. Alicia Garza, "What I Meant When I Said That #Blacklivesmatter: A Birthday Card for a Movement," *Those People*, July 13, 2015.
53. Ibid.
54. See Collins, *Black Feminist Thought.*
55. Cf. Harding, "Rethinking Standpoint Epistemology," 65.
56. Santos, Nunes, and Meneses, "Introduction," xxxiii–xli.
57. Grasswick, "Feminist Social Epistemology," 2.
58. For the meaning of "Third World" and "feminists" see ibid., 17ff.
59. Brooke A. Ackerly, *Political Theory and Feminist Social Criticism* (Cambridge: Cambridge University Press, 2000), 123.
60. Ibid., 77.
61. Ibid., 124–25.
62. Ibid., 27–28.
63. Ibid., 7.
64. Ibid., 199–200.
65. Ackerly, *Just Responsibility*, ch. 4.
66. I think this usage is largely consistent with dialectical thinking in the Marxist tradition, which helps theorists to focus on relationships and processes, to recognize the interpenetration of opposites, to track developments and changes through time and across different contexts, and to understand the interpenetration of opposites; Bertell Ollman, "The Meaning of Dialectics," in *Dance of the Dialectic: Steps in Marx's Method* (Urbana: University of Illinois Press, 2016), https://www.nyu.edu/projects/ollman/books/dd.php.
67. E.g., Risse, "How Does the Global Order Harm." Some important exceptions include Lea Ypi, Robert E. Goodin, and Christian Barry, "Associative Duties, Global Justice, and the Colonies," *Philosophy and Public Affairs* 37, no. 2 (2009); Catherine Lu, "Colonialism as Structural Injustice: Historical Responsibility and Contemporary Redress," *Journal of Political Philosophy* 19, no. 3 (2011). See chapter 2 for a discussion of Pogge's (non)use of history.
68. Spinner-Halev, *Enduring Injustice*, 5–6.
69. Realist political theory also tends to ignore history, in a way that realist international relations does not. I can't account for this oversight except to suggest that realism's descriptive focus gives it a presentist bias.
70. McCarthy, "Liberal Imperialism," 160.
71. Ibid., 168.

72. Ibid., 169.
73. See Dipesh Chakrabarty, *Provincializing Europe: Postcolonial Thought and Historical Difference* (Princeton, NJ: Princeton University Press, 2000).
74. McCarthy, "Liberal Imperialism," 172–73.
75. Ivison, "Indigenous Peoples," 220.
76. Kohn, "Postcolonialism and Global Justice," 192. I regard postcolonial thinking as inherently dialectical, though not all dialectical thinking is necessarily postcolonial.
77. Kohn, "Postcolonialism and Global Justice," 188–89.
78. Spinner-Halev, *Enduring Injustice*, 5–6.
79. See ibid., 156.
80. Young, *Justice and the Politics of Difference*, 5.
81. James Tully, *Public Philosophy in a New Key: Democracy and Civic Freedom*, 2 vols., vol. 1 (New York: Cambridge University Press, 2008), 225.
82. Young, *Justice and the Politics of Difference*, 5.
83. McCarthy, cited in Mills, "Race and Global Justice," 16.
84. Rainer Forst, "Transnational Justice and Non-domination: A Discourse-Theoretical Approach," in Buckinx, Trejo-Mathys, and Waligore, *Domination and Global Political Justice*, 91.
85. Rainer Forst, "Justifying Justification: Reply to My Critics," in *Justice, Democracy, and the Right to Justification* (London: Bloomsbury, 2014), 182.
86. Ibid., 195.
87. Ibid., 198.
88. Nancy Fraser, "Abnormal Justice," *Critical Inquiry* 34, no. 3 (2008): 418. Fraser refers to the "who, what, and how" of justice; subject, scope, and scale don't perfectly track her meaning, but are clearer to readers unfamiliar with her argument.
89. Ibid., 419.
90. Ibid., 422.
91. Fraser, *Scales of Justice*, 96.
92. Bohman is less explicit on normativity, but it's clear that he regards the republican ideal of freedom as nondomination as grounded in the (immanent and transcendent, reconstructed) discourse principle.
93. Bohman, "Critical Theory," 100.
94. Ibid., 101.
95. Bohman, "Domination, Global Harms," 2015.
96. Bohman, *Democracy across Borders: From Dêmos to Dêmoi* (Cambridge, MA: MIT Press, 2007), 27.
97. Ibid., 95ff.
98. Bohman, "Domination, Global Harms," 81.
99. Fraser, *Scales of Justice*, 23.
100. Fraser, "Abnormal Justice," 411, 14ff.
101. Paul Muldoon, "The Injustice of Territoriality," *Critical Review of International Social and Political Philosophy* 15, no. 5 (2012): 641.

102. See, e.g., Boaventura de Sousa Santos, *The Rise of the Global Left: The World Social Forum and Beyond* (London: Zed Books, 2006); Jackie Smith et al., *Global Democracy and the World Social Forums* (Boulder, CO: Paradigm, 2008).
103. Rosalba Icaza and Rolando Vázquez, "Social Struggles as Epistemic Struggles," *Development and Change* 44, no. 3 (2013): 687.
104. Rainer Forst, *The Right to Justification: Elements of a Constructivist Theory of Justice*, trans. Jeffrey Flynn (New York: Columbia University Press, 2012), 256–57.
105. Forst, "Transnational Justice and Non-domination," 103ff.
106. Bohman, *Democracy across Borders*, 101.
107. Bohman, "Domination, Global Harms," 74.
108. Muldoon, "The Injustice of Territoriality," 638. Muldoon makes the point in criticizing Fraser.

CHAPTER 6

1. Ypi, *Global Justice*, 35–36.
2. Ibid., 40, 35.
3. Ibid., 40.
4. Ibid., 62.
5. Ibid.
6. Ibid., 43.
7. Ibid., 37.
8. Ibid., 66.
9. Ibid., 177.
10. Ibid., 178.
11. David Miller, "Lea Ypi on Global Justice and Avant-Garde Political Agency: Some Reflections," *Ethics and Global Politics* 6, no. 2 (2013): 98; cf. Pablo Gilabert, "How Should We Think about the Relation between Principles and Agency?," *Ethics and Global Politics* 6, no. 2 (2013): 79–80; David Owen, "Activist Political Theory and the Question of Power," *Ethics and Global Politics* 6, no. 2 (2013): 88; Rahul Rao, "Listening to the Avant-Garde," *Ethics and Global Politics* 6, no. 2 (2013): 104ff.
12. Miller, "Lea Ypi on Global Justice," 95.
13. Ibid., 98. As Williams wrote (in another context), "there is no way in which theory can get all the way ahead of practice and reach the final determination[;] it cannot ever, in advance, determine very securely what direction might count as 'ahead.'" Williams, *In the Beginning*, 25–26.
14. Miller, "Lea Ypi on Global Justice," 95–96.
15. Ypi is right to think that close alliances with activists are important elements in a realistic approach to political agency; I return to this below.
16. Steve Jones, *Antonio Gramsci* (New York: Routledge, 2006), 41.
17. Ibid., 53–56; Gramsci, *Prison Notebooks*.
18. See Thomas J. Butko, "Gramsci and the 'Anti-globalization' Movement: Think before You Act," *Socialism and Democracy* 20, no. 2 (2006).
19. Dryzek, *Deliberative Global Politics*, 1.
20. Ibid., 3.

21. See also Iris Marion Young, *Responsibility for Justice* (New York: Oxford University Press, 2011), 112.
22. Dryzek, *Deliberative Global Politics*, 85.
23. Ibid., 22, 24.
24. Ibid., 3.
25. http://www.epi.org/minimum-wage-tracker/#/min_wage/Washington%20D.C.
26. E.g., Dryzek, *Deliberative Global Politics*, 126–27.
27. Ibid., 19ff.
28. Laclau and Mouffe, *Hegemony and Socialist Strategy*, 168. Contrast this with the model of activism implied in Thomas Pogge and Luis Cabrera, "Outreach, Impact, Collaboration: Why Academics Should Join to Stand against Poverty," *Ethics and International Affairs* 26, no. 2 (2012).
29. Santos, Nunes, and Meneses, "Introduction," xl.
30. The phrase "a movement of movements" is popularly associated with the World Social Forum process; see Tom Mertes, ed., *A Movement of Movements: Is Another World Really Possible?* (London: Verso, 2004); Jackie Smith, "The World Social Forum and the Challenges of Global Democracy," *Global Networks* 4, no. 4 (2004); Santos, *Rise of the Global Left*.
31. Martin Kirk, "Beyond Charity: Helping NGOs Lead a Transformative New Public Discourse on Global Poverty and Social Justice," *Ethics and International Affairs* 26, no. 2 (2012): 253.
32. Santos, Nunes, and Meneses, "Introduction"; Santos, *Rise of the Global Left*.
33. Santos, *Rise of the Global Left*, 133.
34. Ibid., 138.
35. See Sally Engle Merry, *Human Rights and Gender Violence: Translating International Law into Local Justice* (Chicago: University of Chicago Press, 2006); Mark Goodale and Sally Merry, eds., *The Practice of Human Rights: Tracking Law between the Global and the Local* (Cambridge: Cambridge University Press, 2007).
36. Michael Goodhart and Jeanne Morefield, "Reflection Now! Critique and Solidarity in the Trump Era," *Theory and Event* 20, no. 1 (supplement) (2017): S-79.
37. Santos, *Rise of the Global Left*, 138.
38. Santos, Nunes, and Meneses, "Introduction," xlvii.
39. Santos, *Rise of the Global Left*, 140.
40. Laclau and Mouffe, *Hegemony and Socialist Strategy*, 188ff.
41. Ibid., 190.
42. Working Group Meeting on Globalization and Trade, "*Jemez Principles* for Democratic Organizing," Southwest Network for Environmental and Economic Justice, Jemez, NM, 1996.
43. Goodhart and Morefield, "Reflection Now," S-80; see Toyacoyah Brown, "Veterans at Standing Rock Offer Long Overdue Apology," December 6, 2016, http://www.powwows.com/veterans-standing-rock-offer-long-overdue-apology-native-elders/.
44. Goodhart and Morefield, "Reflection Now," S-80.
45. See Smith et al., *Global Democracy*; Santos, *Rise of the Global Left*.
46. Paul Kingsnorth, *One No, Many Yesses: A Journey to the Heart of the Global Resistance Movement* (London: Free Press, 2003).

47. Robert Nozick, *Anarchy, State, and Utopia* (New York: Basic Books, 1974).
48. Gaus, *Tyranny of the Ideal*, 246.
49. Ibid., 215ff.
50. Ibid., 246.
51. Ibid., 243.
52. Ibid., 243–44.
53. Ibid., 243.
54. Ibid., 211ff.
55. Onora O'Neill, "Global Poverty and the Limits of Academic Expertise," *Ethics and International Affairs* 26, no. 2 (2012): 183.

CHAPTER 7

1. Christian Barry and Thomas W. Pogge, "Introduction," in Barry and Pogge, *Global Institutions and Responsibilities*, 2.
2. For an overview see Anja Görnitz, "Which Policies Do Enhance Global Justice? How Normative Ideals Apply to Real-World Justice Problems," Berlin Graduate School for Transnational Studies, 2012, 41ff.
3. Rüdiger Bittner, "Morality and World Hunger," in Pogge, *Global Justice*, 28ff.; cf. Marion Smiley, *Moral Responsibiity and the Boundaries of Community: Power and Accountability from a Pragmatic Point of View* (Chicago: University of Chicago Press, 1992), 105–6.
4. Samuel Scheffler, "Individual Responsibility in a Global Age," in Pogge and Horton, *Global Ethics*; cf. Smiley, *Moral Responsibiity*, 76ff; Young, *Responsibility for Justice*, 97–98.
5. Smiley, *Moral Responsibiity*, 167.
6. Soran Reader, "Distance, Relationship and Moral Obligation," *The Monist* 86, no. 3 (2003); Joan C. Tronto, "Relational Responsibilities, Partiality, and an Ethics of Care: Thinking about Global Ethics," IDEA Series on Global Ethics, Minneapolis, MN, 2011.
7. Peter Singer, *One World: The Ethics of Globalization* (New Haven, CT: Yale University Press, 2002); "Famine, Affluence, and Morality."
8. Leif Wenar, "Responsibility and Severe Poverty," in Pogge, *Freedom from Poverty*. The point of such designations is to make it wrong for some agent(s) to behave in certain ways—in effect, to create or clarify an obligation for agents such that their failure to fulfill it would be a form of culpable behavior.
9. Bittner, "Morality and World Hunger," 28.
10. Scheffler, "Individual Responsibility," 307.
11. Miller, *National Responsibility and Global Justice*, 81. These are less different concepts than different perspectives on injustice; see Goodhart, "Interpreting Responsibility Politically," *Journal of Political Philosophy* 25, no. 2 (2017).
12. Miller, *National Responsibility and Global Justice*, 89–90, 108.
13. Ibid., 108.
14. Ibid., 84.
15. Sometimes mere causation and forms of strict liability identify agents as remedially responsible in the absence of outcome responsibility; Miller's thinking

here and elsewhere is strongly colored by legal theory, specifically Tony Honoré, *Responsibility and Fault* (Oxford: Hart, 1999).

16. Miller, *National Responsibility and Global Justice*, 108.
17. David Miller, "Distributing Responsibilities," in Kuper, *Global Responsibilities*, 96.
18. Miller, *National Responsibility and Global Justice*, 99ff.
19. Ibid., 107.
20. Ibid., 238–47.
21. Ibid., 273–74.
22. A more cynical view is that this argument is designed to bolster Miller's long-standing claim that justice is purely a domestic or "national" concern.
23. Goodhart, "Interpreting Responsibiilty Politically," offers a somewhat expanded version of this critique.
24. Iris Marion Young, "Responsibility and Global Justice: A Social Connection Model," in *Justice and Global Politics*, ed. Ellen Frankel Paul, Fred D. Miller Jr., and Jeffrey Paul (Cambridge: Cambridge University Press, 2006), 114.
25. Ibid., 118.
26. Young, *Responsibility for Justice*, 100.
27. Young, "Responsibility and Global Justice," 102–3.
28. Ibid., 111–12; cf. *Responsibility for Justice*, 52–64.
29. Young, *Responsibility for Justice*, 56–57.
30. Young, "Responsibility and Global Justice," 114.
31. Young, *Responsibility for Justice*, 63.
32. Ibid., 110. For a recent discussion of this "many hands" problem, see Derrick Darby and Nyla R. Branscombe, "Beyond the Sins of the Fathers: Responsibility for Inequality," *Midwest Studies in Philosophy* 38, no. 1 (2014).
33. Young, *Responsibility for Justice*, 110.
34. Ibid., 109.
35. Ibid., 111.
36. Young, "Responsibility and Global Justice," 123; *Responsibility for Justice*, 112.
37. Young, "Responsibility and Global Justice," 125.
38. Young, *Responsibility for Justice*, 112. My discussion brackets Young's earlier thinking about shared responsibility (which she sometimes called *political* responsibility) because her views evolved significantly. The earlier account was influenced strongly by Arendt's conception of collective responsibility as responsibility that cannot be individuated to the self-conscious acts of individuals; it derives from membership in a collective that no individual's voluntary actions can dissolve ("Responsibility and Global Labor Justice," *Journal of Political Philosophy* 12, no. 4 [2004]: 375). Young followed Onora O'Neill in thinking that we have responsibility to all those assumed by our actions; when we purchase cheap clothing, we make (perhaps unconscious) assumptions about the people who labor in sweatshops and about all of the others involved in the production and distribution of our garments, who constitute an indissoluble community (ibid., 370ff.). Young's later view emphasizes actual (rather than assumed) social connections through which our behavior produces injustice.

Nussbaum argues that, for Young, the "imperative of political responsibility" consists in watching social and governmental institutions, "monitoring their effects to make sure they are not grossly harmful, and maintaining organized public space where such watching and monitoring can occur and citizens can speak publicly and support one another in their efforts to prevent suffering"; Martha C. Nussbaum, "Foreword," in Young, *Responsibility for Justice*, xv. I think this reading overemphasizes Young's early work; it relies heavily on the chapter of Young's posthumously published book dealing with Arendt and German guilt, which remained unrevised at the time of Young's death (see ibid.).

39. Young, "Responsibility and Global Justice," 102.
40. Ibid., 119.
41. Carol Gould has keenly observed that two distinct conceptions of responsibility operate in the social connection model: one is responsibility that arises from causing or contributing to some harmful action or process; the other is responsibility to or for someone, a sense of responsibility to do things for or with respect to others; Carol C. Gould, "Varieties of Global Responsibility: Social Connection, Human Rights and Transnational Solidarity," in *Dancing with Iris: The Philosophy of Iris Marion Young*, ed. Ann Ferguson and Mechthild Nagel (Oxford: Oxford University Press, 2009), 204. Young often (con)fuses these two conceptions of responsibility. Her insistence that agents share responsibility because of their connection to injustice remains distinctly past-oriented, but shared responsibility arising from a sense that we should do something for others is clearly forward looking (cf. Christopher Kutz, *Complicity: Ethics and Law for a Collective Age* [Cambridge: Cambridge University Press, 2000] and the critical discussion in Young, *Responsibility for Justice*).
42. Smiley, *Moral Responsibiity*, 106ff., 227ff.
43. Ibid., 144–45, 64.
44. Young, "Responsibility and Global Justice," 149.
45. Nussbaum, "Foreword," xx–xxiv; cf. "Iris Young's Last Thoughts on Responsibility for Global Justice," in Ferguson and Nagel, *Dancing with Iris*.
46. E.g., Young, *Responsibility for Justice*, 113.
47. Ibid., 3–26.
48. Ibid., 131.
49. Ibid., 132–33.
50. Ibid., 148.
51. Ibid., 143.
52. Ibid., 144.
53. Ibid., 144–47; "Responsibility and Global Justice," 127ff.
54. Young, *Responsibility for Justice*, 52.
55. This may be because, despite her attention to structures, Young seems primarily concerned with the ethical behavior and dilemmas of individuals.
56. Barnett and Duvall, "Power in Global Governance," 3.
57. Ibid., 10.
58. Young, *Responsibility for Justice*, 52.

59. Harvey, "Neoliberalism as Creative Destruction"; *A Brief History of Neoliberalism*; Klein, *The Shock Doctrine*; cf. Karl Polanyi, *The Great Transformation* (New York: Octagon Books, 1975).
60. See http://law2.wlu.edu/powellarchives/page.asp?pageid=1251. For a broader history, see Daniel Stedman Jones, *Masters of the Universe: Hayek, Friedman, and the Birth of Neoliberal Politics* (Princeton, NJ: Princeton University Press, 2012).
61. Smiley, *Moral Responsibiity*, 110.
62. E.g., Lauren Berlant, *Cruel Optimism* (Durham, NC: Duke University Press, 2011); Santos, Nunes, and Meneses, "Introduction."
63. Young uses the example to make a point about connections.
64. Cf. Butko, "Gramsci."
65. Young, *Responsibility for Justice*, 89ff.
66. Young cannot argue, as Reader or Tronto might, that the fact of their being neighbors established a relation that entailed or amounted to responsibility (see ibid., 90–91); for Young, the connection must *contribute* to causing the injustice in some way.

BIBLIOGRAPHY

Abizadeh, Arash. "Cooperation, Pervasive Impact and Coercion: On the Site (Not Scope) of Distributive Justice." *Philosophy and Public Affairs* 35, no. 4 (2007): 318–58.

Ackerly, Brooke A. *Just Responsibility: A Human Rights Theory of Global Justice*. New York: Oxford University Press, 2018.

———. *Political Theory and Feminist Social Criticism*. Cambridge: Cambridge University Press, 2000.

———. *Universal Human Rights in a World of Difference*. Cambridge: Cambridge University Press, 2008.

Amdur, Robert. "Rawls' Theory of Justice: Domestic and International Perspectives." *World Politics* 29, no. 3 (April 1977): 438–61.

Anderson, Elizabeth. "What Is the Point of Equality?" *Ethics* 109, no. 2 (January 1999): 287–337.

Appiah, K. Anthony. "Grounding Human Rights." In *Human Rights as Politics and Idolatry*, edited by Amy Gutmann, 101–16. Princeton, NJ: Princeton University Press, 2001.

Arblaster, Anthony. *Democracy*. 2nd ed. Minneapolis: University of Minnesota Press, 1994.

Barnett, Michael, and Raymond Duvall. "Power in Global Governance." In *Power in Global Governance*, edited by Michael Barnett and Raymond Duvall, 1–32. Cambridge: Cambridge University Press, 2005.

Barry, Brian. "Humanity and Justice in Global Perspective." In *Ethics, Economics, and the Law: Nomos 24*, edited by J. Roland Pennock and John W. Chapman, 219–52. New York: New York University Press, 1982.

———. *The Liberal Theory of Justice*. Oxford: Clarendon Press, 1973.

Barry, Christian, and Gerhard Øverland. "The Feasible Alternatives Thesis: Kicking Away the Livelihoods of the Global Poor." *Politics, Philosophy, and Economics* 11, no. 1 (2012): 97–119.

Barry, Christian, and Thomas W. Pogge. "Introduction." In *Global Institutions and Responsibilities: Achieving Global Justice*, edited by Christian Barry and Thomas W. Pogge, 1–2. Oxford: Blackwell, 2005.

Beitz, Charles R. "Cosmopolitan Ideals and National Sentiment." *Journal of Philosophy* 80, no. 10 (October 1983): 591–600.

———. "Economic Rights and Distributive Justice in Developing Societies." *World Politics* 33, no. 3 (April 1981): 321–46.

———. *Political Theory and International Relations*. Princeton, NJ: Princeton University Press, 1979.

———. "Rawls's Law of Peoples." *Ethics* 110, no. 4 (July 2000): 669–96.

———."Social and Cosmopolitan Liberalism." *International Affairs* 75, no. 3 (1999): 515–29.

Bell, Duncan. "Political Realism and International Relations." *Philosophy Compass* 12, no. 2 (2017), e12403.

———. "Realist Challenges." In *Handbook of International Political Theory*, edited by Chris Brown and Robin Eckersly. Oxford: Oxford University Press, forthcoming.

Bellamy, Richard. "Dirty Hands and Clean Gloves: Liberal Ideals and Real Politics." *European Journal of Political Theory* 9, no. 4 (2010): 412–30.

Benhabib, Seyla. "Another Cosmopolitanism." In *Another Cosmopolitanism*, edited by Robert Post, 13–80. Oxford: Oxford University Press, 2006.

———. *Dignity in Adversity: Human Rights in Troubled Times*. Cambridge, MA: Polity Press, 2011.

Berlant, Lauren. *Cruel Optimism*. Durham, NC: Duke University Press, 2011.

Bittner, Rüdiger. "Morality and World Hunger." In *Global Justice*, edited by Thomas W. Pogge, 24–31. Oxford: Blackwell, 2001.

Blake, Michael. "Distributive Justice, State Coercion, and Autonomy." *Philosophy and Public Affairs* 30, no. 3 (Summer 2001): 257–96.

Bohman, James. "Critical Theory, Republicanism, and the Priority of Injustice: Transnational Republicanism as a Nonideal Theory." *Journal of Social Philosophy* 43, no. 2 (Summer 2012): 97–112.

———. *Democracy across Borders: From Dêmos to Dêmoi*. Cambridge, MA: MIT Press, 2007.

———. "Domination, Global Harms, and the Priority of Injustice: Expanding Transnational Republicanism." In *Domination and Global Political Justice: Conceptual, Historical, and Institutional Perspectives*, edited by Barbara Buckinx, Jonathan Trejo-Mathys, and Timothy Waligore, 71–87. New York: Routledge, 2015.

———. "Republican Cosmopolitanism." *Journal of Political Philosophy* 12, no. 3 (2004): 336–52.

Bowles, Samuel, and Herbert Gintis. *Democracy and Capitalism: Property, Community, and the Contradictions of Modern Social Thought*. New York: Basic Books, 1986.

Brock, Gillian. *Global Justice: A Cosmopolitan Account*. Oxford: Oxford University Press, 2009.

Brown, Chris. "On Amartya Sen and *The Idea of Justice*." *Ethics and International Affairs* 24, no. 3 (2010): 309–18.

Brown, Toyacoyah. "Veterans at Standing Rock Offer Long Overdue Apology." December 6, 2016. http://www.powwows.com/veterans-standing-rock-offer-long-overdue-apology-native-elders/.

Brown, Wendy. *Undoing the Demos: Neoliberalism's Stealth Revolution*. Boston: Zone Books, 2015.

Buchanan, Allen. "Rawls's Law of Peoples: Rules for a Vanished Westphalian World." *Ethics* 110, no. 4 (July 2000): 697–721.

Buckinx, Barbara. "Global Actors and Public Power." *Critical Review of International Social and Political Philosophy* 15, no. 5 (2012): 535–51.

Buckinx, Barbara, Jonathan Trejo-Mathys, and Timothy Waligore. "Domination across Borders: An Introduction." In *Domination and Global Political Justice: Conceptual, Historical, and Institutional Perspectives*, edited by Barbara Buckinx, Jonathan Trejo-Mathys, and Timothy Waligore, 1–33. New York: Routledge, 2015.

Bufacchi, Vittorio. *Social Injustice: Essays in Political Philosophy*. Basingstoke, UK: Palgrave Macmillan, 2012.

Butko, Thomas J. "Gramsci and the 'Anti-globalization' Movement: Think before You Act." *Socialism and Democracy* 20, no. 2 (2006): 79–102.

Cabrera, Luis, ed. *Global Governance, Global Government: Institutional Visions for an Evolving World System*. Albany: State University of New York Press, 2011.

———. *Political Theory of Global Justice: A Cosmopolitan Case for the World State*. New York: Routledge, 2004.

Caney, Simon. "Addressing Poverty and Climate Change: The Varieties of Social Engagement." *Ethics and International Affairs* 26, no. 2 (2012): 191–216.

———. *Justice beyond Borders: A Global Political Theory*. Oxford: Oxford University Press, 2005.

Chakrabarty, Dipesh. *Provincializing Europe: Postcolonial Thought and Historical Difference*. Princeton, NJ: Princeton University Press, 2000.

Chang, Ha-Joon. *Bad Samaritans: The Myth of Free Trade and the Secret History of Capitalism*. New York: Bloomsbury Press, 2008.

Chappell, Richard Yetter. "Truth and Relativism." *Philosophy, et cetera*, July 10, 2004. http://www.philosophyetc.net/2004/07/truth-and-relativism.html.

Cohen, G. A. "Facts and Principles." *Philosophy and Public Affairs* 31, no. 3 (2003): 211–45.

Cohen, Joshua, and Charles Sabel. "Extra Rempublicam Nulla Justitia?" *Philosophy and Public Affairs* 34, no. 2 (2006): 147–75.

Collins, Patricia Hill. *Black Feminist Thought: Knowledge, Consciousness, and the Politics of Empowerment*. Boston: Unwin Hyman, 1990.

Crenshaw, Kimberlé. "Mapping the Margins: Intersectionality, Identity Politics, and Violence against Women of Color." *Stanford Law Review* 43, no. 6 (July 1991): 1241–99.

Dahl, Robert. "The Concept of Power." *Behavioral Science* 2, no. 3 (July 1957): 201–15.

Darby, Derrick, and Nyla R. Branscombe. "Beyond the Sins of the Fathers: Responsibility for Inequality." *Midwest Studies in Philosophy* 38, no. 1 (2014): 121–37.

Das, Bhagirath Lal. *The WTO Agreements: Deficiencies, Imbalances, and Required Changes*. New York: Zed Books, 1998.

De Bres, Helena. "The Many, Not the Few: Pluralism about Global Distributive Justice." *Journal of Political Philosophy* 20, no. 3 (2012): 314–40.

Dryzek, John S. *Deliberative Global Politics: Discourse and Democracy in a Divided World*. Cambridge: Polity Press, 2006.

Dworkin, Ronald. *Freedom's Law: The Moral Reading of the American Constitution*. Cambridge, MA: Harvard University Press, 1996.

Eddy, Katherine. "Against Ideal Rights." *Social Theory and Practice* 34, no. 3 (July 2008): 463–81.

Erman, Eva, and Niklas Möller. "Political Legitimacy in the Real Normative World: The Priority of Morality and the Autonomy of the Political." *British Journal of Political Science* 45, no. 1 (2015): 215–33.

———. "Three Failed Charges against Ideal Theory." *Social Theory and Practice* 39, no. 1 (January 2013): 19–44.

Estlund, David. "Utopophobia." *Philosophy and Public Affairs* 42, no. 2 (2014): 113–34.

Finlay, Stephen, and Mark Schroeder. "Reasons for Action: Internal vs. External." In *Stanford Encyclopedia of Philosophy*, edited by Edward N. Zalta, Fall 2017 ed.

Finlayson, Lorna. "With Radicals Like These, Who Needs Conservatives? Doom, Gloom, and Realism in Political Theory." *European Journal of Political Theory* 16, no. 3 (2017): 264–82.

Flikschuh, Katrin. "The Idea of Philosophical Fieldwork: Global Justice, Moral Ignorance, and Intellectual Attitudes." *Journal of Social Philosophy* 22, no. 1 (2014): 1–26.

Føllesdal, Andreas. "The Distributive Justice of a Global Basic Structure: A Category Mistake?" *Politics, Philosophy and Economics* 10, no. 1 (2011): 46–65.

Foot, Philippa. "Morality as a System of Hypothetical Imperatives." *Philosophical Review* 81, no. 3 (July 1972): 305–16.

Forst, Rainer. "Justifying Justification: Reply to My Critics." In *Justice, Democracy, and the Right to Justification*, 169–216. London: Bloomsbury, 2014.

———. *The Right to Justification: Elements of a Constructivist Theory of Justice*. Translated by Jeffrey Flynn. New York: Columbia University Press, 2012.

———. "Toward a Critical Theory of Transnational Justice." In *Global Justice*, edited by Thomas W. Pogge, 169–87. Oxford: Blackwell, 2001.

———. "Transnational Justice and Non-domination: A Discourse-Theoretical Approach." In *Domination and Global Political Justice: Conceptual, Historical, and Institutional Perspectives*, edited by Barbara Buckinx, Jonathan Trejo-Mathys, and Timothy Waligore, 88–110. New York: Routledge, 2015.

Foucault, Michel. *The Birth of Biopolitics: Lectures at the Collège de France, 1978–1979*. New York: Picador, 2010.

———. "The Subject and Power." *Critical Inquiry* 8, no. 4 (Summer 1982): 777–95.

Fraser, Nancy. "Abnormal Justice." *Critical Inquiry* 34, no. 3 (Spring 2008): 393–422.

———. *Scales of Justice: Reimagining Political Space in a Globalizing World*. New York: Columbia University Press, 2008.

Freeden, Michael. *Ideologies and Political Theory: A Conceptual Approach*. Oxford: Oxford University Press, 1996.

———. "Interpretative Realism and Prescriptive Realism." *Journal of Political Ideologies* 17, no. 1 (2012): 1–11.

———. "What Should the 'Political' in Political Theory Explore?" *Journal of Political Philosophy* 13, no. 2 (June 2005): 113–34.

Fukuda-Parr, Sakiko, and Proochista Ariana. "Health Impact Fund—Raising Issues of Distribution, IP Rights and Alliances." *Intellectual Property Watch*, September 26, 2011. https://www.ip-watch.org/2011/09/26/health-impact-fund-%e2%80%93-raising-issues-of-distribution-ip-rights-and-alliances/.

Gallie, W. B. "Essentially Contested Concepts." *Proceedings of the Aristotelian Society* 56 (1955–56): 167–98.

Galston, William A. "Realism in Political Theory." *European Journal of Political Theory* 9, no. 4 (2010): 385–411.

Garza, Alicia. "What I Meant When I Said That #Blacklivesmatter: A Birthday Card for a Movement." *Those People*, July 13, 2015.

Gaus, Gerald. *The Tyranny of the Ideal: Justice in a Diverse Society*. Princeton, NJ: Princeton University Press, 2016.

Geertz, Clifford. "Distinguished Lecture: Anti Anti-relativism." *American Anthropologist* 86, no. 2 (1984): 263–78.

Getachew, Adom. *Worldmaking after Empire: The Rise and Fall of Self-Determination*. Princeton, NJ: Princeton University Press, forthcoming.

Geuss, Raymond. *History and Illusion in Politics*. Cambridge: Cambridge University Press, 2001.

———. *Philosophy and Real Politics*. Princeton, NJ: Princeton University Press, 2008.

———. "Realism and the Relativity of Judgement." *International Relations* 29, no. 1 (2015): 3–22.

Gilabert, Pablo. "Comparative Assessments of Justice, Political Feasibility and Ideal Theory." *Ethical Theory and Moral Practice* 15, no. 1 (2011): 39–56.

———. "How Should We Think about the Relation between Principles and Agency?" *Ethics and Global Politics* 6, no. 2 (2013): 75–83.

Gilabert, Pablo, and Holly Lawford-Smith. "Political Feasibility: A Conceptual Exploration." *Political Studies* 60, no. 4 (2012): 809–25.

Goodale, Mark, and Sally Merry, eds. *The Practice of Human Rights: Tracking Law between the Global and the Local*. Cambridge: Cambridge University Press, 2007.

Goodhart, Michael. "Constructing Global Justice: A Critique." *Ethics and Global Politics* 5, no. 1 (2012): 1–26.

———. *Democracy as Human Rights: Freedom and Equality in the Age of Globalization*. New York: Routledge, 2005.

———. "Democratic Accountability in Global Politics: Norms, Not Agents." *Journal of Politics* 73, no. 1 (2011): 45–60.

———. "Europe's Democratic Deficits through the Looking Glass: The European Union as a Challenge for Democracy." *Perspectives on Politics* 5, no. 3 (September 2007): 567–84.

———. "Global Democracy through Transnational Human Rights." In *Global Democracy and Its Difficulties*, edited by Anthony Langlois and Karol Edward Soltan, 54–67. London: Routledge, 2009.

———. "Human Rights and Global Democracy." *Ethics and International Affairs* 22, no. 4 (2008): 395–420.

———. "Human Rights and the Politics of Contestation." In *Human Rights at the Crossroads*, edited by Mark Goodale, 31–44. Oxford: Oxford University Press, 2013.

———. "Interpreting Responsibility Politically." *Journal of Political Philosophy* 25, no. 2 (2017): 173–95.

———. "'None So Poor That He Is Compelled to Sell Himself': Democracy, Subsistence, and Basic Income." In *Economic Rights: Conceptual, Measurement and Policy*

Issues, edited by Shareen Hertel, Alanson Minkler, and Richard A. Wilson, 94–114. Cambridge: Cambridge University Press, 2007.

———. "Origins and Universality in the Human Rights Debates: Cultural Essentialism and the Challenge of Globalization." *Human Rights Quarterly* 25, no. 4 (November 2003): 935–64.

Goodhart, Michael, Patrick Manning, John Markoff, and Jackie Smith. "Introduction: Unthinking the World-System." In *Social Movements and World-System Transformation*, edited by Jackie Smith, Michael Goodhart, Patrick Manning, and John Markoff, 1–5. New York: Routledge, 2016.

Goodhart, Michael, and Jeanne Morefield. "Reflection Now! Critique and Solidarity in the Trump Era." *Theory and Event* 20, no. 1 (supplement) (2017): 68–85.

Görnitz, Anja. "Which Policies Do Enhance Global Justice? How Normative Ideals Apply to Real-World Justice Problems." Berlin Graduate School for Transnational Studies, 2012.

Gould, Carol C. "Varieties of Global Responsibility: Social Connection, Human Rights and Transnational Solidarity." In *Dancing with Iris: The Philosophy of Iris Marion Young*, edited by Ann Ferguson and Mechthild Nagel, 199–211. Oxford: Oxford University Press, 2009.

Gramsci, Antonio. *Selections from the Prison Notebooks of Antonio Gramsci*. Translated by Quintin Hoare and Geoffrey Nowell Smith. New York: International Publishers, 1971.

Grasswick, Heidi. "Feminist Social Epistemology." In *The Stanford Encyclopedia of Philosophy*, edited by Edward N. Zalta, Winter 2016 ed.

Grewal, David Singh. "Network Power and Global Standardization: The Controversy over the Multilateral Agreement on Investment." In *Global Institutions and Responsibilities: Achieving Global Justice*, edited by Christian Barry and Thomas W. Pogge, 124–40. Oxford: Blackwell, 2005.

Hall, Edward, and Matt Sleat. "Ethics, Morality and the Case for Realist Political Theory." *Critical Review of International Social and Political Philosophy* 20, no. 3 (2017): 278–95.

Hampshire, Stuart. *Justice Is Conflict*. Princeton, NJ: Princeton University Press, 2000.

Haraway, Donna. "Situated Knowledges: The Science Question in Feminism and the Privilege of Partial Perspective." *Feminist Studies* 14, no. 3 (1988): 575–99.

Harding, Sandra. "Rethinking Standpoint Epistemology: What Is 'Strong Objectivity'?" In *Feminist Epistemologies*, edited by Linda Alcoff and Elizabeth Potter, 49–82. London: Routledge, 1993.

Harvey, David. *A Brief History of Neoliberalism*. Oxford: Oxford University Press, 2005.

———. "Neoliberalism as Creative Destruction." *Geografiska Annaler: Series B, Human Geography* 88, no. 2 (June 2006): 145–58.

Hayward, Clarissa Rile. *De-facing Power*. Cambridge: Cambridge University Press, 2000.

Held, David. *Models of Democracy*. 2nd ed. Stanford, CA: Stanford University Press, 1996.

Honig, Bonnie. *Political Theory and the Displacement of Politics*. Ithaca, NY: Cornell University Press, 1993.

Honoré, Tony. *Responsibility and Fault*. Oxford: Hart, 1999.

Horton, John. "Realism, Liberal Moralism and a Political Theory of Modus Vivendi." *European Journal of Political Theory* 9, no. 4 (2010): 431–48.

Horton, Keith. "How Academics Can Help People Make Better Decisions Concerning Global Poverty." *Ethics and International Affairs* 26, no. 2 (2012): 265–78.

Hurrell, Andrew. "Global Inequality and International Institutions." *Metaphilosophy* 32, nos. 1–2 (2001): 34–57.

Hurrell, Andrew, and Terry Macdonald. "Global Public Power: The Subject of Principles of Global Political Legitimacy." *Critical Review of International Social and Political Philosophy* 15, no. 5 (2012): 553–71.

Icaza, Rosalba, and Rolando Vázquez. "Social Struggles as Epistemic Struggles." *Development and Change* 44, no. 3 (2013): 683–704.

Ivison, Duncan. "Indigenous Peoples, Injustice, and Global Politics." In *Domination and Global Political Justice: Conceptual, Historical, and Institutional Perspectives*, edited by Barbara Buckinx, Jonathan Trejo-Mathys, and Timothy Waligore, 206–23. New York: Routledge, 2015.

Jain, Devaki. "To Be or Not to Be: Problems of Locating Women in Public Policy." *Economic and Political Weekly* 42, no. 8 (2007): 691–96.

Jones, Charles. *Global Justice: Defending Cosmopolitanism*. Oxford: Oxford University Press, 1999.

Jones, Daniel Stedman. *Masters of the Universe: Hayek, Friedman, and the Birth of Neoliberal Politics*. Princeton, NJ: Princeton University Press, 2012.

Jones, Steve. *Antonio Gramsci*. New York: Routledge, 2006.

Jubb, Robert. "Tragedies of Non-ideal Theory." *European Journal of Political Theory* 11, no. 3 (2012): 229–46.

Kaldor, Mary. "Transnational Civil Society." In *Human Rights in Global Politics*, edited by Tim Dunne and Nicholas J. Wheeler, 195–213. Cambridge: Cambridge University Press, 1999.

Kariel, Henry, ed. *Frontiers of Democratic Theory*. New York: Random House, 1970.

Kingsnorth, Paul. *One No, Many Yesses: A Journey to the Heart of the Global Resistance Movement*. London: Free Press, 2003.

Kirk, Martin. "Beyond Charity: Helping NGOs Lead a Transformative New Public Discourse on Global Poverty and Social Justice." *Ethics and International Affairs* 26, no. 2 (2012): 245–63.

Klein, Naomi. *The Shock Doctrine: The Rise of Disaster Capitalism*. New York: Metropolitan Books, 2007.

Kohn, Margaret. "Postcolonialism and Global Justice." *Journal of Global Ethics* 9, no. 2 (2013): 187–200.

Kuhn, Thomas S. *The Structure of Scientific Revolutions*. 3rd ed. Chicago: University of Chicago Press, 1996.

Kutz, Christopher. *Complicity: Ethics and Law for a Collective Age*. Cambridge: Cambridge University Press, 2000.

Laborde, Cécile. "Republicanism and Global Justice: A Sketch." *European Journal of Political Theory* 9, no. 1 (2010): 48–69.

Laclau, Ernesto, and Chantal Mouffe. *Hegemony and Socialist Strategy*. 2nd ed. London: Verson, 2001.

Lawford-Smith, Holly. "Ideal Theory—a Reply to Valentini." *Journal of Political Philosophy* 18, no. 3 (2010): 357–68.

———. "Understanding Political Feasibility." *Journal of Political Philosophy* 21, no. 3 (2013): 243–59.

Lu, Catherine. "Colonialism as Structural Injustice: Historical Responsibility and Contemporary Redress." *Journal of Political Philosophy* 19, no. 3 (2011): 261–81.

Macdonald, Terry. "Antipower, Agency, and the Republican Case for Global Institutional Pluralism." In *Domination and Global Political Justice: Conceptual, Historical, and Institutional Perspectives*, edited by Barbara Buckinx, Jonathan Trejo-Mathys, and Timothy Waligore, 291–312. New York: Routledge, 2015.

Macdonald, Terry, and Miriam Ronzoni. "Introduction: The Idea of Global Political Justice." *Critical Review of International Social and Political Philosophy* 15, no. 5 (2012): 521–33.

Mann, Michael. *The Sources of Social Power.* Vol. 1: *A History of Power from the Beginning to A.D. 1760*. Cambridge: Cambridge University Press, 1986.

Mannheim, Karl. *Ideology and Utopia: An Introduction to the Sociology of Knowledge.* Translated by Louis Wirth and Edward Shils. San Diego: Harvest/Harcourt, 1955.

Markoff, John. "A Moving Target: Democracy." *European Journal of Sociology* 52, no. 2 (2011): 239–76.

McCarthy, Thomas. "Liberal Imperialism and the Dilemma of Development." In *Domination and Global Political Justice: Conceptual, Historical, and Institutional Perspectives*, edited by Barbara Buckinx, Jonathan Trejo-Mathys, and Timothy Waligore, 157–80. New York: Routledge, 2015.

———. "Political Philosophy and Racial Injustice: From Normative to Critical Theory." In *Pragmatism, Critique, Judgement: Essays for Richard J. Bernstein*, edited by Seyla Benhabib and Nancy Fraser, 149–70. Cambridge, MA: MIT Press, 2004.

Merry, Sally Engle. *Human Rights and Gender Violence: Translating International Law into Local Justice*. Chicago: University of Chicago Press, 2006.

Mertes, Tom, ed. *A Movement of Movements: Is Another World Really Possible?* London: Verso, 2004.

Milanovich, Branko. *The Haves and the Have Nots: A Brief and Idiosyncratic History of Global Inequality* New York: Basic Books, 2011.

Miller, David. "Distributing Responsibilities." In *Global Responsibilities: Who Must Deliver on Human Rights?*, edited by Andrew Kuper, 95–115. New York: Routledge, 2005.

———. "Justice and Global Inequality." In *Inequality, Globalization, and World Politics*, edited by Andrew Hurrell and Ngaire Woods, 187–210. Oxford: Oxford University Press, 1999.

———. "Lea Ypi on Global Justice and Avant-Garde Political Agency: Some Reflections." *Ethics and Global Politics* 6, no. 2 (2013): 93–99.

———. *National Responsibility and Global Justice*. Oxford: Oxford University Press, 2007.

Mills, Charles W. "'Ideal Theory' as Ideology." *Hypatia* 20, no. 3 (Summer 2005): 165–84.

———. "Race and Global Justice". In *Domination and Global Political Justice: Conceptual, Historical, and Institutional Perspectives*, edited by Barbara Buckinx, Jonathan Trejo-Mathys, and Timothy Waligore, 181–205. New York: Routledge, 2015.

Moellendorf, Darrel. *Cosmopolitan Justice*. Boulder, CO: Westview Press, 2002.

Monbiot, George. "Neoliberalism—the Ideology at the Root of All Our Problems." *The Guardian*, April 15, 2016. https://www.theguardian.com/books/2016/apr/15/neoliberalism-ideology-problem-george-monbiot.

Moore, Barrington, Jr. *Reflections on the Causes of Human Misery and upon Certain Proposals to Eliminate Them*. Boston: Beacon Press, 1970.

Morefield, Jeanne. *Empires without Imperialism: Anglo-American Decline and the Politics of Deflection*. New York: Oxford University Press, 2014.

Muldoon, Paul. "The Injustice of Territoriality." *Critical Review of International Social and Political Philosophy* 15, no. 5 (2012): 631–48.

Murphy, Liam B. *Moral Demands in Nonideal Theory*. Oxford: Oxford University Press, 2000.

Nagel, Thomas. "The Problem of Global Justice." *Philosophy and Public Affairs* 33, no. 2 (2005): 113–47.

Nardin, Terry. "The New Realism and the Old." *Critical Review of International Social and Political Philosophy* 20, no. 3 (2017): 314–30.

Newey, Glen. "Two Dogmas of Liberalism." *European Journal of Political Theory* 9, no. 4 (2010): 449–65.

North, Richard. "Political Realism: Introduction." *European Journal of Political Theory* 9, no. 4 (2010): 381–84.

Nozick, Robert. *Anarchy, State, and Utopia*. New York: Basic Books, 1974.

Nussbaum, Martha C. "Beyond the Social Contract: Capabilities and Global Justice." *Oxford Development Studies* 32, no. 1 (March 2004): 3–18.

———. "Capabilities and Human Rights." *Fordham Law Review* 66, no. 2 (November 1997): 273–300.

———. "Capabilities as Fundamental Entitlements: Sen and Social Justice." *Feminist Economics* 9, nos. 2–3 (2003): 33–59.

———. "Foreword." In *Responsibility for Justice*. Oxford: Oxford University Press, 2011.

———. "Human Functioning and Social Justice: In Defense of Aristotelian Essentialism." *Political Theory* 20, no. 2 (May 1992): 202–46.

———. "Iris Young's Last Thoughts on Responsibility for Global Justice." In *Dancing with Iris: The Philosophy of Iris Marion Young*, edited by Ann Ferguson and Mechthild Nagel, 133–45. Oxford: Oxford University Press, 2009.

O'Neill, Onora. "Bounded and Cosmopolitan Justice." *Review of International Studies* 26 (2000): 45–60.

———. *Bounds of Justice*. Cambridge: Cambridge University Press, 2000.

———. "Global Poverty and the Limits of Academic Expertise." *Ethics and International Affairs* 26, no. 2 (2012): 183–89.

O'Neill, Shane. "Struggles against Injustice: Contemporary Critical Theory and Political Violence." *Journal of Global Ethics* 6, no. 2 (2010): 127–39.

Ollman, Bertell. "The Meaning of Dialectics." In *Dance of the Dialectic: Steps in Marx's Method*. Urbana: University of Illinois Press, 2016. https://www.nyu.edu/projects/ollman/books/dd.php.

Owen, David. "Activist Political Theory and the Question of Power." *Ethics and Global Politics* 6, no. 2 (2013): 85–91.

Pateman, Carole. *The Sexual Contract*. Stanford, CA: Stanford University Press, 1988.

Pettit, Philip. *Republicanism: A Theory of Freedom and Government*. Oxford: Oxford University Press, 1997.

Pevnick, Ryan. "Political Coercion and the Scope of Distributive Justice." *Political Studies* 56, no. 2 (June 2008): 399–413.

Phillips, Anne. "Egalitarians and the Market: Dangerous Ideals." *Social Theory and Practice* 34, no. 3 (July 2008): 439–62.

Phillips, Michael. "Reflections on the Transition from Ideal to Non-ideal Theory." *Noûs* 19, no. 4 (1985): 551–70.

Philp, Mark. "What Is to Be Done? Political Theory and Political Realism." *European Journal of Political Theory* 9, no. 4 (2010): 466–84.

Pierson, Paul. *Politics in Time: History, Institutions and Social Analysis*. Princeton, NJ: Princeton University Press, 2004.

Pierson, Paul, and Theda Skocpol. "Historical Institutionalism in Contemporary Political Science." In *Political Science: State of the Discipline*, edited by Ira Katznelson and Helen V. Milner, 693–721. New York: Norton, 2002.

Piketty, Thomas. *Capital in the Twenty-First Century*. Trans. Arthur Goldhammer. Cambridge, MA: Belknap Press of Harvard University Press, 2014.

Pogge, Thomas W. "Achieving Democracy." *Ethics and International Affairs* 15, no. 1 (2001): 3–23.

———. "'Assisting' the Global Poor." In *Global Ethics: Seminal Essays*, edited by Thomas Pogge and Keith Horton, 531–63. St. Paul, MN: Paragon House, 2008.

———. "The Health Impact Fund: Enhancing Justice and Efficiency in Global Health." *Journal of Human Development and Capabilities* 13, no. 4 (2012): 537–59.

———. "The Influence of the Global Order on the Prospects for Genuine Democracy in Developing Countries." *Ratio Juris* 14, no. 3 (September 2001): 326–43.

———. *Realizing Rawls*. Ithaca, NY: Cornell University Press, 1989.

———. "Severe Poverty as a Human Rights Violation." In *Freedom from Poverty as a Human Right: Who Owes What to the Very Poor?*, edited by Thomas W. Pogge, 11–53. New York: Oxford University Press / UNESCO, 2007.

———. *World Poverty and Human Rights*. 2nd ed. Cambridge: Polity Press, 2008.

Pogge, Thomas W., and Luis Cabrera. "Outreach, Impact, Collaboration: Why Academics Should Join to Stand against Poverty." *Ethics and International Affairs* 26, no. 2 (2012): 163–82.

Polanyi, Karl. *The Great Transformation*. New York: Octagon Books, 1975.

Prinz, Janosch. "Raymond Geuss' Radicalization of Realism in Political Theory." *Philosophy and Social Criticism* 42, no. 8 (2016): 777–96.

Prinz, Janosch, and Enzo Rossi. "Political Realism as Ideology Critique." *Critical Review of International Social and Political Philosophy* 20, no. 3 (2017): 348–65.

Quinn, Joanna R. "Transitional Justice." In *Human Rights: Politics and Practice*, 3rd ed., edited by Michael Goodhart, 328–43. Oxford: Oxford University Press, 2016.

Rao, Rahul. "Listening to the Avant-Garde." *Ethics and Global Politics* 6, no. 2 (2013): 101–7.

Rawls, John. "Kantian Constructivism in Moral Theory." *Journal of Philosophy* 77, no. 9 (September 1980): 515–72.

———. *The Law of Peoples; with, "the Idea of Public Reason Revisited"* Cambridge, MA: Harvard University Press, 1999.
———. *Political Liberalism*. New York: Columbia University Press, 1993.
———. *A Theory of Justice*. Cambridge, MA: Harvard University Press, 1971.
———. *A Theory of Justice*. Rev. ed. Cambridge, MA: Harvard University Press, 1999.
Reader, Soran. "Distance, Relationship and Moral Obligation." *The Monist* 86, no. 3 (2003): 367–81.
Risse, Mathias. "Do We Owe the Global Poor Assistance or Rectification?" *Ethics and International Affairs* 19, no. 1 (Spring 2005): 9–18.
———. "How Does the Global Order Harm the Poor?" *Philosophy and Public Affairs* 33, no. 4 (2005): 349–76.
———. *On Global Justice*. Princeton, NJ: Princeton University Press, 2012.
———. "What We Owe to the Global Poor." *Journal of Ethics* 9, nos. 1–2 (2005): 81–117.
Robeyns, Ingrid. "Ideal Theory in Theory and Practice." *Social Theory and Practice* 34, no. 3 (July 2008): 341–62.
Rogowski, Ronald. *Commerce and Coalitions: How Trade Affects Domestic Political Alignments*. Princeton, NJ: Princeton University Press, 1989.
Ronzoni, Miriam. "Two Conceptions of State Sovereignty and Their Implications for Global Institutional Design." *Critical Review of International Social and Political Philosophy* 15, no. 5 (2012): 573–91.
Rorty, Richard. "The Priority of Democracy to Philosophy." In *The Virginia Statute for Religious Freedom*, edited by Merrill D. Peterson and Robert C. Vaughn, 257–82. Cambridge: Cambridge University Press, 1988.
Rossi, Enzo. "Review: Reality and Imagination in Political Theory and Practice: On Raymond Geuss's Realism." *European Journal of Political Theory* 9, no. 4 (2010): 504–12.
Said, Edward W. *Humanism and Democratic Criticism*. New York: Columbia University Press, 2004.
Sangiovanni, Andrea. "Justice and the Priority of Politics to Morality." *Journal of Political Philosophy* 16, no. 2 (2008): 137–64.
Santos, Boaventura de Sousa. *The Rise of the Global Left: The World Social Forum and Beyond*. London: Zed Books, 2006.
Santos, Boaventura de Sousa, João Arriscado Nunes, and Maria Paula Meneses. "Introduction: Opening Up the Canon of Knowledge and Recognition of Difference." In *Another Epistemology Is Possible: Beyond Northern Epistemologies*, edited by Boaventura de Sousa Santos, xix–lxii. London: Verso, 2007.
Scheffler, Samuel. "Individual Responsibility in a Global Age." In *Global Ethics: Seminal Essays*, edited by Thomas Pogge and Keith Horton, 291–311. St. Paul, MN: Paragon House, 2008.
Scheuerman, William E. "The Realist Revival in Political Philosophy, Or: Why New Is Not Always Improved." *International Politics* 50, no. 6 (2013): 798–814.
Scholte, Jan Aart. *Democratising the Global Economy: The Role of Civil Society*, University of Warwick: Centre for the Study of Globalisation and Regionalisation, 2003.
Schwartzman, Lisa H. "Abstraction, Idealization, and Oppression." *Metaphilosophy* 37, no. 5 (October 2006): 565–88.

Seliger, Martin. *Ideology and Politics*. London: Allen and Unwin, 1976.
Sen, Amartya. *Development as Freedom*. New York: Alfred A. Knopf, 1999.
———. *The Idea of Justice*. Cambridge, MA: Belknap Press of Harvard University Press, 2009.
———. *Inequality Re-examined*. Cambridge, MA: Harvard University Press, 1992.
———. "Open and Closed Impartiality." In *Global Responsibilities: Who Must Deliver on Human Rights?*, edited by Andrew Kuper, 53–76. New York: Routledge, 2005.
———. "What Do We Want from a Theory of Justice?" *Journal of Philosophy* 103, no. 5 (May 2006): 215–38.
Shapiro, Ian. *Democratic Justice*. New Haven, CT: Yale University Press, 1999.
———. "Review: The Idea of Justice." *Journal of Economic Literature* 49, no. 4 (2011): 1251–63.
Shelby, Tommie. "Justice, Deviance, and the Dark Ghetto." *Philosophy and Public Affairs* 35, no. 2 (2007): 127–60.
Shklar, Judith N. *The Faces of Injustice*. New Haven, CT: Yale University Press, 1990.
———. "The Liberalism of Fear." In *Political Thought and Political Thinkers*, edited by Stanley Hoffmann, 3–20. Chicago: University of Chicago Press, 1998.
Simmons, A. John. "Ideal and Nonideal Theory." *Philosophy and Public Affairs* 38, no. 1 (2010): 5–36.
Singer, Peter. "Famine, Affluence, and Morality." *Philosophy and Public Affairs* 1, no. 3 (Spring 1972): 229–43.
———. *One World: The Ethics of Globalization*. New Haven, CT: Yale University Press, 2002.
Sklair, Leslie. *The Transnational Capitalist Class*. Oxford: Wiley-Blackwell, 2000.
Sleat, Matt. "Bernard Williams and the Possibility of a Realist Political Theory." *European Journal of Political Theory* 9, no. 4 (2010): 485–503.
———. "What Is a Political Value? Political Philosophy and Fidelity to Reality." *Social Philosophy and Policy* 33, nos. 1–2 (2016): 252–72.
Smiley, Marion. *Moral Responsibility and the Boundaries of Community: Power and Accountability from a Pragmatic Point of View*. Chicago: University of Chicago Press, 1992.
Smith, Jackie. "Global Civil Society? Transnational Social Movement Organizations and Social Capital." *American Behavioral Scientist* 42, no. 1 (September 1998): 93–107.
———. "The World Social Forum and the Challenges of Global Democracy." *Global Networks* 4, no. 4 (2004): 413–21.
Smith, Jackie, et al. *Global Democracy and the World Social Forums*. Boulder, CO: Paradigm, 2008.
Spinner-Halev, Jeff. *Enduring Injustice*. Cambridge: Cambridge University Press, 2012.
Stammers, Neil. "Social Movements and the Social Construction of Human Rights." *Human Rights Quarterly* 21, no. 4 (November 1999): 980–1008.
Steger, Manfred. *Globalization: A Very Short Introduction*. 3rd ed. Oxford: Oxford University Press, 2013.
Stemplowska, Zofia. "What's Ideal about Ideal Theory?" *Social Theory and Practice* 34, no. 3 (July 2008): 319–40.

Swift, Adam. "The Value of Philosophy in Nonideal Circumstances." *Social Theory and Practice* 34, no. 3 (July 2008): 363–87.

Taylor, P. J. "Embedded Statism and the Social Sciences: Opening Up to New Spaces." *Environment and Planning A* 28 (1996): 1917–28.

Tronto, Joan C. "Relational Responsibilities, Partiality, and an Ethics of Care: Thinking about Global Ethics." IDEA Series on Global Ethics. Minneapolis, MN, 2011.

Tully, James. *Public Philosophy in a New Key: Democracy and Civic Freedom*. 2 vols. Vol. 1. New York: Cambridge University Press, 2008.

Valentini, Laura. "Assessing the Global Order: Justice, Legitimacy, or Political Justice?" *Critical Review of International Social and Political Philosophy* 15, no. 5 (2012): 593–612.

———. *Justice in a Globalized World: A Normative Framework*. Oxford: Oxford University Press, 2011.

———. "On the Apparent Paradox of Ideal Theory." *Journal of Political Philosophy* 17, no. 3 (September 2009): 332–55.

Wacquant, Loïc. *Punishing the Poor: The Neoliberal Government of Social Insecurity*. Durham, NC: Duke University Press, 2009.

Wall, Steven. "Freedom, Interference and Domination." *Political Studies* 49, no. 2 (June 2001): 216–30.

Walzer, Michael. *Spheres of Justice: A Defense of Pluralism and Equality*. New York: Basic Books, 1983.

Wannheden, Emil. "Justice and the Capability Approach." In *Human Development and International Cooperation*, 1–11. University of Florence, 2013. https://www.academia.edu/16157371/Justice_and_the_Capability_Approach?auto=download

Weldon, S. Laurel. "Inclusion and Understanding: A Collective Methodology for Feminist International Relations." In *Feminist Methodologies for International Relations*, edited by Brooke A. Ackerly, Maria Stern, and Jacqui True, 62–87. Cambridge: Cambridge University Press, 2006.

Wenar, Leif. "Responsibility and Severe Poverty." In *Freedom from Poverty as a Human Right: Who Owes What to the Very Poor?*, edited by Thomas W. Pogge, 255–74. New York: Oxford University Press / UNESCO, 2007.

———. "What We Owe to Distant Others." *Politics, Philosophy, and Economics* 2, no. 3 (2003): 283–304.

Wiens, David. "Prescribing Institutions without Ideal Theory." *Journal of Political Philosophy* 20, no. 1 (March 2011): 45–70.

Williams, Bernard. *In the Beginning Was the Deed: Realism and Moralism in Political Argument*. Edited by Geoffrey Hawthorn. Princeton, NJ: Princeton University Press, 2005.

Williamson, John, ed. *The Political Economy of Policy Reform*. Washington, DC: Institute for International Economics, 1994.

———. "What Washington Means by Policy Reform." In *Latin American Adjustment: How Much Has Happened?*, edited by John Williamson, 5–20. Washington, DC: Institute for International Economics, 1990.

Working Group Meeting on Globalization and Trade. "*Jemez Principles* for Democratic Organizing." Southwest Network for Environmental and Economic Justice, Jemez, NM, 1996.

Yack, Bernard. "Putting Injustice First: An Alternative Approach to Liberal Pluralism." *Social Research* 66, no. 4 (Winter 1999): 1103–20.

Young, Iris Marion. *Justice and the Politics of Difference*. Princeton, NJ: Princeton University Press, 1990.

———. "Responsibility and Global Justice: A Social Connection Model." In *Justice and Global Politics*, edited by Ellen Frankel Paul, Fred D. Miller Jr., and Jeffrey Paul, 102–30. Cambridge: Cambridge University Press, 2006.

———. "Responsibility and Global Labor Justice." *Journal of Political Philosophy* 12, no. 4 (December 2004): 365–88.

———. *Responsibility for Justice*. New York: Oxford University Press, 2011.

Ypi, Lea. *Global Justice and Avant Garde Political Agency*. Oxford: Oxford University Press, 2011.

———. "On the Confusion between Ideal and Non-ideal in Recent Debates on Global Justice." *Political Studies* 58, no. 3 (2010): 536–55.

Ypi, Lea, Robert E. Goodin, and Christian Barry. "Associative Duties, Global Justice, and the Colonies." *Philosophy and Public Affairs* 37, no. 2 (2009): 103–35.

Zivi, Karen. *Making Rights Claims: A Practice of Democratic Citizenship*. New York: Oxford University Press, 2012.

INDEX

The manufacturer's authorised representative in the EU for product safety is Oxford University Press España S.A. of El Parque Empresarial San Fernando de Henares, Avenida de Castilla, 2 - 28830 Madrid (www.oup.es/en or product.safety@oup.com). OUP España S.A. also acts as importer into Spain of products made by the manufacturer.
Printed and bound by CPI Group (UK) Ltd, Croydon, CR0 4YY
14/09/2026
02216306-0018